# Studies in
# ETHNOMETHODOLOGY

## HAROLD GARFINKEL

### University of California, Los Angeles

POLITY PRESS

Copyright © Prentice-Hall Inc., 1967

First published in America, 1967
This edition published 1984 by Polity Press in association with
Blackwell Publishers Ltd.

Reprinted 1987, 1989, 1990, 1992, 1994, 1996, 1999, 2002

*Editorial office*:
Polity Press
65 Bridge Street
Cambridge CB2 1UR, UK

*Marketing and production*:
Blackwell Publishers Ltd
108 Cowley Road
Oxford OX4 1JF, UK

*Published in the USA by*
Blackwell Publishers Inc.
Commerce Place
350 Main Street
Malden MA 02148, USA

ISBN 0–7456–0005–0  (pbk)

A catalogue record for this book is available from the British Library and the Library
of Congress.

Printed in Great Britain by MPG Books, Bodmin, Cornwall

TO ABRAHAM GARFINKEL

# Preface

In doing sociology, lay and professional, every reference to the "real world," even where the reference is to physical or biological events, is a reference to the organized activities of everyday life. Thereby, in contrast to certain versions of Durkheim that teach that the objective reality of social facts is sociology's fundamental principle, the lesson is taken instead, and used as a study policy, that the objective reality of social facts *as* an ongoing accomplishment of the concerted activities of daily life, with the ordinary, artful ways of that accomplishment being by members known, used, and taken for granted, is, for members doing sociology, a fundamental phenomenon. Because, and in the ways it is practical sociology's fundamental phenomenon, it is the prevailing topic for ethnomethodological study. Ethnomethodological studies analyze everyday activities as members' methods for making those same activities visibly-rational-and-reportable-for-all-practical-purposes, i.e., "accountable," as organizations of commonplace everyday activities. The reflexivity of that phenomenon is a singular feature of practical actions, of practical circumstances, of common sense knowledge of social structures, and of practical sociological reasoning. By permitting us to locate and examine their occurrence the reflexivity of that phenomenon establishes their study.

Their study is directed to the tasks of learning how members' actual, ordinary activities consist of methods to make practical actions, practical circumstances, common sense knowledge of social structures, and practical sociological reasoning analyzeable; and of discovering the formal properties of commonplace, practical common sense actions, "from within" actual settings, as ongoing accomplishments of those settings. The formal properties obtain their guarantees from no other source, and in no other way. Because this is so, our study tasks cannot be accomplished by free invention, constructive analytic theorizing, mock-ups, or book reviews, and so no special interest is paid to them aside from an interest in their varieties as organizationally situated methods of practical reasoning. Similarly, there can be nothing to quarrel with or to correct about practical sociological reasoning, and so, because professional sociological inquiries are practical through and through, except that quarrels between those doing professional inquiries and ethnomethodology may be of interest as phenomena for ethnomethodological studies, these quarrels need not be taken seriously.

Ethnomethodological studies are not directed to formulating or arguing correctives. They are useless when they are done as ironies. Although they are directed to the preparation of manuals on sociological methods, these are in *no way* supplements to "standard" procedure, but are distinct from them. They do not formulate a remedy for practical actions, as if it was being found about practical actions that they were better or worse than they are usually cracked up to be. Nor are they in search of humanistic arguments, nor do they engage in or encourage permissive discussions of theory.

Over the past ten years a group of increasing size has been doing ethnomethodological studies as day to day concerns: Egon Bittner, Aaron V. Cicourel, Lindsey Churchill, Craig MacAndrew, Michael Moerman, Edward Rose, Harvey Sacks, Emmanuel Schegloff, David Sudnow, D. Lawrence Wieder, and Don Zimmerman. Harvey Sacks must be mentioned particularly because his extraordinary writings and lectures have served as critical resources.

Through their studies methods have been made available whose use has established a domain of sociological phenomena: the formal properties of common sense activities as a practical organizational accomplishment. An early body of work of considerable size is now either in print or in press. This volume is a part of that early corpus.

A later, very large set of materials is currently circulating prior to publication. Findings and methods are becoming available at an increasing rate, and it is pointless any longer to doubt that an immense, hitherto unknown domain of social phenomena has been uncovered.

The studies in this volume were written over the last twelve years. I regret a certain unity in the collection that was obtained by pondering and rearranging texts. I am saddened by that practice for in the way it assures to the collected articles an overall "good sense" it will certainly have sacrificed news. The articles originated from my studies of the writings of Talcott Parsons, Alfred Schutz, Aron Gurwitsch, and Edmund Husserl. For twenty years their writings have provided me with inexhaustible directives into the world of everyday activities. Parsons' work, particularly, remains awesome for the penetrating depth and unfailing precision of its practical sociological reasoning on the constituent tasks of the problem of social order and its solutions.

The completion of these studies was made materially possible by the following grants and fellowships. Studies reported in the papers on routine grounds, the documentary method, and passing were supported by a Senior Research Fellowship, SF-81, from the U.S. Public Health Service. Investigations of common understandings and coding practices were supported by Senior Research Fellowship SF-81 from the U.S. Public Health Service, Grant Q-2 from the Research Section of the California State Department of Mental Hygiene, and Project Af-AFOSR-757-65 of the Behavioral Sciences Division of the Air Force Office of Scientific Research.

The work upon which the paper on the rationalities is based was initiated while the author was a member of the Organizational Behavior Project, Princeton University, and was completed under a Senior Research Fellowship, SF-81, from the U.S. Public Health Service. The author is indebted to the Interdisciplinary Program in the Behavioral Sciences at the University of New Mexico, Summer, 1958, under project AF 49(638)-33 of the Behavioral Sciences Division, Air Force Office of Scientific Research, ARDC, and the Society for the Investigation of Human Ecology.

I was privileged to spend the academic year 1963-1964 as a Fellow in the Center for the Scientific Study of Suicide of the Los

Angeles Suicide Prevention Center. I am indebted to Drs. Edwin S. Shneidman, Norman L. Farberow, and Robert E. Litman for their hospitality.

The investigations of the work of the Psychiatric Outpatient Clinic of the U.C.L.A. Neuropsychiatric Institute were supported by Grants A-7 and Q-2 from the Research Section of the California State Department of Mental Hygiene, and Senior Research Fellowship SF-81 from the U.S. Public Health Service.

The investigation of staff uses of clinic folders was supported by Grant Q-2 from the Research Section of the California State Department of Mental Hygiene, the senior author's Senior Research Fellowship SF-81 from the U.S. Public Health Service, and the Conferences on Ethnomethodology under Grant AF-AFOSR-278-62 of the Behavioral Sciences Division of the Air Force Office of Scientific Research. Harry R. Brickman, M.D., and Eugene Pumpian-Mindlin, M.D., former Directors of the Psychiatric Outpatient Clinic of the Neuropsychiatric Institute at the University of California, Los Angeles, greatly facilitated the inquiries. Drs. Leon Epstein and Robert Ross, encouraged the clinic studies and administered Grants A-7 and Q-2 from the California Department of Mental Hygiene when they directed its Research Section.

Particular gratitude is extended to Dr. Charles E. Hutchinson, Chief of the Behavioral Sciences Division, Air Force Office of Scientific Research, whose Division supported the Conferences on Ethnomethodology with Grant AF-AFOSR-278-62 to Edward Rose and me, and Studies of Decision Making in Common Sense Situations of Choice with Grants AF-AFOSR-757-65, and AF-AFOSR-757-66 to Harvey Sacks, Lindsey Churchill and me.

The study of methodological adequacy benefited in many important ways from the criticisms of Drs. Richard J. Hill, Elliot G. Mishler, Eleanor B. Sheldon, and Stanton Wheeler. Thanks are due to Egon Bittner, when he was my research assistant, for coding the cases, and to Michael R. Mend for the calculations. The paper required the advice of Professor Charles F. Mosteller, Department of Statistics, Harvard University, and the inventiveness of Professor Wilfred J. Dixon, School of Public Health, University of California, Los Angeles. Professor Dixon devised the method for using chi-square to evaluate data involving conditional probabilities. With his permission the method is reported in Appendix I. Only I am responsible for the paper's shortcomings.

I am grateful to my students Michael R. Mend and Patricia Allen for their assistance with the clinic and reliability studies. Peter McHugh, when he was a graduate student at U.C.L.A., assisted me with the "counseling" experiment. David Sudnow worked to the limits of his patience to improve the writing. Robert J. Stoller, Egon Bittner, and Saul Mendlovitz collaborated in the studies that cite them as co-authors. The study of jurors is based on interviews with jurors done by Mendlovitz and me when we were affiliated with the Jury Project of the Law School of the University of Chicago.

Debts are owed to very particular persons: to James H. Clark, friend and editor; and to old friends: William C. Beckwith, Joseph Bensman, Heinz and Ruth Ellersieck, Erving Goffman, Evelyn Hooker, Duncan MacRae, Jr., Saul Mendlovitz, Elliot G. Mishler, Henry W. Riecken, Jr., William S. Robinson, Edward Rose, Edwin S. Shneidman, Melvin Seeman, and Eleanor B. Sheldon.

My lovely wife knows this book with me.

HAROLD GARFINKEL

# Acknowledgments

Chapters One (in part), Two, Three, and Eight were previously published. Chapter One includes material from "Practical Sociological Reasoning: Some Features in the Work of the Los Angeles Suicide Prevention Center," in *Essays in Self Destruction*, edited by Edwin S. Shneidman, International Science Press, 1967, in press. Chapter Two is reprinted with revisions from *Social Problems*, Winter, 1964, Vol. 11, No. 3, pp. 225-250. Chapter Three is reprinted with permission of the Macmillan Company from *Theories of the Mind*, edited by Jordan M. Scher, the Free Press of Glencoe, Inc., New York, 1962, pp. 689-712. Chapter Eight originally appeared in *Behavioral Science*, Vol. 5, No. 1, January, 1960, pp. 72-83. It also appeared in *Decisions, Values, and Groups*, Vol. 2, edited by Norman F. Washburne, Pergamon Press, Inc., New York, 1962, pp. 304-324. I am indebted to these sources for their permission to reprint. I wish also to thank the RAND Corporation for permission to reprint the detailed excerpt from the monograph by Olaf Helmer and Nicholas Rescher, *On the Epistemology of the Inexact Sciences*, P-1513 Santa Monica, California: RAND Corporation, October 13, 1958, pp. 8-14.

Chapter Seven, "Methodological Adequacy in the Quantitative Study of Selection Criteria and Selection Practices in Psychiatric Outpatient Clinics," was drafted in March, 1960. No updating of the list of studies was done after the original list was assembled in March, 1960 and so several studies are conspicuously absent, e.g., Elliot Mishler and Nancy E. Waxler's study, "Decision Processes in Psychiatric Hospitalization," *American Sociological Review*, Vol. 28, No. 4, August, 1963, pp. 576-587; and the long series by Anita Bahn and her associates at the National Institute of Mental Health. A review of studies was done originally in order to discover the "parameters" of the selection problem and to enrich their discussion. At the time the paper was written the task of reporting what had been found out about admissions to psychiatric clinics was of secondary interest, and is now immaterial.

# Contents

ONE

What is ethnomethodology?                                    1

TWO

Studies of the routine grounds
of everyday activities                                      35

THREE

Common sense knowledge of social structures:
the documentary method of interpretation
in lay and professional fact finding                       76

FOUR

Some rules of correct decisions
that jurors respect                                        104

FIVE

Passing and the managed achievement
of sex status in an intersexed person,
part 1                                                          116


SIX

"Good organizational reasons
for 'bad' clinic records"                                       186


SEVEN

Methodological adequacy in the
quantitative study of selection criteria
and selection practices
in psychiatric outpatient clinics                              208


EIGHT

The rational properties of scientific
and common sense activities                                    262


Appendix to chapter five                                      285

# ONE

# What is ethnomethodology?

The following studies seek to treat practical activities, practical circumstances, and practical sociological reasoning as topics of empirical study, and by paying to the most commonplace activities of daily life the attention usually accorded extraordinary events, seek to learn about them as phenomena in their own right. Their central recommendation is that the activities whereby members produce and manage settings of organized everyday affairs are identical with members' procedures for making those settings "account-able." The "reflexive," or "incarnate" character of accounting practices and accounts makes up the crux of that recommendation. When I speak of accountable my interests are directed to such matters as the following. I mean observable-and-reportable, *i.e.* available to members as situated practices of looking-and-telling. I mean, too, that such practices consist of an endless, ongoing, contingent accomplishment; that they are carried on under the auspices of, and are made to happen as events in, the same ordinary affairs that in organizing they describe; that the practices are done by parties to those settings whose skill with, knowledge of, and entitlement to the detailed work of that accomplishment—whose competence—they obstinately depend upon, recognize, use, and take for granted; and *that* they take their competence for granted itself furnishes parties with a setting's distinguishing and particular features, and of course it furnishes them as well as resources, troubles, projects, and the rest.

Some structurally equivocal features of the methods and results by persons doing sociology, lay and professional, of making practical activities observable were epitomized by Helmer and Rescher.[1] When members' accounts of everyday activities are used as prescriptions with which to locate, to identify, to analyze, to classify, to make recognizable, or to find one's way around in comparable occasions, the prescriptions, they observe, are law-like, spatiotemporally restricted, and "loose." By "loose" is meant that though they are intendedly conditional in their logical form, "the nature of the conditions is such that they can often not be spelled out completely or fully." The authors cite as an example a statement about sailing fleet tactics in the 18th century. They point out the statement carries as a test condition reference to the state of naval ordnance.

> In elaborating conditions (under which such a statement would hold) the historian delineates what is typical of the place and period. The full implications of such reference may be vast and inexhaustible; for instance . . . ordnance soon ramifies *via* metal working technology into metallurgy, mining, etc. Thus, the conditions which are operative in the formulation of an historical law may only be indicated in a general way, and are not necessarily, indeed, in most cases cannot be expected to be exhaustively articulated. This characteristic of such laws is here designed as *looseness*. . . .
>
> A consequence of the looseness of historical laws is that they are not universal, but merely quasi-general in that they admit of exceptions. Since the conditions delimiting the area of application of the law are often not exhaustively articulated, a supposed violation of the law may be explicable by showing that a legitimate, but as yet unformulated, precondition of the law's applicability is not fulfilled in the case under consideration.

Consider that this holds in every *particular* case, and holds not by reason of the meaning of "quasi-law," but because of investigators' actual, particular practices.

[1] Olaf Helmer and Nicholas Rescher, *On the Epistemology of the Inexact Sciences*, P-1513 (Santa Monica, California: RAND Corporation, October 13, 1958), pp. 8-14.

Further, Helmer and Rescher point out,

> The laws may be taken to contain a tacit caveat of the "usually" or "other things being equal" type. An historical law is thus not strictly universal in that it must be taken as applicable to all cases falling within the scope of its explicitly formulated or formulable conditions; rather, it may be thought to formulate relationships which obtain generally, or better, which obtain "as a rule."
>
> Such a "law" we will term *quasi-law*. In order for the law to be valid it is not necessary that no apparent exceptions occur. It is only necessary that, if an apparent exception should occur, an adequate explanation be forthcoming, an explanation demonstrating the exceptional characteristic of the case in hand by establishing the violation of an appropriate, if hitherto unformulated, condition of the law's applicability.

These and other features can be cited for the cogency with which they describe members' accounting practices. Thus: (1) Whenever a member is required to demonstrate that an account analyzes an actual situation, he invariably makes use of the practices of "et cetera," "unless," and "let it pass" to demonstrate the rationality of his achievement. (2) The definite and sensible character of the matter that is being reported is settled by an assignment that reporter and auditor make to each other that each will have furnished whatever unstated understandings are required. Much therefore of what is actually reported is not mentioned. (3) Over the time for their delivery accounts are apt to require that "auditors" be willing to wait for what will have been said in order that the present significance of what has been said will have become clear. (4) Like conversations, reputations, and careers, the particulars of accounts are built up step by step over the actual uses of and references to them. (5) An account's materials are apt to depend heavily for sense upon their serial placement, upon their relevance to the auditor's projects, or upon the developing course of the organizational occasions of their use.

In short, *recognizable* sense, or fact, or methodic character, or impersonality, or objectivity of accounts are not independent of the socially organized occasions of their use. Their rational features *consist* of what members do with, what they "make of" the accounts in the socially organized actual occasions of their use. Members' accounts are reflexively and essentially tied for their rational features to the socially organized occasions of their use for they are *features* of the socially organized occasions of their use.

That tie establishes the central topic of our studies: the rational accountability of practical actions as an ongoing, practical accomplishment. I want to specify the topic by reviewing three of its constituent, problematic phenomena. Wherever studies of practical action and practical reasoning are concerned, these consist of the following: (1) the unsatisfied programmatic distinction between and substitutability of objective (context free) for indexical expressions; (2) the "uninteresting" essential reflexivity of accounts of practical actions; and (3) the analyzability of actions-in-context as a practical accomplishment.

### The unsatisfied programmatic distinction between and substitutability of objective for indexical expressions

Properties that are exhibited by accounts (by reason of their being features of the socially organized occasions of their use) are available from studies by logicians as the properties of indexical expressions and indexical sentences. Husserl [2] spoke of expressions whose sense cannot be decided by an auditor without his necessarily knowing or assuming something about the biography and the purposes of the user of the expression, the circumstances of the utterance, the previous course of the conversation, or the particular relationship of actual or potential interaction that exists between the expressor and the auditor. Russell [3] observed that descriptions involving them apply on each occasion of use to only one thing, but to different things on different occasions. Such expressions, wrote Goodman,[4] are used to make unequivocal statements that nevertheless seem to change in truth value. Each of their utterances, "tokens," constitutes a word and refers to a cer-

[2] In Marvin Farber, *The Foundation of Phenomenology* (Cambridge, Massachusetts: Harvard University Press, 1943), pp. 237-238.

[3] Bertrand Russell, *Inquiry into Meaning and Truth* (New York: W. W. Norton & Company, Inc., 1940), pp. 134-143.

[4] Nelson Goodman, *The Structure of Appearance* (Cambridge, Massachusetts: Harvard University Press, 1951), pp. 287-298.

tain person, time, or place, but names something not named by some replica of the word. Their denotation is relative to the speaker. Their use depends upon the relation of the user to the object with which the word is concerned. Time for a temporal indexical expression is relevant to what it names. Similarly, just what region a spatial indexical expression names depends upon the location of its utterance. Indexical expressions and statements containing them are not freely repeatable; in a given discourse, not all their replicas therein are also translations of them. The list can be extended indefinitely.

Virtually unanimous agreement exists among students of practical sociological reasoning, laymen and professionals, about the properties of indexical expressions and indexical actions. Impressive agreement exists as well (1) that although indexical expressions "are of enormous utility" they are "awkward for formal discourse"; (2) that a distinction between objective expressions and indexical expressions is not only procedurally proper but unavoidable for whosoever would do science; (3) that without the distinction between objective and indexical expressions, and without the preferred use of objective expressions the victories of generalizing, rigorous, scientific inquiries—logic, mathematics, some of the physical sciences—are unintelligible, the victories would fail, and the inexact sciences would have to abandon their hopes; (4) that the exact sciences are distinguishable from the inexact sciences by the fact that in the case of the exact sciences the distinction between and substitution of objective for indexical expressions for problem formulation, methods, findings, adequate demonstration, adequate evidence and the rest is both an actual task and an actual achievement, whereas in the case of the inexact sciences the availability of the distinction and substitutability to actual tasks, practices, and results remains unrealizably programmatic; (5) that the distinction between objective and indexical expressions, insofar as the distinction consists of inquirers' tasks, ideals, norms, resources, achievements, and the rest describes the difference between sciences and arts—e.g., between biochemistry and documentary filming; (6) that terms and sentences can be distinguished as one or the other in accordance with an assessment procedure that makes decidable their character as indexical or objective expressions; and (7) that in any particular case only practical difficulties prevent the substitution by an objective expression for an indexical expression.

Features of indexical expressions motivate endless methodological studies directed to their remedy. Indeed, attempts to rid the practices of a science of these nuisances lends to each science its distinctive character of preoccupation and productivity with methodological issues. Research practitioners' studies of practical activities of a science, whatever their science, afford them endless occasions to deal rigorously with indexical expressions.

Areas in the social sciences where the promised distinction and promised substitutability occurs are countless. The promised distinction and substitutability are supported by and themselves support immense resources directed to developing methods for the strong analysis of practical actions and practical reasoning. Promised applications and benefits are immense.

Nevertheless, *wherever practical actions are topics of study* the promised distinction and substitutability of objective for indexical expressions remains programmatic in every *particular* case and in every *actual* occasion in which the distinction or substitutability must be demonstrated. In every actual case without exception, conditions will be cited that a competent investigator will be required to recognize, such that in *that* particular case the terms of the demonstration can be relaxed and nevertheless the demonstration be counted an adequate one.

We learn from logicians and linguists, who are in virtually unanimous agreement about them, what some of these conditions are. For "long" texts, or "long" courses of action, for events where members' actions are features of the events their actions are accomplishing, or wherever tokens are not used or are not suitable as proxies for indexical expressions, the program's claimed demonstrations are satisfied as matters of practical social management.

Under such conditions indexical expressions, by reason of their prevalence and other properties, present immense, obstinate, and irremediable nuisances to the tasks of dealing rigorously with the phenomena of structure and relevance in theories of consistency proofs and computability, and in attempts to recover actual as compared with supposed common conduct and common talk with full structural particulars. Drawing upon their experience in the uses of sample surveys, and the design and application of measurements of practical actions, statistical analyses, mathematical models, and computer simulations of social processes, professional sociologists are able to document endlessly the ways in which the programmatic distinction and substitutability is satisfied in, and depends upon, professional practices of socially managed demonstration.

In short, wherever studies of practical actions are involved, the distinction and substitutability is always accomplished *only* for all practical purposes. Thereby, the first problematic phenomenon is recommended to consist of the reflexivity of the practices and attainments of sciences in and of the organized activities of everyday life, which is an essential reflexivity.

## The "uninteresting" essential reflexivity of accounts

For members engaged in practical sociological reasoning—as we shall see in later studies, for staff personnel at the Los Angeles Suicide Prevention Center, for staff users of psychiatric clinic folders at U.C.L.A., for graduate student coders of psychiatric records, for jurors, for an intersexed person managing a sex change, for professional sociological researchers—their concerns are for what is decidable "for practical purposes," "in light of this situation," "given the nature of actual circumstances," and the like. Practical circumstances and practical actions refer for them to many organizationally important and serious matters: to resources, aims, excuses, opportunities, tasks, and of course to grounds for arguing or foretelling the adequacy of procedures and of the findings they yield. One matter, however, is excluded from their interests: practical actions and practical circumstances are not in themselves *a* topic, let alone a sole topic of their inquiries; nor are their inquiries, addressed to the tasks of sociological theorizing, undertaken to formulate what these tasks consist of as practical actions. In no case is the investigation of practical actions undertaken in order that personnel might be able to recognize and describe what they are doing in the first place. Least of all are practical actions investigated in order to explain to practitioners their own talk about what they are doing. For example personnel at the Los Angeles Suicide Prevention Center found it altogether incongruous to consider seriously that they be so engaged in the work of certifying mode of death that a person seeking to commit suicide, and they could concert their efforts to assure the unequivocal recognition of "what really happened."

To say they are "not interested" in the study of practical actions is not to complain, nor to point to an opportunity they miss, nor is it a disclosure of error, nor is it an ironic comment. Neither is it the case that because members are "not interested" that they are "precluded" from sociological theorizing. Nor do their inquiries preclude the use of the rule of doubt, nor are they precluded from making the organized activities of everyday life scientifically problematical, nor does the comment insinuate a difference between "basic" and "applied" interests in research and theorizing.

What does it mean then to say that they are "not interested" in studying practical actions and practical sociological reasoning? And what is the import of such a statement?

There is a feature of members' accounts that for them is of such singular and prevailing relevance that it controls other features in their specific character as recognizable, rational features of practical sociological inquiries. The feature is this. With respect to the problematic character of practical actions and to the practical adequacy of their inquiries, members take for granted that a member must at the outset "know" the settings in which he is to operate if his practices are to serve as measures to bring particular, located features of these settings to recognizable account. They treat as the most passing matter of fact that members' accounts, of every sort, in all their logical modes, with all of their uses, and for every method for their assembly are constituent features of the settings they make observable. Members know, require, count on, and make use of this reflexivity to produce, accomplish, recognize, or demonstrate rational-adequacy-for-all-practical-purposes of their procedures and findings.

Not only do members—the jurors and the others—take that reflexivity for granted, but they recognize, demonstrate, and make observable for each other the rational character of their actual, and that means their occasional, practices while respecting that reflexivity as an unalterable and unavoidable condition of their inquiries.

When I propose that members are "not interested" in studying practical actions, I do not mean that members will have none, a little, or a lot of it. That they are "not interested" has to do with reasonable practices, with plausible argument, and with reasonable findings. It has to do with treating "accountable-for-all-practical-purposes" as a discoverable matter, exclusively, only, and entirely. For members to be "interested" would consist of their undertaking to make the "reflexive" character of practical activities observable; to examine the artful practices of rational inquiry as organizational phenomena without thought for correctives or irony. Members of the Los Angeles Suicide Prevention Center are like members wherever they engage in practical sociological inquiries: though they would, they *can* have none of it.

### The analyzability of actions-in-context as a practical accomplishment

In indefinitely many ways members' inquiries are constituent features of the settings they analyze. In the same ways, their inquiries are made recognizable to members as adequate-for-all-practical-purposes. For example, at the Los Angeles Suicide Prevention Center, that deaths are made accountable-for-all-practical-purposes are practical organizational accomplishments. Organizationally, the Suicide Prevention Center consists of practical procedures for accomplishing the rational accountability of suicidal deaths as recognizable features of the settings in which that accountability occurs.

In the actual occasions of interaction that accomplishment is for members omnipresent, unproblematic, and commonplace. For members doing sociology, to make that accomplishment a topic of practical sociological inquiry seems unavoidably to require that they treat the rational properties of practical activities as "anthropologically strange." By this I mean to call attention to "reflexive" practices such as the following: that by his accounting practices the member makes familiar, commonplace activities of everyday life recognizable *as* familiar, commonplace activities; that on each occasion that an account of common activities is used, that they be recognized for "another first time"; that the member treat the processes and attainments of "imagination" as continuous with the *other* observable features of the settings in which they occur; and of proceeding in such a way that at the same time that the member

"in the midst" of witnessed actual settings recognizes that witnessed settings have an *accomplished* sense, an accomplished facticity, an accomplished objectivity, an accomplished familiarity,
an accomplished accountability, for the member the organizational
hows of these accomplishments are unproblematic, are known
vaguely, and are known only in the doing which is done skillfully,
reliably, uniformly, with enormous standardization and as an un-
accountable matter.

That accomplishment consists of members doing, recognizing,
and using ethnographies. In unknown ways that accomplishment
is for members a commonplace phenomenon. And in the unknown
ways that the accomplishment is commonplace it is for our interests, an awesome phenomenon, for in its unknown ways it consists
(1) of members' uses of concerted everyday activities as methods
with which to recognize and demonstrate the isolatable, typical,
uniform, potential repetition, connected appearance, consistency,
equivalence, substitutability, directionality, anonymously describ-
able, planful—in short, the rational properties of indexical expressions and indexical actions. (2) The phenomenon consists, too, of
the analyzability of actions-in-context given that not only does no
concept of context-in-general exist, but every use of "context" without exception is itself essentially indexical.

The *recognizedly* rational properties of their common sense inquiries—their recognizedly consistent, or methodic, or uniform, or
planful, etc. character—are *somehow* attainments of members' concerted activities. For Suicide Prevention Center staff, for coders,
for jurors the rational properties of their practical inquiries *somehow* consist in the concerted work of making evident from frag-
ments, from proverbs, from passing remarks, from rumors, from
partial descriptions, from "codified" but essentially vague cata-
logues of experience and the like how a person died in society, or
by what criteria patients were selected for psychiatric treatment,
or which among the alternative verdicts was correct. *Somehow* is
the problematic crux of the matter.

### What is ethnomethodology?

The earmark of practical sociological reasoning, wherever it occurs, is that it seeks to remedy the indexical properties of members'

talk and conduct. Endless methodological studies are directed to the tasks of providing members a remedy for indexical expressions in members' abiding attempts, with rigorous uses of ideals to demonstrate the observability of organized activities in actual occasions with situated particulars of talk and conduct.

The properties of indexical expressions and indexical actions are ordered properties. These consist of organizationally demonstrable sense, or facticity, or methodic use, or agreement among "cultural colleagues." Their ordered properties consist of organizationally demonstrable rational properties of indexical expressions and indexical actions. Those ordered properties are ongoing achievements of the concerted commonplace activities of investigators. The demonstrable rationality of indexical expressions and indexical actions retains over the course of its managed production by members the character of ordinary, familiar, routinized practical circumstances. As process and attainment the produced rationality of indexical expressions consists of practical tasks subject to every exigency of organizationally situated conduct.

I use the term "ethnomethodology" to refer to the investigation of the rational properties of indexical expressions and other practical actions as contingent ongoing accomplishments of organized artful practices of everyday life. The papers of this volume treat that accomplishment as the phenomenon of interest. They seek to specify its problematic features, to recommend methods for its study, but above all to consider what we might learn definitely about it. My purpose in the remainder of this chapter is to characterize ethnomethodology, which I have done by presenting three studies of the work of that accomplishment together with a concluding recitation of study policies.

### PRACTICAL SOCIOLOGICAL REASONING: DOING ACCOUNTS IN "COMMON SENSE SITUATIONS OF CHOICE"

The Los Angeles Suicide Prevention Center (SPC) and the Los Angeles Medical Examiner-Coroner's Office joined forces in 1957 to furnish Coroner's Death Certificates the warrant of scientific authority "within the limits of practical certainties imposed by the state of the art." Selected cases of "sudden, unnatural death" that were equivocal between "suicide" and other modes of death were referred by the Medical Examiner-Coroner to the SPC with the request that an inquiry, called a "psychological autopsy," [5] be done.

The practices and concerns by SPC staff to accomplish their inquiries in common sense situations of choice repeated the features of practical inquiries that were encountered in other situations: studies of jury deliberations in negligence cases; clinic staff in selecting patients for out-patient psychiatric treatment; graduate students in sociology coding the contents of clinic folders into a coding sheet by following detailed coding instructions; and countless professional procedures in the conduct of anthropological, linguistic, social psychiatric, and sociological inquiry. The following features in the work at SPC were recognized by staff with frank acknowledgement as prevailing conditions of their work and as matters to consider when assessing the efficacy, efficiency, or intelligibility of their work—and added SPC testimony to that of jurors, survey researchers, and the rest:

(1) An abiding concern on the part of all parties for the temporal concerting of activities; (2) a concern for the practical question *par excellence*: "What to do next?"; (3) a concern on the inquirer's part to give evidence of his grasp of "What Anyone Knows" about how the settings work in which he had to accomplish his inquiries, and his concern to do so in the actual occasions in which the decisions were to be made by his exhibitable conduct in choosing; (4) matters which at the level of talk might be spoken of as "production programs," "laws of conduct," "rules of rational

---

[5] The following references contain reports on the "psychological autopsy" procedure developed at the Los Angeles Suicide Prevention Center: Theodore J. Curphey, "The Forensic Pathologist and the Multi-Disciplinary Approach to Death," in *Essays in Self-Destruction,* ed. Edwin S. Shneidman (International Science Press, 1967), in press; Theodore J. Curphey, "The Role of the Social Scientist in the Medico-Legal Certification of Death from Suicide," in *The Cry for Help,* ed. Norman L. Farberow and Edwin S. Shneidman (New York: McGraw-Hill Book Company, 1961); Edwin S. Shneidman and Norman L. Farberow, "Sample Investigations of Equivocal Suicidal Deaths," in *The Cry for Help;* Robert E. Litman, Theodore J. Curphey, Edwin S. Shneidman, Norman L. Farberow, and Norman D. Tabachnick, "Investigations of Equivocal Suicides," *Journal of the American Medical Association,* 184 (1963), 924-929; and Edwin S. Shneidman, "Orientations Toward Death: A Vital Aspect of the Study of Lives," in *The Study of Lives,* ed. Robert W. White (New York: Atherton Press, 1963), reprinted in the *International Journal of Psychiatry,* 2 (1966), 167-200.

decision-making," "causes," "conditions," "hypothesis testing," "models," "rules of inductive and deductive inference" in the actual situation were taken for granted and were depended upon to consist of recipes, proverbs, slogans, and partially formulated plans of action; (5) inquirers were required to know and be skilled in dealing with situations "of the sort" for which "rules of rational decision-making" and the rest were intended in order to "see" or by what they did to insure the objective, effective, consistent, completely, empirically adequate, *i.e.*, rational character of recipes, prophecies, proverbs, partial descriptions in an actual occasion of the use of rules; (6) for the practical decider the "actual occasion" as a phenomenon in its own right exercised overwhelming priority of relevance to which "decision rules" or theories of decision-making were without exception subordinated in order to assess their rational features rather than *vice versa*; (7) finally, and perhaps most characteristically, all of the foregoing features, together with an inquirer's "system" of alternatives, his "decision" methods, his information, his choices, and the rationality of his accounts and actions were constituent parts of the same practical circumstances in which inquirers did the work of inquiry—a feature that inquirers if they were to claim and recognize the practicality of their efforts knew of, required, counted on, took for granted, used, and glossed.

The work by SPC members of conducting their inquiries was part and parcel of the day's work. Recognized by staff members as constituent features of the day's work, their inquiries were thereby intimately connected to the terms of employment, to various internal and external chains of reportage, supervision, and review, and to similar organizationally supplied "priorities of relevances" for assessments of what "realistically," "practically," or "reasonably" needed to be done and could be done, how quickly, with what resources, seeing whom, talking about what, for how long, and so on. Such considerations furnished "We did what we could, and for all reasonable interests here is what we came out with" its features of organizationally appropriate sense, fact, impersonality, anonymity of authorship, purpose, reproducibility— *i.e.*, of a *properly* and *visibly* rational account of the inquiry.

Members were required in their occupational capacities to formulate accounts of how a death *really*-for-all-practical-purposes-happened. "Really" made unavoidable reference to daily, ordinary, occupational workings. Members alone were entitled to invoke such workings as appropriate grounds for recommending the reasonable character of the result *without necessity for furnishing specifics*. On occasions of challenge, ordinary occupational workings would be cited explicitly, in "relevant part." Otherwise those features were disengaged from the product. In their place an account of how the inquiry was done made out the how-it-was-actually-done as appropriate to usual demands, usual attainments, usual practices, *and* to usual talk by SPC personnel talking as *bona fide* professional practitioners about usual demands, usual attainments, and usual practices.

One of several titles (relating to mode of death) had to be assigned to each case. The collection consisted of legally possible combinations of four elementary possibilities—natural death, accident, suicide, and homicide.[6] *All* titles were so administered as to not only withstand the varieties of equivocation, ambiguity, and improvisation that arose in every actual occasion of their use, but these titles were so administered as to *invite* that ambiguity, equivocality, and improvisation. It was part of the work not *only* that equivocality is a trouble—is *perhaps* a trouble—but also the practitioners were directed to those circumstances in order to *invite* the ambiguity or the equivocality, to invite the improvisation, or to invite the temporizing, and the rest. It is not that the investigator, having a list of titles performed an inquiry that proceeded stepwise to establish the grounds for electing among them. The formula was not, "Here is what we did, and among the titles as goals of our research *this* title finally interprets in a best fashion what we found out." Instead titles were continually postdicted and foretold. An inquiry was apt to be heavily guided by the inquirer's use of imagined settings in which the title will have been "used" by one or another interested party, including the deceased, and this was done by the inquirers in order to decide, using whatever "datum" might have been searched out, that *that* "datum" could be

---

[6] The possible combinations include the following: natural; accident; suicide; homicide; possible accident; possible suicide; possible natural; (between) accident or suicide, undetermined; (between) natural or suicide, undetermined; (between) natural or accident, undetermined; and (among) natural or accident or suicide, undetermined.

used to mask if masking needed to be done, or to equivocate, or gloss, or lead, or exemplify if they were needed. The prevailing feature of an inquiry was that nothing about it remained assured aside from the organized occasions of its uses. Thus a routine inquiry was one that the investigator used particular contingencies to accomplish, and depended upon particular contingencies to recognize and to recommend the practical adequacy of his work. When assessed by a member, *i.e.* viewed with respect to actual practices for making it happen, a routine inquiry is not one that is accomplished by rule, or according to rules. It seemed much more to consist of an inquiry that is openly recognized to have fallen short, but in the same ways it falls short its adequacy is acknowledged and for which no one is offering or calling particularly for explanations.

What members are *doing* in their inquiries is always somebody else's business in the sense that particular, organizationally located, locatable persons acquire an interest in light of the SPC member's account of whatever it is that will have been reported to have "really happened." Such considerations contributed heavily to the perceived feature of investigations that they were directed in their course by an account for which the claim will have been advanced that for all practical purposes it is correct. Thus over the path of his inquiry the investigator's task consisted of an account of how a particular person died in society that is adequately told, sufficiently detailed, clear, etc., for all practical purposes.

"What really happened," over the course of arriving at it, as well as after the "what really happened" has been inserted into the file and the title has been decided, may be chronically reviewed as well as chronically foretold in light of what might have been done, or what will have been·done with those decisions. It is hardly news that on the way to a decision what a decision will have come to was reviewed and foretold in light of the anticipated consequences of a decision. *After* a recommendation had been made and the coroner had signed the death certificate the result can yet be, as they say, "revised." It can still be made a decision which needs to be reviewed "once more."

Inquirers wanted very much to be able to assure that they could come out at the end with an account of how the person died that would permit the coroner and his staff to withstand claims arguing that that account was incomplete or that the death happened differently than—or in contrast to or in contradiction of—what the members to the arrangement "claimed." The reference is neither only nor entirely to the complaints of the survivors. Those issues are dealt with as a succession of episodes, most being settled fairly quickly. The great contingencies consisted of enduring processes that lay in the fact that the coroner's office is a political office. The coroner's office activities produce continuing records of his office's activities. These records are subject to review as the products of the scientific work of the coroner, his staff, and his consultant. Office activities are methods for accomplishing reports that are scientific-for-all-practical-purposes. This involved "writing" as a warranting procedure in that a report, by reason of being written, is put into a file. That the investigator "does" a report is thereby made a matter for public record for the use of only partially identifiable other persons. Their interests in why or how or what the inquirer did would have in some relevant part to do with his skill and entitlement as a professional. But investigators know too that other interests will inform the "review," for the inquirer's work will be scrutinized to see its scientific-adequacy-for-all-practical-purposes as professionals' socially managed claims. Not only for investigators, but on all sides there is the relevance of "What was really found out for-all-practical-purposes?" which consists unavoidably of how much can you find out, how much can you disclose, how much can you gloss, how much can you conceal, how much can you hold as none of the business of some important persons, *investigators* included. All of them acquired an interest by reason of the fact that investigators, as a matter of occupational duty, were coming up with written reports of how, for-all-practical-purposes persons-really-died-and-are-really-dead-*in*-the-society.

Decisions had an unavoidable consequentiality. By this is meant that investigators needed to say *in so many words,* "What really happened?" The important words were the titles that were assigned to a text to recover that text as the title's "explication." But what an assigned title consists of as an "explicated" title is at any particular time for no one to say with any finality even when it is proposed "in so many words." In fact, *that* it is proposed "in so many words," *that* for example a written text was inserted "into the file of the case," furnishes entitling grounds that can be invoked in order to make something of the "so many words" that will have been used as an account of the death. Viewed with respect to patterns of use, titles and their accompanying texts have an open set of consequences. Upon any occasion of the use of texts it can remain to be seen what can be done with them, or what they will have come to, or what remains done "for the time being" pending the ways in which the environment of that decision may organize itself to "reopen the case," or "issue a complaint," or "find an issue" and so on. Such ways for SPC'ers are, as patterns, certain; but as particular processes for making them happen are in every actual occasion indefinite.

SPC inquiries begin with a death that the coroner finds equivocal as to *mode* of death. That death they use as a precedent with which various ways of living in society that could have terminated with that death are searched out and read "in the remains"; in the scraps of this and that like the body and its trappings, medicine bottles, notes, bits and pieces of clothing, and other memorabilia—stuff that can be photographed, collected, and packaged. Other "remains" are collected too: rumors, passing remarks, and stories—materials in the "repertoires" of whosoever might be consulted via the common work of conversations. These *whatsoever* bits and pieces that a story or a rule or a proverb might make intelligible are used to formulate a recognizably coherent, standard, typical, cogent, uniform, planful, *i.e.*, a professionally defensible, and thereby, for members, a *recognizably* rational account of how the society worked to produce those remains. This point will be easier to make if the reader will consult any standard textbook in forensic pathology. In it he will find the inevitable photograph of a victim with a slashed throat. Were the coroner to use that "sight" to recommend the equivocality of the mode of death he might say something like this: "In the case where a body looks like the one in that picture, you are looking at a suicidal death because the wound shows the 'hesitation cuts' that accompany the great wound. One can imagine these cuts are the remains of a procedure whereby the victim first made several preliminary trials of a hesitating sort and then performed the lethal slash. Other courses of action are imaginable, too, and so cuts that look like hesitation cuts can be produced by other mechanisms. One needs to start with the actual display and imagine how different courses of actions could have been organized such that *that* picture would be compatible with it. One might think of the photographed display as a phase-of-the-action. In any actual display is there a course of action with which that phase is uniquely compatible? *That* is the coroner's question."

The coroner (and SPC'ers) ask this with respect to each *particular* case, and thereby their work of achieving practical decidability seems almost unavoidably to display the following prevailing and important characteristic. SPC'ers must accomplish that decidability with respect to the "this's": they have to start with *this* much; *this* sight; *this* note; *this* collection of whatever is at hand. And *whatever* is there is good enough in the sense that *whatever* is there not only *will* do, but *does*. One makes whatever is there *do*. I do not mean by "making do" that an SPC investigator is too easily content, or that he does not look for more when he should. Instead, I mean: the *whatever* it is that he has to deal with, *that* is what will have been used to have found out, to have made decidable, the way in which the society operated to have produced *that* picture, to have come to *that* scene as its end result. In this way the remains on the slab serve not only as a precedent but as a goal of SPC inquiries. *Whatsoever* SPC members are faced with must serve as the precedent with which to read the remains so as to see how the society could have operated to have produced what it is that the inquirer has "in the end," "in the final analysis," and "in *any* case." What the inquiry can come to is what the death came to.

### PRACTICAL SOCIOLOGICAL REASONING: FOLLOWING CODING INSTRUCTIONS

Several years ago my co-workers and I undertook to analyze the experience of the U.C.L.A. Outpatient Clinic in order to answer the questions "By what criteria are its applicants selected for treatment?" To formulate and to answer this question we used a version of a method of cohort analysis that Kramer and his associates [7] had used to describe load and flow characteristics of patients in mental hospitals. (Chapters Six and Seven report further aspects of this re-

[7] M. Kramer, H. Goldstein, R. H. Israel, and N. A. Johnson, "Applications of Life Table Methodology to the Study of Mental Hospital Populations," *Psychiatric Research Reports of the American Psychiatric Association,* June, 1956, pp. 49-76.

search.) Successive activities of "first contact," "intake interview," "psychological testing," "intake conference," "in-treatment," and "termination" were conceived with the use of the tree diagram of Figure 1. Any path from first contact to termination was called a "career."

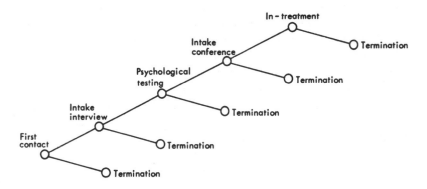

**FIGURE 1.** Career paths of patients of a psychiatric clinic

We wished to know what characteristics of patients, of clinical personnel, of their interactions, and of the tree were associated with which careers. Clinic records were our sources of information, the most important of which were intake application forms and case folder contents. In order to obtain a continuing record of patient-clinic case transactions from the time of a patient's initial contact until he terminated a "Clinic Career Form" was designed and inserted into case folders. Because clinic folders contain records that clinic personnel provide of their own activities, almost all of these sources of data were the results of self-reporting procedures.

Two graduate students in Sociology at UCLA examined 1,582 clinic folders for the information to complete the items of a Coding Sheet. A conventional reliability procedure was designed and conducted with the aim of determining the amount of agreement between coders and between successive trials of their coding. According to conventional reasoning, the amount of agreement furnishes one set of grounds for lending credence to coded events as actual clinic events. A critical feature of conventional reliability assessments is that the agreement between coders consists of agreement on the end results.

To no one's surprise, preliminary work showed that in order to accomplish the coding, coders were assuming knowledge of the very organized ways of the clinic that their coding procedures were intended to produce descriptions of. More interestingly, such presupposed knowledge seemed necessary and was most deliberately consulted whenever, for whatever reasons, the coders needed to be satisfied that they had coded "what really happened." *This was so regardless of whether or not they had encountered "ambiguous" folder contents.* Such a procedure undermined any claim that actuarial methods for interrogating the folder contents had been used, no matter how apparently clear the coding instructions were. Agreement in coding results was being produced by a contrasting procedure with unknown characteristics.

To find out more about the procedure that our students used, the reliability procedure was treated as a problematic activity in its own right. The "reliability" of coded results was addressed by asking how the coders had actually brought folder contents under the jurisdiction of the Coding Sheet's item. Via what practices had actual folder contents been assigned the status of answers to the researcher's questions? What actual activities made up those coders' practices called "following coding instruction"?

A procedure was designed that yielded conventional reliability information so that the original interests of the study were preserved. At the same time the procedure permitted the study of how any amount of agreement or disagreement had been produced by the actual ways that the two coders had gone about treating folder contents as answers to the questions formulated by the Coding Sheet. But, instead of assuming that coders, proceeding in whatever ways they did, might have been in error, in greater or lesser amount, the assumption was made that *whatever* they did could be counted correct procedure in *some* coding "game." The question was, what were these "games"? How *ever* coders did it, it was sufficient to produce whatever they got. How did they do it to get what they got?

We soon found the essential relevance to the coders, in their work of interrogating folder contents for answers to their questions, of such considerations as "et cetera," "unless," "let it pass," and "factum valet" (*i.e.*, an action that is otherwise prohibited by a rule is counted correct once it is done). For convenience let me call these "*ad hoc*" considerations, and call their practice "*ad hocing.*" Coders used the same *ad hoc* considerations in order to recognize the relevance of the coding instructions to the organized activities of the clinic. Only when this relevance was clear were the coders satisfied that the coding instructions analyzed actually encountered folder contents so as to permit the coders to treat folder contents as reports of "real events." Finally, *ad hoc* considerations were invariant features of the practices of "following coding instructions." Attempts to suppress them while retaining an unequivocal sense to the instructions produced bewilderment on their part.

Various facets of the "new" reliability study were then developed, at first in order to see if these results could be firmly established, and after it was clear, to my satisfaction, that they could, to exploit their consequences for the general sociological character of the coders' methods of interrogation (as well as contrasting methods) as well as for the work that is involved in recognizing or claiming that something had been done by rule—that an action had followed or had been "governed" by instructions.

*Ad hoc* considerations are invariably relevant considerations in deciding the fit between what could be read from the clinic folders and what the coder inserted into the coding sheet. No matter how definitely and elaborately instructions had been written, and despite the fact that strict actuarial coding rules [8] *could* be formulated for every item, and with which folder contents *could* be mapped into the coding sheet, insofar as the claim had to be advanced that Coding Sheet entries reported real events of the clinic's activities, then in every instance, and for every item, "et cetera," "unless," "let it pass" and "factum valet" accompanied the coder's grasp of the coding instructions as ways of analyzing actual folder contents. Their use made it possible, as well, for the coder to read a folder's contents as a report about the events that the Coding Sheet provided and formulated as events of the processing tree.

Ordinarily researchers treat such *ad hoc* procedures as flawed

[8] David Harrah's model of an information-matching game was taken to define the meaning of "strict actuarial method for interrogating." See David Harrah, "A Logic of Questions and Answers," *Philosophy of Science*, 28, No. 1 (January, 1961), 40-46.

ways of writing, recognizing, or following coding instructions. The prevailing view holds that good work requires researchers, by extending the number and explicitness of their coding rules, to minimize or even eliminate the occasions in which "et cetera" and other such *ad hocing* practices would be used.

To treat instructions as though *ad hoc* features in their use were a nuisance, or to treat their presence as grounds for complaint about the incompleteness of instructions, is very much like complaining that if the walls of a building were only gotten out of the way one could see better what was keeping the roof up. Our studies showed that *ad hoc* considerations are essential features of coding procedures. *Ad hocing* is required if the researcher is to grasp the relevance of the instructions to the particular and actual situation they are intended to analyze. For every particular and actual occasion of search, detection, and assignment of folder contents to a "proper" category—which is to say, over the course of actually coding—such *ad hoc* considerations have irremediable priority over the usually talked about "necessary and sufficient" criteria. It is not the case that the "necessary and sufficient" criteria are procedurally defined by coding instructions. Nor is it the case that *ad hoc* practices such as "et cetera" or "let it pass" are controlled or eliminated in their presence, use, number, or occasions of use by making coding instructions as definite as possible. Instead *ad hoc* considerations are consulted by coders and *ad hocing* practices are *used in order to recognize what the instructions are definitely talking about*. *Ad hoc* considerations are consulted by coders in order to recognize coding instructions as "operational definitions" of coding categories. They operate as the grounds for and as methods to advance and secure researchers' claims to have coded in accordance with "necessary and sufficient" criteria.

*Ad hocing* occurs (without, I believe, any possibility of remedy), whenever the coder assumes the position of a socially competent member of the arrangement that he seeks to assemble an account of and, when from this "position," he treats actual folder contents as standing in a relationship of trusted signification to the "system" in the clinic activities. Because the coder assumes the "position" of a competent member to the arrangements that he seeks to give an account of, he can "see the system" in the actual content of the folder. This he accomplishes in something like the way that one must know the orderly ways of English usage in order to recognize an utterance as a word-in-English or know the rules of a game to make out a move-in-a-game, given that alternative ways of making out an utterance or a board play are always imaginable. Thereby, the coder recognizes the folder content for "what it actually is," or can "see what a note in the folder 'is really talking about.' "

Given this, if the coder has to be satisfied that he has detected a real clinic occurrence, he must treat actual folder contents as standing proxy for the social-order-in-and-of-clinic-activities. Actual folder contents stand to the socially ordered ways of clinic activities as *representations* of them; they do not describe the order, nor are they evidences of the order. It is the coder's use of folder documents as *sign-functions* to which I mean to be pointing in saying that the coder must know the order of the clinic's activities that he is looking at in order to recognize the actual content as an appearance-of-the-order. Once the coder can "see the system" in the content, it is possible for the coder to extend and to otherwise interpret the coding instructions—to *ad hoc* them—so as to maintain the relevance of the coding instructions to the actual contents, and in this way to formulate the sense of actual content so that its meaning, even though it is transformed by the coding, is preserved in the coder's eyes as a real event of the clinic's actual activities.

There are several important consequences:

(1) Characteristically, coded results would be treated as if they were disinterested descriptions of clinic events, and coding rules are presumed to back up the claim of disinterested description. But if the work of *ad hocing* is required to make such claims intelligible, it can always be argued—and so far I do not see a defensible reply—that the coded results consist of a persuasive version of the socially organized character of the clinic's operations, regardless of what the actual order is, perhaps independently of what the actual order is, and even without the investigator having detected the actual order. Instead of our study of patients' clinic careers (as well as the multitude of studies of various social arrangements that have been carried out in similarly conventional ways) having described the order of the clinic's operations, the account may be argued to consist of a socially invented, persuasive, and proper way of talking about the clinic as an orderly enterprise, since "after all" the account was produced by "scientific procedures." The account

would be itself part of the actual order of the clinic's operations, in much the same way that one might treat a person's report on his own activities as a feature of his activities. *The actual order would remain to be described.*

(2) Another consequence arises when we ask what is to be made of the care that nevertheless is so assiduously exercised in the design and use of coding instructions for interrogating actual contents and transforming them into the language of the coding sheet? If the resulting account is itself a feature of the clinic's activities, then perhaps one ought not read the coding instructions as a way of obtaining a scientific description of the clinic's activities, since this assumes that the coding language, in what it is talking *about*, is independent of the interests of the members that are being served in using it. Coding instructions ought to be read instead as consisting of a grammar of rhetoric; they furnish a "social science" way of talking so as to persuade consensus and action within the practical circumstances of the clinic's organized daily activities, a grasp of which members are expected to have as a matter of course. By referring to an account of the clinic that was obtained by following coding instructions, it is possible for members with different interests to persuade each other and to reconcile their talk about clinic affairs in an impersonal way, while the matters that are really being talked *about* retain their sense, for the "discussants," as a legitimate, or illegitimate, a desirable or undesirable, an advantaged or disadvantaged state of affairs for the "discussants" in their occupational lives. It furnishes an impersonal way of characterizing their affairs without the members relinquishing important organizationally determined interests in what the account, in their eyes, is "after all" all about. What it is all about is the clinic order whose real features, as any member knows that Anyone Knows, are always none of somebody-else-in-that-organization's business.

### PRACTICAL SOCIOLOGICAL REASONING: COMMON UNDERSTANDING

Sociologists distinguish the "product" from the "process" meanings of a common understanding. As "product," a common understanding is thought to consist of a shared agreement on substantive matters; as "process," it consists of various methods whereby something that a person says or does is recognized to accord with a rule. With his concepts of *Begreifen* and *Verstehen*, each with its distinct character as method and knowledge, Weber provided sociologists an authority for this distinction.

An analysis of students' experiences in reporting commonplace conversation suggests that for either case, for "product" or process," a common understanding consists of an inner-temporal course of interpretive work. Their experiences suggest some strange consequences of the facts that *in either case* a common understanding has necessarily an operational structure.

In Chapter Two research is reported in which students were asked to report common conversations by writing on the left side of a sheet what the parties actually said, and on the right side what they and their partners understood they were talking about. The following colloquy is reported there:

| | |
|---|---|
| HUSBAND: Dana succeeded in putting a penny in a parking meter today without being picked up. | This afternoon as I was bringing Dana, our four-year-old son, home from the nursery school, he succeeded in reaching high enough to put a penny in a parking meter when we parked in a meter zone, whereas before he had always had to be picked up to reach that high. |
| WIFE: Did you take him to the record store? | Since he put a penny in a meter that means that you stopped while he was with you. I know that you stopped at the record store either on the way to get him or on the way back. Was it on the way back, so that he was with you or did you stop there on the way to get him and somewhere else on the way back? |
| HUSBAND: No, to the shoe repair shop. | No, I stopped at the record store on the way to get him and stopped at the shoe repair shop on the way home when he was with me. |

| | |
|---|---|
| WIFE:    What for? | I know of one reason why you might have stopped at the shoe repair shop. Why did you in fact? |
| HUSBAND: I got some new shoe laces for my shoes. | As you will remember I broke a shoe lace on one of my brown oxfords the other day so I stopped to get some new laces. |
| WIFE:    Your loafers need new heels badly. | Something else you could have gotten that I was thinking of. You could have taken in your black loafers which need heels badly. You'd better get them taken care of pretty soon. |

Students filled out the left side of the sheet quickly and easily, but found the right side incomparably more difficult. When the assignment was made, many asked how much I wanted them to write. As I progressively imposed accuracy, clarity, and distinctness, the task became increasingly laborious. Finally, when I required that they assume I would know what they had actually talked about only from reading literally what they wrote literally, they gave up with the complaint that the task was impossible.

Although their complaints were concerned with the laboriousness of having to write "more," the frustrating "more" was not made up of the large labor of having to reduce a mountain with buckets. It was not their complaint that what was talked about consisted of bounded contents made so vast by pedantry that they lacked sufficient time, stamina, paper, drive, or good reason to write "all of it." Instead, the complaint and its circumstances seemed to consist of this: *if*, for whatever a student wrote, I was able to persuade him that it was not yet accurate, distinct, or clear enough, and *if* he remained willing to repair the ambiguity, then he returned to the task with the complaint that the writing itself developed the conversation as a branching texture of relevant matters. The very *way* of accomplishing the task multiplied its features.

What task had I set them such that it required that they write "more"; such that the progressive imposition of accuracy, clarity, and literalness made it increasingly difficult and finally impossible;

and such that the way of accomplishing the task multiplied its features? If a common understanding consisted of shared agreement on substantive matters, their task would have been identical with one that professional sociologists supposedly address. The task would have been solved as professional sociologists are apt to propose its solution, as follows:

Students would first distinguish *what* was said from *what* was talked about, and set the two contents into a correspondence of sign and referent. *What the parties said* would be treated as a sketchy, partial, incomplete, masked, elliptical, concealed, ambiguous, or misleading version of *what the parties talked about*. The task would consist of filling out the sketchiness of what was said. What was talked about would consist of elaborated and corresponding contents of what the parties said. Thus the format of left and right hand columns would accord with the "fact" that the contents of what was said were recordable by writing what a tape recorder would pick up. The right hand column would require that something "more" be "added." Because the sketchiness of what was said was its defect, it would be necessary for students to look elsewhere than to what was said in order (a) to find the corresponding contents, and (b) to find the grounds to argue—because they would need to argue—for the correctness of the correspondence. Because they were reporting the actual conversation of particular persons, they would look for these further contents in what the conversationalists had "in mind," or what they were "thinking," or what they "believed," or what they "intended." Furthermore, they would need to be assured that they had detected what the conversationalists actually, and not supposedly, hypothetically, imaginably, or possibly had in mind. That is to say, they would need to cite observed actions—observed ways that the parties conducted themselves—in order to furnish grounds for the claim of "actually." This assurance would be obtained by seeking to establish the presence, in the conversationalists' relationship, of warranting virtues such as their having spoken honestly, openly, candidly, sincerely, and the like. All of which is to say that students would invoke their knowledge of the community of understandings, and their knowledge of shared agreements to recommend the adequacy of their accounts of what the parties had been talking about, *i.e.*, what the parties understood in common. Then, for anything the

students wrote, they could assume that I, as a competent co-
member of the same community (the conversations were after all
commonplace) should be able to see the correspondence and its
grounds. If I did not see the correspondence or if I made out the
contents differently than they did, then as long as they could continue to assume my competence—*i.e.*, as long as my alternative
interpretations did not undermine my right to claim that such alternatives needed to be taken seriously by them and by me—I could
be made out by the students as insisting that they furnish me with
finer detailing than practical considerations required. In such a
case, they should have charged me with blind pedantry and should
have complained that because "anyone can see" when, for all practical purposes, enough is enough, none are so blind as those who
*will* not see.

This version of their task accounts for their complaints of having
to write "more." It also accounts for the task's increasing laboriousness when clarity and the like were progressively imposed. But it
does not account very well for the final impossibility, for it explains
one facet of the task's "impossibility" as students' unwillingness to
go any further, but it does not explain an accompanying sense,
namely, that students somehow saw that the task was, in principle,
unaccomplishable. Finally, this version of their task does not explain at all their complaint that the way of accomplishing the task
multiplied its features.

An alternative conception of the task may do better. Although
it may at first appear strange to do so, suppose we drop the assumption that in order to describe a usage as a feature of a community
of understandings we must at the outset know what the substantive
common understandings consist of. With it, drop the assumption's
accompanying theory of signs, according to which a "sign" and "referent" are respectively properties of something said and something talked about, and which in this fashion proposes sign and
referent to be related as corresponding contents. By dropping such
a theory of signs we drop as well, thereby, the possibility that an
invoked shared agreement on substantive matters explains a usage.

If these notions are dropped, then what the parties talked about
could not be distinguished from *how* the parties were speaking. An
explanation of what the parties were talking about would then consist entirely of describing how the parties had been speaking; of

furnishing a method for saying whatever is to be said, like talking synonymously, talking ironically, talking metaphorically, talking cryptically, talking narratively, talking in a questioning or answering way, lying, glossing, double-talking, and the rest.

In the place of and in contrast to a concern for a difference between *what* was said and *what* was talked about, the appropriate difference is between a language-community member's recognition that a person is saying something, *i.e.*, that he was *speaking*, on the one hand, and *how* he was speaking on the other. Then the recognized sense of what a person said consists only and entirely in recognizing the method of his speaking, of *seeing how he spoke*.

I suggest that one not read the right hand column as corresponding contents of the left, and that the students' task of explaining what the conversationalists talked about did not involve them in elaborating the contents of what the conversationalists said. I suggest, instead, that their written explanations consisted of their attempts to instruct me in how to use what the parties said as a method for seeing what the conversationalists said. I suggest that I had asked the students to furnish me with instructions for recognizing what the parties were actually and certainly saying. By persuading them of alternative "interpretations," by insisting that ambiguity still remained, I had persuaded them that they had demonstrated to me only what the parties were supposedly, or probably, or imaginably, or hypothetically saying. *They took this to mean that their instructions were incomplete; that their demonstrations failed by the extent to which their instructions were incomplete; and that the difference between claims of "actually" and "supposedly" depended on the completeness of the instructions.*

We now see what the task was that required them to write "more," that they found increasingly difficult and finally impossible, and that became elaborated in its features by the very procedures for doing it. I had set them the task of formulating these instructions so as to make them "increasingly" accurate, clear, distinct, and finally literal where the meanings of "increasingly" and of clarity, accuracy, distinctness, and literalness were supposedly explained in terms of the properties of the instructions themselves and the instructions alone. I had required them to take on the impossible task of "repairing" the essential incompleteness of *any* set of instructions no matter how carefully or elaborately written they might be. I had required them to formulate the method that the parties had used in speaking as rules of procedure to follow in order to say what the parties said, rules that would withstand every exigency of situation, imagination, and development. I had asked them to describe the parties' methods of speaking as if these methods were isomorphic with actions in strict compliance with a rule of procedure that formulated the method as an instructable matter. To recognize *what* is said *means* to recognize how a person is speaking, *e.g.*, to recognize that the wife in saying "your shoes need heels badly" was speaking narratively, or metaphorically, or euphemistically, or double-talking.

They stumbled over the fact that the question of how a person is speaking, the task of describing a person's method of speaking, is not satisfied by, and is not the same as showing that what he said accords with a rule for demonstrating consistency, compatibility, and coherence of meanings.

For the conduct of their everyday affairs, persons take for granted that what is said will be made out according to methods that the parties use to make out what they are saying for its clear, consistent, coherent, understandable, or planful character, *i.e.*, as subject to some rule's jurisdiction—in a word, as rational. To see the "sense" of what is said is to accord to what was said its character "as a rule." *"Shared agreement" refers to various social methods for accomplishing the member's recognition that something was said-according-to-a-rule and not the demonstrable matching of substantive matters. The appropriate image of a common understanding is therefore an operation rather than a common intersection of overlapping sets.*

A person doing sociology, be it lay or professional sociology, can treat a common understanding as a shared agreement on substantive matters by taking for granted that what is said will be made out in accordance with methods that need not be specified, which is to say that need only be specified on "special" occasions.

Given the discovering character of what the husband and wife were talking about, its recognizable character for both entailed the use by each and the attribution by each to the other of work whereby what was said is or will have been understood to have accorded with their relationship of interaction as an invokable rule of their agreement, as an intersubjectively used grammatical scheme for analyzing each other's talk whose use provided that they *would* understand each other in ways that they *would* be understood. It provides that neither one was entitled to call upon the other to specify how it was being done; neither one was entitled to claim that the other needed to "explain" himself.

In short, a common understanding, entailing as it does an "inner" temporal course of interpretive work, necessarily has an operational structure. For the analyst to disregard its operational structure, is to use common sense knowledge of the society in exactly the ways that members use it when they must decide what persons are really doing or really "talking about," *i.e.*, to use common sense knowledge of social structures as *both* a topic and a resource of inquiry. An alternative would be to assign exclusive priority to the study of the methods of concerted actions and methods of common understanding. Not *a* method of understanding, but immensely various methods of understanding are the professional sociologist's proper and hitherto unstudied and critical phenomena. Their multitude is indicated in the endless list of ways that persons speak. Some indication of their character and their differences occurs in the socially available glosses of a multitude of sign functions as when we take note of marking, labeling, symbolizing, emblemizing, cryptograms, analogies, anagrams, indicating, miniaturizing, imitating, mocking-up, simulating—in short, in recognizing, using, and producing the orderly ways of cultural settings from "within" those settings.[9]

### Policies

That practical actions are problematic in ways not so far seen; how they are problematical; how to make them accessible to study; what we might learn about them—these are proposed tasks. I use the term "ethnomethodology" to refer to the study of practical actions according to policies such as the following, and to the

[9] This note was touched off by Monroe Beardsley's remark in "The Metaphorical Twist," *Philosophy and Phenomenological Research*, March, 1962, to the effect that we do not decide that a word is used metaphorically because we know what a person is thinking; rather we know what he is thinking because we see that a word is used metaphorically. Taking poetry for his case, Beardsley points out that "the clues of this fact must somehow be in the poem itself, or we should seldom be able to read poetry."

phenomena, issues, findings, and methods that accompany their use.

(1) An indefinitely large domain of appropriate settings can be located if one uses a search policy that *any occasion whatsoever* be examined for the feature that "choice" among alternatives of sense, of facticity, of objectivity, of cause, of explanation, of communality *of practical actions* is a project of members' actions. Such a policy provides that inquiries of every imaginable kind, from divination to theoretical physics, claim our interest as socially organized artful practices. That the social structures of everyday activities furnish contexts, objects, resources, justifications, problematic topics, etc. to practices and products of inquiries establishes the eligibility for our interest of every way of doing inquiries without exception.

No inquiries can be excluded no matter where or when they occur, no matter how vast or trivial their scope, organization, cost, duration, consequences, whatever their successes, whatever their repute, their practitioners, their claims, their philosophies or philosophers. Procedures and results of water witching, divination, mathematics, sociology—whether done by lay persons or professionals—are addressed according to the policy that every feature of sense, of fact, of method, for every particular case of inquiry without exception, is the managed accomplishment of organized settings of practical actions, and that particular determinations in members' practices of consistency, planfulness, relevance, or reproducibility of their practices and results—from witchcraft to topology—are acquired and assured only through particular, located organizations of artful practices.

(2) Members to an organized arrangement are continually engaged in having to decide, recognize, persuade, or make evident the rational, *i.e.*, the coherent, or consistent, or chosen, or planful, or effective, or methodical, or knowledgeable character of such activities of their inquiries as counting, graphing, interrogation, sampling, recording, reporting, planning, decision-making, and the rest. It is not satisfactory to describe how actual investigative procedures, as constituent features of members' ordinary and organized affairs, are accomplished by members as recognizedly rational actions *in actual occasions* of organizational circumstances by saying that members invoke some rule with which to define the

coherent or consistent or planful, *i.e.*, rational, character of their actual activities. Nor is it satisfactory to propose that the rational properties of members' inquiries are produced by members' compliance to rules of inquiry. Instead, "adequate demonstration," "adequate reporting," "sufficient evidence," "plain talk," "making too much of the record," "necessary inference," "frame of restricted alternatives," in short, every topic of "logic" and "methodology," including these two titles as well, are glosses for organizational phenomena. These phenomena are contingent achievements of organizations of common practices, and as contingent achievements they are variously available to members as norms, tasks, troubles. Only in these ways rather than as invariant categories or as general principles do they define "adequate inquiry and discourse."

(3) Thus, a leading policy is to refuse serious consideration to the prevailing proposal that efficiency, efficacy, effectiveness, intelligibility, consistency, planfulness, typicality, uniformity, reproducibility of activities—*i.e.*, that rational properties of practical activities—be assessed, recognized, categorized, described by using a rule or a standard obtained outside actual settings within which such properties are recognized, used, produced, and talked about by settings' members. All procedures whereby logical and methodological properties of the practices and results of inquiries are assessed in their general characteristics by rule are of interest as *phenomena* for ethnomethodological study but not otherwise. Structurally differing organized practical activities of everyday life are to be sought out and examined for the production, origins, recognition, and representations of rational practices. All "logical" and "methodological" properties of action, every feature of an activity's sense, facticity, objectivity, accountability, communality is to be treated as a contingent accomplishment of socially organized common practices.

(4) The policy is recommended that any social setting be viewed as self-organizing with respect to the intelligible character of its own appearances as either representations of or as evidences-of-a-social-order. Any setting organizes its activities to make its properties as an organized environment of practical activities detectable, countable, recordable, reportable, tell-a-story-aboutable, analyzable—in short, *accountable*.

Organized social arrangements consist of various methods for accomplishing the accountability of a settings' organizational ways as a concerted undertaking. Every claim by practitioners of effectiveness, clarity, consistency, planfulness, or efficiency, and every consideration for adequate evidence, demonstration, description, or relevance obtains its character as a *phenomenon* from the corporate pursuit of this undertaking and from the ways in which various organizational environments, by reason of their characteristics as organizations of activities, "sustain," "facilitate," "resist," etc. these methods for making their affairs accountable-matters-for-all-practical-purposes.

In exactly the ways that a setting is organized, it *consists* of members' methods for making evident that settings' ways as clear, coherent, planful, consistent, chosen, knowable, uniform, reproducible connections,—*i.e.*, rational connections. In exactly the way that persons are members to organized affairs, they are engaged in serious and practical work of detecting, demonstrating, persuading through displays in the ordinary occasions of their interactions the appearances of consistent, coherent, clear, chosen, planful arrangements. In exactly the ways in which a setting is organized, it *consists* of methods whereby its members are provided with accounts of the setting as countable, storyable, proverbial, comparable, picturable, representable—*i.e.*, accountable events.

(5) Every kind of inquiry without exception consists of organized artful practices whereby the rational properties of proverbs, partially formulated advice, partial description, elliptical expressions, passing remarks, fables, cautionary tales, and the like are made evident, are demonstrated.

The demonstrably rational properties of indexical expressions and indexical actions is an ongoing achievement of the organized activities of everyday life. Here is the heart of the matter. The managed production of this phenomenon in every aspect, from every perspective, and in every stage retains the character for members of serious, practical tasks, subject to every exigency of organizationally situated conduct. Each of the papers in this volume, in one way or another, recommends that phenomenon for professional sociological analysis.

# TWO

# Studies of the routine grounds of everyday activities

### The problem

For Kant the moral order "within" was an awesome mystery; for sociologists the moral order "without" is a technical mystery. From the point of view of sociological theory the moral order consists of the rule governed activities of everyday life. A society's members encounter and know the moral order as perceivedly normal courses of action—familiar scenes of everyday affairs, the world of daily life known in common with others and with others taken for granted.

They refer to this world as the "natural facts of life" which, for members, are through and through moral facts of life. For members not only are matters so about familiar scenes, but they are so because it is morally right or wrong that they are so. Familiar scenes of everyday activities, treated by members as the "natural facts of life," are massive facts of the members' daily existence both as a real world and as the product of activities in a real world. They furnish the "fix," the "this is it" to which the waking state returns one, and are the points of departure and return for every modification of the world of daily life that is achieved in play, dreaming, trance, theater, scientific theorizing, or high ceremony.

In every discipline, humanistic or scientific, the familiar common sense world of everyday life is a matter of abiding interest. In the social sciences, and in sociology particularly, it is a matter of essential preoccupation. It makes up sociology's problematic subject matter, enters the very constitution of the sociological attitude, and exercises an odd and obstinate sovereignty over sociologists' claims to adequate explanation.

Despite the topic's centrality, an immense literature contains little data and few methods with which the essential features of socially recognized "familiar scenes" may be detected and related to dimensions of social organization. Although sociologists take socially structured scenes of everyday life as a point of departure they rarely see,[1] as a task of sociological inquiry in its own right, the general question of how any such common sense world is possible. Instead, the possibility of the everyday world is either settled by theoretical representation or merely assumed. As a topic and methodological ground for sociological inquiries, the definition of the common sense world of everyday life, though it is appropriately a project of sociological inquiry, has been neglected. My purposes in this paper are to demonstrate the essential relevance, to sociological inquiries, of a concern for common sense activities as a topic of inquiry in its own right and, by reporting a series of studies, to urge its "rediscovery."

### Making commonplace scenes visible

In accounting for the stable features of everyday activities sociologists commonly select familiar settings such as familial households or work places and ask for the variables that contribute to their stable features. Just as commonly, one set of considerations are unexamined: the socially standardized and standardizing, "seen but unnoticed," expected, background features of everyday scenes. The member of the society uses background expectancies as a scheme of interpretation. With their use actual appearances are for him recognizable and intelligible as the appearances-of-familiar-events. Demonstrably he is responsive to this background,

---

[1] The work of Alfred Schutz, cited in footnote 2, is a magnificent exception. Readers who are acquainted with his writings will recognize how heavily this paper is indebted to him.

while at the same time he is at a loss to tell us specifically of what the expectancies consist. When we ask him about them he has little or nothing to say.

For these background expectancies to come into view one must either be a stranger to the "life as usual" character of everyday scenes, or become estranged from them. As Alfred Schutz pointed out, a "special motive" is required to make them problematic. In the sociologists' case this "special motive" consists in the programmatic task of treating a societal member's practical circumstances, which include from the member's point of view the morally necessary character of many of its background features, as matters of theoretic interest. The seen but unnoticed backgrounds of everyday activities are made visible and are described from a perspective in which persons live out the lives they do, have the children they do, feel the feelings, think the thoughts, enter the relationships they do, all in order to permit the sociologist to solve his theoretical problems.

Almost alone among sociological theorists, the late Alfred Schutz, in a series of classical studies [2] of the constitutive phenomenology of the world of everyday life, described many of these seen but unnoticed background expectancies. He called them the "attitude of daily life." He referred to their scenic attributions as the "world known in common and taken for granted." Schutz' fundamental work makes it possible to pursue further the tasks of clarifying their nature and operation, of relating them to the processes of concerted actions, and assigning them their place in an empirically imaginable society.

The studies reported in this paper attempt to detect some expectancies that lend commonplace scenes their familiar, life-as-usual character, and to relate these to the stable social structures of everyday activities. Procedurally it is my preference to start with familiar scenes and ask what can be done to make trouble. The operations that one would have to perform in order to multiply the senseless features of perceived environments; to produce and

---

[2] Alfred Schutz, *Der Sinnhafte Aufbau Der Sozialen Welt* (Wein: Verlag von Julius Springer, 1932); *Collected Papers I: The Problem of Social Reality*, ed. Maurice Natanson (The Hague: Martinus Nijhoff, 1962); *Collected Papers II: Studies in Social Theory*, ed. Arvid Broderson (The Hague: Martinus Nijhoff, 1964); *Collected Papers III: Studies in Phenomenological Philosophy*, ed. I. Schutz (The Hague: Martinus Nijhoff, 1966).

sustain bewilderment, consternation, and confusion; to produce the socially structured affects of anxiety, shame, guilt, and indignation; and to produce disorganized interaction should tell us something about how the structures of everyday activities are ordinarily and routinely produced and maintained.[3]

A word of reservation. Despite their procedural emphasis, my studies are not properly speaking experimental. They are demonstrations, designed, in Herbert Spiegelberg's phrase, as "aids to a sluggish imagination." I have found that they produce reflections through which the strangeness of an obstinately familiar world can be detected.

## Some essential features of common understandings

Various considerations dictate that common understandings cannot possibly consist of a measured amount of shared agreement among persons on certain topics. Even if the topics are limited in number and scope and every practical difficulty of assessment is forgiven, the notion that we are dealing with an amount of shared agreement remains essentially incorrect. This may be demonstrated as follows.

Students were asked to report common conversations by writing on the left side of a sheet what the parties actually said and on the right side what they and their partners understood that they were talking about. A student reported the following colloquy between himself and his wife.

| HUSBAND: | Dana succeeded in putting a penny in a parking meter today without being picked up. | This afternoon as I was bringing Dana, our four-year-old son, home from the nursery school, he succeeded in reaching high enough to put a penny in a parking meter when we parked in a meter parking zone, whereas before he has always had to be picked up to reach that high. |

---

[3] Obversely, a knowledge of how the structures of everyday activities are routinely produced should permit us to tell how we might proceed for the effective production of desired disturbances.

| WIFE: | Did you take him to the record store? | Since he put a penny in a meter that means that you stopped while he was with you. I know that you stopped at the record store either on the way to get him or on the way back. Was it on the way back, so that he was with you or did you stop there on the way to get him and somewhere else on the way back? |
|---|---|---|
| HUSBAND: | No, to the shoe repair shop. | No, I stopped at the record store on the way to get him and stopped at the shoe repair shop on the way home when he was with me. |
| WIFE: | What for? | I know of one reason why you might have stopped at the shoe repair shop. Why did you in fact? |
| HUSBAND: | I got some new shoe laces for my shoes. | As you will remember I broke a shoe lace on one of my brown oxfords the other day so I stopped to get some new laces. |
| WIFE: | Your loafers need new heels badly. | Something else you could have gotten that I was thinking of. You could have taken in your black loafers which need heels badly. You'd better get them taken care of pretty soon. |

An examination of the colloquy reveals the following. (a) There were many matters that the partners understood they were talking about that they did not mention. (b) Many matters that the partners understood were understood on the basis not only of what was actually said but what was left unspoken. (c) Many matters were understood through a process of attending to the temporal series of utterances as documentary evidences of a developing conversation rather than as a string of terms. (d) Matters that the two understood in common were understood only in and through a course of understanding work that consisted of treating an actual linguistic event as "the document of," as "pointing to," as standing on behalf of an underlying pattern of matters that each already supposed to be the matters that the person, by his speaking, could be telling the other about. The underlying pattern was not only derived from a course of individual documentary evidences but the documentary evidences in their turn were interpreted on the basis of "what was known" and anticipatorily knowable about the underlying patterns.[4] Each was used to elaborate the other. (e) In attending to the utterances as events-in-the-conversation each party made references to the biography and prospects of the present interaction which each used and attributed to the other as a common scheme of interpretation and expression. (f) Each waited for something more to be said in order to hear what had previously been talked about, and each seemed willing to wait.

Common understandings would consist of a measured amount of shared agreement if the common understandings consisted of events coordinated with the successive positions of the hands of the clock, i.e., of events in standard time. The foregoing results, because they deal with the exchanges of the colloquy as events-in-a-conversation, urge that one more time parameter, at least, is required: the role of time as it is constitutive of "the matter talked about" as a developing and developed event over the course of action that produced it, as both the process and product were known *from within* this development by both parties, each for himself as well as on behalf of the other.

The colloquy reveals additional features. (1) Many of its expressions are such that their sense cannot be decided by an auditor unless he knows or assumes something about the biography and the purposes of the speaker, the circumstances of the utterance, the previous course of the conversation, or the particular relationship of actual or potential interaction that exists between user and auditor. The expressions do not have a sense that remains identical through the changing occasions of their use. (2) The events that were talked about were specifically vague. Not only do they not

---

[4] Karl Mannheim, in his essay "On the Interpretation of 'Weltanschauung' " (in *Essays on the Sociology of Knowledge,* trans. and ed. Pául Kecskemeti [New York: Oxford University Press, 1952], pp. 33-83), referred to this work as the "documentary method of interpretation." Its features are detailed in Chapter Three.

frame a clearly restricted set of possible determinations but the depicted events include as their essentially intended and sanctioned features an accompanying "fringe" of determinations that are open with respect to internal relationships, relationships to other events, and relationships to retrospective and prospective possibilities. (3) For the sensible character of an expression, upon its occurrence each of the conversationalists as auditor of his own as well as the other's productions had to assume as of any present accomplished point in the exchange that by waiting for what he or the other person might have said at a later time the present significance of what had already been said would have been clarified. Thus many expressions had the property of being progressively realized and realizable through the further course of the conversation. (4) It hardly needs to be pointed out that the sense of the expressions depended upon where the expression occurred in serial order, the expressive character of the terms that comprised it, and the importance to the conversationalists of the events depicted.

These properties of common understandings stand in contrast to the features they would have if we disregarded their temporally constituted character and treated them instead as precoded entries on a memory drum, to be consulted as a definite set of alternative meanings from among which one was to select, under predecided conditions that specified in which of some set of alternative ways one was to understand the situation upon the occasion that the necessity for a decision arose. The latter properties are those of strict rational discourse as these are idealized in the rules that define an adequate logical proof.

For the purposes of *conducting their everyday affairs* persons refuse to permit each other to understand "what they are really talking about" in this way. The anticipation that persons *will* understand, the occasionality of expressions, the specific vagueness of references, the retrospective-prospective sense of a present occurrence, waiting for something later in order to see what was meant before, are sanctioned properties of common discourse. They furnish a background of seen but unnoticed features of common discourse whereby actual utterances are recognized as events of common, reasonable, understandable, plain talk. Persons require these properties of discourse as conditions under which they are themselves entitled and entitle others to claim that they know what they are talking about, and that what they are saying is understandable and ought to be understood. In short, their seen but unnoticed presence is used to entitle persons to conduct their common conversational affairs without interference. Departures from such usages call forth immediate attempts to restore a right state of affairs.

The sanctioned character of these properties is demonstrable as follows. Students were instructed to engage an acquaintance or a friend in an ordinary conversation and, without indicating that what the experimenter was asking was in any way unusual, to insist that the person clarify the sense of his commonplace remarks. Twenty-three students reported twenty-five instances of such encounters. The following are typical excerpts from their accounts.

### CASE 1

The subject was telling the experimenter, a member of the subject's car pool, about having had a flat tire while going to work the previous day.

(S) I had a flat tire.

(E) What do you mean, you had a flat tire?

She appeared momentarily stunned. Then she answered in a hostile way: "What do you mean, 'What do you mean?' A flat tire is a flat tire. That is what I meant. Nothing special. What a crazy question!"

### CASE 2

(S) Hi, Ray. How is your girl friend feeling?

(E) What do you mean, "How is she feeling?" Do you mean physical or mental?

(S) I mean how is she feeling? What's the matter with you? (He looked peeved.)

(E) Nothing. Just explain a little clearer what do you mean?

(S) Skip it. How are your Med School applications coming?

(E) What do you mean, "How are they?"

(S) You know what I mean.

(E) I really don't.
(S) What's the matter with you? Are you sick?

## CASE 3

"On Friday night my husband and I were watching television. My husband remarked that he was tired. I asked, 'How are you tired? Physically, mentally, or just bored?'"

(S) I don't know, I guess physically, mainly.
(E) You mean that your muscles ache or your bones?
(S) I guess so. Don't be so technical.
   (*After more watching*)
(S) All these old movies have the same kind of old iron bed-stead in them.
(E) What do you mean? Do you mean all old movies, or some of them, or just the ones you have seen?
(S) What's the matter with you? You know what I mean.
(E) I wish you would be more specific.
(S) You know what I mean! Drop dead!

## CASE 4

During a conversation (with the E's female fiancee) the E questioned the meaning of various words used by the subject . . .

> For the first minute and a half the subject responded to the questions as if they were legitimate inquiries. Then she responded with "Why are you asking me those questions?" and repeated this two or three times after each question. She became nervous and jittery, her face and hand movements . . . uncontrolled. She appeared bewildered and complained that I was making her nervous and demanded that I "Stop it". . . . The subject picked up a magazine and covered her face. She put down the magazine and pretended to be engrossed. When asked why she was looking at the magazine she closed her mouth and refused any further remarks.

## CASE 5

My friend said to me, "Hurry or we will be late." I asked him what did he mean by late and from what point of view did it have reference. There was a look of perplexity and cynicism on his face. "Why are you asking me such silly questions? Surely I don't have to explain such a statement. What is wrong with you today? Why should I have to stop to analyze such a statement? Everyone understands my statements and you should be no exception!"

### CASE 6

The victim waved his hand cheerily.
(S) How are you?
(E) How am I in regard to what? My health, my finances, my school work, my peace of mind, my . . . ?
(S) (Red in the face and suddenly out of control.) Look! I was just trying to be polite. Frankly, I don't give a damn how you are.

### CASE 7

My friend and I were talking about a man whose overbearing attitude annoyed us. My friend expressed his feeling.
(S) I'm sick of him.
(E) Would you explain what is wrong with you that you are sick?
(S) Are you kidding me? You know what I mean.
(E) Please explain your ailment.
(S) (He listened to me with a puzzled look.) What came over you? We never talk this way, do we?

### Background understandings and "adequate" recognition of commonplace events

What kinds of expectancies make up a "seen but unnoticed" background of common understandings, and how are they related to persons' recognition of stable courses of interpersonal transactions? Some information can be obtained if we first ask how a person will look at an ordinary and familiar scene and what will he see in it if we require of him that he do no more than look at it as something that for him it "obviously" and "really" is not.

Undergraduate students were assigned the task of spending from fifteen minutes to an hour in their homes viewing its activities while assuming that they were boarders in the household. They were instructed not to act out the assumption. Thirty-three students reported their experiences.

In their written reports students "behaviorized" the household scenes. Here is an excerpt from one account to illustrate my meaning.

> A short, stout man entered the house, kissed me on the cheek and asked, "How was school?" I answered politely. He walked into the kitchen, kissed the younger of the two women, and said hello to the other. The younger woman asked me, "What do you want for dinner, honey?" I answered, "Nothing." She shrugged her shoulders and said no more. The older woman shuffled around the kitchen muttering. The man washed his hands, sat down at the table, and picked up the paper. He read until the two women had finished putting the food on the table. The three sat down. They exchanged idle chatter about the day's events. The older woman said something in a foreign language which made the others laugh.

Persons, relationships, and activities were described without respect for their history, for the place of the scene in a set of developing life circumstances, or for the scenes as texture of relevant events for the parties themselves. References to motives, propriety, subjectivity generally, and the socially standardized character of the events were omitted. Descriptions might be thought of as those of a keyhole observer who puts aside much of what he knows in common with subjects about the scenes he is looking at, as if the writer had witnessed the scenes under a mild amnesia for his common sense knowledge of social structures.

Students were surprised to see the ways in which members' treatments of each other were personal. The business of one was treated as the business of the others. A person being criticized was unable to stand on dignity and was prevented by the others from taking offense. One student reported her surprise at how freely she had the run of the house. Displays of conduct and feeling occurred without apparent concern for the management of impressions. Table manners were bad, and family members showed each other little politeness. An early casualty in the scene was the family news of the day which turned into trivial talk.

Students reported that this way of looking was difficult to sustain. Familiar objects—persons obviously, but furniture and room arrangements as well—resisted students' efforts to think of themselves as strangers. Many became uncomfortably aware of how habitual movements were being made; of *how* one was handling the silverware, or *how* one opened a door or greeted another member. Many reported that the attitude was difficult to sustain because with it quarreling, bickering, and hostile motivations became discomfitingly visible. Frequently an account that recited newly visible troubles was accompanied by the student's assertion that his account of family problems was not a "true" picture; the family was *really* a very happy one. Several students reported a mildly oppressive feeling of "conforming to a part." Several students attempted to formulate the "real me" as activities governed by rules of conduct but gave it up as a bad job. They found it more convincing to think of themselves in "usual" circumstances as "being one's real self." Nevertheless one student was intrigued with how deliberately and successfully he could predict the other's responses to his actions. He was not troubled by this feeling.

Many accounts reported a variation on the theme: "I was glad when the hour was up and I could return to the real me."

Students were convinced that the view from the boarder's attitude was not their real home environment. The boarder's attitude produced appearances which they discounted as interesting incongruities of little and misleading practical import. How had the familiar ways of looking at their home environments been altered? How did their looking differ from usual?

Several contrasts to the "usual" and "required" way of looking are detectable from their accounts. (1) In looking at their homes as boarders they replaced the mutually recognized texture of events with a rule of interpretation which required that this mutual texture be *temporarily* disregarded. (2) The mutually recognized texture was brought under the jurisdiction of the new attitude as a definition of the essential structures of this texture. (3) This was done by engaging in interaction with others with an attitude whose nature and purpose only the user knew about, that remained undisclosed, that could be either adopted or put aside at a time of the user's own choosing, and was a matter of willful election. (4) The attitude as an intention was sustained as a matter of personal and willed compliance with an explicit and single rule, (5) in which, like a game, the goal of the intention was identical with looking at things under the auspices of the single rule itself. (6) Above all, looking was not bound by any necessity for gearing one's interests within the attitude to the actions of others. These were the matters that students found strange.

When students used these background expectancies not only as ways of looking at familial scenes but as grounds for acting in them, the scenes exploded with the bewilderment and anger of family members.

In another procedure students were asked to spend from fifteen minutes to an hour in their homes imagining that they were boarders and acting out this assumption. They were instructed to conduct themselves in a circumspect and polite fashion. They were to avoid getting personal, to use formal address, to speak only when spoken to.

In nine of forty-nine cases students either refused to do the assignment (five cases) or the try was "unsuccessful" (four cases). Four of the "no try" students said they were afraid to do it; a fifth said she preferred to avoid the risk of exciting her mother who had a heart condition. In two of the "unsuccessful" cases the family treated it as a joke from the beginning and refused despite the continuing actions of the student to change. A third family took the view that something undisclosed was the matter, but what it might be was of no concern to them. In the fourth family the father and mother remarked that the daughter was being "extra nice" and undoubtedly wanted something that she would shortly reveal.

In the remaining four-fifths of the cases family members were stupefied. They vigorously sought to make the strange actions intelligible and to restore the situation to normal appearances. Reports were filled with accounts of astonishment, bewilderment, shock, anxiety, embarrassment, and anger, and with charges by various family members that the student was mean, inconsiderate, selfish, nasty, or impolite. Family members demanded explanations: What's the matter? What's gotten into you? Did you get fired? Are you sick? What are you being so superior about? Why are you mad? Are you out of your mind or are you just stupid? One student acutely embarrassed his mother in front of her friends by asking if she minded if he had a snack from the refrigerator. "Mind if you have a little snack? You've been eating little snacks around here for years without asking me. What's gotten into you?" One mother, infuriated when her daughter spoke to her only when she was spoken to, began to shriek in angry denunciation of the daughter for her disrespect and insubordination and refused to be calmed by the student's sister. A father berated his daughter for being insufficiently concerned for the welfare of others and of acting like a spoiled child.

Occasionally family members would first treat the student's action as a cue for a joint comedy routine which was soon replaced by irritation and exasperated anger at the student for not knowing when enough was enough. Family members mocked the "politeness" of the students—"Certainly Mr. Herzberg!"—or charged the student with acting like a wise guy and generally reproved the "politeness" with sarcasm.

Explanations were sought in previous, understandable motives of the student: the student was "working too hard" in school; the student was "ill"; there had been "another fight" with a fiancee. When offered explanations by family members went unacknowledged, there followed withdrawal by the offended member, attempted isolation of the culprit, retaliation, and denunciation. "Don't bother with him, he's in one of his moods again"; "Pay no attention but just wait until he asks me for something"; "You're cutting me, okay I'll cut you and then some"; "Why must you always create friction in our family harmony?" Many accounts reported versions of the following confrontation. A father followed his son into the bedroom. "Your Mother is right. You don't look well and you're not talking sense. You had better get another job that doesn't require such late hours." To this the student replied that he appreciated the consideration, but that he felt fine and only wanted a little privacy. The father responded in a high rage, "I don't want any more of *that* out of *you* and if you can't treat your mother decently you'd better move out!"

There were no cases in which the situation was not restorable upon the student's explanation. Nevertheless, for the most part family members were not amused and only rarely did they find the experience instructive as the student argued that it was supposed to have been. After hearing the explanation a sister replied coldly on behalf of a family of four, "Please, no more of these experiments. We're not rats, you know." Occasionally an explanation was accepted but still it added offense. In several cases students reported that the explanations left them, their families, or both wondering how much of what the student had said was "in character" and how much the student "really meant."

Students found the assignment difficult to complete. But in contrast with on-lookers' accounts students were likely to report that difficulties consisted in not being treated as if they were in the role that they were attempting to play, and of being confronted with situations but not knowing how a boarder would respond.

There were several entirely unexpected findings. (1) Although many students reported extensive rehearsals in imagination, very few mentioned anticipatory fears or embarrassment. (2) On the other hand, although unanticipated and nasty developments frequently occurred, in only one case did a student report serious regrets. (3) Very few students reported heartfelt relief when the hour was over. They were much more likely to report partial relief. They frequently reported that in response to the anger of others they became angry in return and slipped easily into subjectively recognizable feelings and actions.

In contrast to the reports of the on-looking "boarders" very few reports "behaviorized" the scene.

## Background understandings and social affects

Despite the interest in social affects that prevails in the social sciences, and despite the extensive concern that clinical psychiatry pays them, surprisingly little has been written on the socially structured conditions for their production. The role that a background of common understandings plays in their production, control, and recognition is, however, almost *terra incognita*. This lack of attention from experimental investigators is all the more remarkable if one considers that it is precisely this relationship that persons are concerned with in their common sense portrayals of how to conduct one's daily affairs so as to solicit enthusiasm and friendliness or avoid anxiety, guilt, shame, or boredom. The relationship between the common understandings and social affects may be illustrated by thinking of the acting out student-boarders' procedure as one that involved the production of bewilderment and anger by treating an important state of affairs as something that it "obviously," "naturally," and "really," is not.

The existence of a definite and strong relationship between common understandings and social affects can be demonstrated and some of its features explored by the deliberate display of distrust, a procedure that for us produced highly standardized effects. The rationale was as follows:

One of the background expectancies Schutz described concerns the sanctioned use of doubt as a constituent feature of a world that is being understood in common. Schutz proposed that for the *conduct of his everyday affairs* the person assumes, assumes the other person assumes as well, and assumes that as he assumes it of the other person, the other person assumes it of him, that a relationship of undoubted correspondence is the sanctioned relationship between the actual appearances of an object and the intended object that appears in a particular way. For the person conducting his everyday affairs, objects, for him as he expects for others, are as they appear to be. To treat this relationship under a *rule* of doubt requires that the necessity and motivation for such a rule be justified.

We anticipated that because of the differing relationship of an exhibited rule of doubt (distrust) [5] that the other person was as he appeared to be to the legitimate texture of common expectancies, there should be different affective states for the doubter and the doubted. On the part of the person distrusted there should be

---

[5] The concepts of "trust" and "distrust" are elaborated in my paper, "A Conception of and Experiments with 'Trust' as a Condition of Stable Concerted Actions," in *Motivation and Social Interaction*, ed. O. J. Harvey (New York: The Ronald Press Company, 1963, pp. 187-238). The term "trust" is used there to refer to a person's compliance with the expectancies of the attitude of daily life as a morality. Acting in accordance with a rule of doubt directed to the correspondence between appearances and the objects that appearances are appearances of is only one way of specifying "distrust." Modifications of each of the other expectancies that make up the attitude of everyday life, as well as their various sub-sets, furnish variations on the central theme of treating a world that one is required to know in common and take for granted as a problematic matter. See footnote 2 for references to Schutz' discussion of the attitude of daily life. The attitude's constituent expectancies are briefly enumerated on pages 55-56.

the demand for justification, and when it was not forthcoming, as "anyone could see" it could not be, anger. For the experimenter we expected embarrassment to result from the disparity, under the gaze of his victim, between the lesser thing that the experimenter's challenges of "what anyone could see" made him out to be and the competent person he with others knew himself "after all" to be but which the procedure required that he could not claim.

Like Santayana's clock, this formulation was neither right nor wrong. Although the procedure produced what we anticipated, it also furnished us and the experimenters with more than we had bargained for.

Students were instructed to engage someone in conversation and to imagine and act on the assumption that what the other person was saying was directed by hidden motives which were his real ones. They were to assume that the other person was trying to trick them or mislead them.

In only two of thirty-five accounts did students attempt the assignment with strangers. Most students were afraid that such a situation would get out of hand so they selected friends, roommates, and family members. Even so they reported considerable rehearsal in imagination, much review of possible consequences, and deliberate selections among persons.

The attitude was difficult to sustain and carry through. Students reported acute awareness of being "in an artificial game," of being unable "to live the part," and of frequently being "at a loss as to what to do next." In the course of listening to the other person, experimenters would lose sight of the assignment. One student spoke for several when she said she was unable to get any results because so much of her effort was directed to maintaining an attitude of distrust that she was unable to follow the conversation. She said she was unable to imagine how her fellow conversationalists might be deceiving her because they were talking about such inconsequential matters.

With many students the assumption that the other person was not what he appeared to be and was to be distrusted was the same as the attribution that the other person was angry with them and hated them. On the other hand many victims, although they complained that the student had no reason to be angry with them, offered unsolicited attempts at explanation and conciliation. When this was of no avail there followed frank displays of anger and "disgust."

Anticipated and acute embarrassment swiftly materialized for the two students who attempted the procedure with strangers. After badgering a bus driver for assurances that the bus would pass the street that she wanted and receiving several assurances in return that indeed the bus did pass the street, the exasperated bus driver shouted so that all passengers overheard, "Look lady, I told you once, didn't I? How many times do I have to tell you!" She reported, "I shrank to the back of the bus to sink as low as I could in the seat. I had gotten a good case of cold feet, a flaming face, and a strong dislike for my assignment."

There were very few reports of shame or embarrassment from students who tried it with friends and family. Instead they were surprised, and so were we, to find as one student reported that "once I started acting the role of a hated person I actually came to feel somewhat hated and by the time I left the table I was quite angry." Even more surprising to us, many reported that they found the procedure enjoyable and this included the real anger not only of others but their own.

Although students' explanations easily restored most situations, some episodes "turned serious" and left a residue of disturbance for one or both parties that offered explanation did not resolve. This can be illustrated in the report of a student housewife who, at the conclusion of dinner, and with some trepidation, questioned her husband about having worked late the night before and raised a question about his actually having played poker as he claimed on an evening of the week before. Without asking him what he had actually done she indicated an explanation was called for. He replied sarcastically, "You seem to be uneasy about something. Do you know what it might be? This conversation would no doubt make more sense if I knew too." She accused him of deliberately avoiding the subject, although the subject had not been mentioned. He insisted that *she* tell *him* what the *subject* was. When she did not say, he asked directly, "Okay, what's the joke?" Instead of replying, "I gave him a long, hurt look." He became visibly upset, became very solicitous, gentle, and persuasive. In response she acknowledged the experiment. He stalked off obviously unhappy and for the remainder of the evening was sullen and suspicious. She, in the meanwhile, remained at the table piqued and unsettled about the remarks that her statements had drawn forth about his not being bored at work "with all the insinuations it might or could mean," particularly the insinuation that he was not bored at work but he *was* bored with her and at home. She wrote, "I was actually bothered by his remarks. . . . I felt more upset and worried than he did throughout the experiment . . . about how imperturbable he seemed to be." Neither one attempted nor wanted to discuss the matter further. The following day the husband confessed that he had been considerably disturbed and had the following reactions in this order: determination to remain calm; shock at his wife's "suspicious nature"; surprise to find that cheating on her was liable to be hard; a determination to make her figure out her own answers to her questions without any denial or help from him; extreme relief when the encounter was revealed to have been experimentally contrived; but finally a residue of uneasy feelings which he characterized as "his shaken ideas of my (the wife's) nature which remained for the rest of the evening."

## Background understandings and bewilderment

Earlier the argument was made that the possibility of common understanding does not consist in demonstrated measures of shared knowledge of social structure, but consists instead and entirely in the enforceable character of actions in compliance with the expectancies of everyday life as a morality. Common sense knowledge of the facts of social life for the members of the society is institutionalized knowledge of the real world. Not only does common sense knowledge portray a real society for members, but in the manner of a self fulfilling prophecy the features of the real society are produced by persons' motivated compliance with these background expectancies. Hence the stability of concerted actions should vary directly with whatsoever are the real conditions of social organization that guarantee persons' motivated compliance with this background texture of relevances as a legitimate order of beliefs about life in society seen "from within" the society. Seen from the person's point of view, his commitments to motivated compliance consist of his grasp of and subscription to the "natural facts of life in society."

Such considerations suggest that the firmer a societal member's grasp of What Anyone Like Us Necessarily Knows, the more severe should be his disturbance when "natural facts of life" are impugned for him as a depiction of his real circumstances. To test this suggestion a procedure would need to modify the *objective* structure of the familiar, known-in-common environment by rendering the background expectancies inoperative. Specifically, this modification would consist of subjecting a person to a breach of the background expectancies of everyday life while (a) making it difficult for the person to interpret his situation as a game, an experiment, a deception, a play, *i.e.*, as something other than the one known according to the attitude of everyday life as a matter of enforceable morality and action, (b) making it necessary that he reconstruct the "natural facts" but giving him insufficient time to manage the reconstruction with respect to required mastery of practical circumstances for which he must call upon his knowledge of the "natural facts," and (c) requiring that he manage the reconstruction of the natural facts by himself and without consensual validation.

Presumably he should have no alternative but to try to normalize the resultant incongruities within the order of events of everyday life. Under the developing effort itself, events should lose their perceivedly normal character. The member should be unable to recognize an event's status as typical. Judgments of likelihood should fail him. He should be unable to assign present occurrences to similar orders of events he has known in the past. He should be unable to assign, let alone to "see at a glance," the conditions under which the events can be reproduced. He should be unable to order these events to means-ends relationships. The conviction should be undermined that the moral authority of the familiar society compels their occurrence. Stable and "realistic" matchings of intentions and objects should dissolve, by which I mean that the ways, otherwise familiar to him, in which the objective perceived environment serves as both the motivating grounds of feelings and is motivated by feelings directed to it, should become obscure. In short, the members' real perceived environment on losing its known-in-common background should become "specifically senseless." [6] Ideally speaking, behaviors directed to such a senseless environment should be those of bewilderment, uncertainty, internal conflict, psycho-social isolation, acute, and nameless anxiety along with various symptoms of acute depersonalization. Structures of interaction should be correspondingly disorganized.

This is expecting quite a lot of a breach of the background expectancies. Obviously we would settle for less if the results of a procedure for their breach was at all encouraging about this formulation. As it happens, the procedure produced convincing and easily detected bewilderment and anxiety.

To begin with, it is necessary to specify just what expectancies we are dealing with. Schutz reported that the feature of a scene, "known in common with others," was compound and consisted of several constituents. Because they have been discussed elsewhere [7] I shall restrict discussion to brief enumeration.

According to Schutz, the person assumes, assumes that the other person assumes as well, and assumes that as he assumes it of the other person the other person assumes the same for him:

1. That the determinations assigned to an event by the witness are required matters that hold on grounds that specifically disregard personal opinion or socially structured circumstances of particular witnesses, *i.e.*, that the determinations are required as matters of "objective necessity" or "facts of nature."

2. That a relationship of undoubted correspondence is the sanctioned relationship between the-presented-appearance-of-the-object and the-intended-object-that-presents-itself-in-the-perspective-of-the-particular-appearance.

3. That the event that is known in the manner that it is known can actually and potentially affect the witness and can be affected by his action.

[6] The term is borrowed from Max Weber's essay, "The Social Psychology of the World Religions," in *From Max Weber: Essays in Sociology*, trans. H. H. Gerth and C. Wright Mills (New York: Oxford University Press, 1946), pp. 267-301. I have adapted its meaning.

[7] Schutz, "Common Sense and Scientific Interpretations of Human Action," in *Collected Papers I: The Problem of Social Reality*, pp. 3-96; and "On Multiple Realities," pp. 207-259. Garfinkel, Chapter Eight, and "Common Sense Knowledge of Social Structures," *Transactions of the Fourth World Congress of Sociology*, 4 (Milan, 1959), 51-65.

4. That the meanings of events are products of a socially standardized process of naming, reification, and idealization of the user's stream of experience, *i.e.*, are the products of a language.

5. That present determinations of an event, whatsoever these may be, are determinations that were intended on previous occasions and that may be again intended in identical fashion on an indefinite number of future occasions.

6. That the intended event is retained as the temporally identical event throughout the stream of experience.

7. That the event has as its context of interpretation: (a) a commonly entertained scheme of interpretation consisting of a standardized system of symbols, and (b) "What Anyone Knows," *i.e.*, a preestablished corpus of socially warranted knowledge.

8. That the actual determinations that the event exhibits for the witness are the potential determinations that it would exhibit for the other person were they to exchange positions.

9. That to each event there corresponds its determinations that originate in the witness's and in the other person's particular biography. From the witness's point of view such determinations are irrelevant for the purposes at hand of either, and both he and the other have selected and interpreted the actual and potential determinations of events in an empirically identical manner that is sufficient for all their practical purposes.

10. That there is a characteristic disparity between the publicly acknowledged determinations and the personal, withheld determinations of events, and this private knowledge is held in reserve, *i.e.*, that the event means for both the witness and the other more than the witness can say.

11. That alterations of this characteristic disparity remain within the witness's autonomous control.

It is *not* the case that what an event exhibits as a distinctive determination is a condition of its membership in a known-in-the-manner-of-common-sense-environment. Instead the conditions of its membership are the attributions that its determinations, *whatever they might substantively consist of,* could be seen by the other person if their positions were exchanged, or that its features are not assigned as matters of personal preference but are to be seen by anyone, *i.e.*, the previously enumerated features. These and only these enumerated features *irrespective* of any other determinations of an event define the common sense character of an event. Whatever other determinations an event of everyday life may exhibit—whether its determinations are those of persons' motives, their life histories, the distributions of income in the population, kinship obligations, the organization of an industry, or what ghosts do when night falls—if and only if the event has for the witness the enumerated determinations is it an event in an environment "known in common with others."

Such attributions are features of witnessed events that are seen without being noticed. They are demonstrably relevant to the common sense that the actor makes of what is going on about him. They inform the witness about any particular appearance of an interpersonal environment. They inform the witness as to the real objects that actual appearances are the appearances of, but without these attributed features necessarily being recognized in a deliberate or conscious fashion.

Since each of the expectancies that make up the attitude of daily life assigns an expected feature to the actor's environment, it should be possible to breach these expectancies by deliberately modifying scenic events so as to disappoint these attributions. By definition, surprise is possible with respect to each of these expected features. The nastiness of surprise should vary directly with the extent to which the person as a matter of moral necessity complies with their use as a scheme for assigning witnessed appearances their status as events in a perceivedly normal environment. In short, the realistic grasp by a collectivity member of the natural facts of life, and his commitment to a knowledge of them as a condition of self-esteem as a bona-fide and competent collectivity member,[8] is the condition that we require in order to maximize his

---

[8] I use the term "competence" to mean the claim that a collectivity member is entitled to exercise that he is capable of managing his everyday affairs without interference. That members can take such claims for granted I refer to by speaking of a person as a "bona-fide" collectivity member. More extensive discussion of the relationships between "competence" and "common sense knowledge of social structures" will be found in the Ph.D. dissertation by Egon Bittner, "Popular Interests in Psychiatric Remedies: A Study in Social Control," University of California, Los Angeles, 1961. The terms, "collectivity" and "collectivity membership" are intended in strict accord with Talcott Parsons' usage in *The Social System* (New York: The Free Press of Glencoe, Inc., 1951) and in the general introduction to *Theories of Society*, by Talcott Parsons, Edward Shils, Kaspar D. Naegele, and Jesse R. Pitts (New York: The Free Press of Glencoe, Inc., 1961).

confusion upon the occasion that the grounds of this grasp are made a source of irreducible incongruity.

I designed a procedure to breach these expectancies while satisfying the three conditions under which their breach would presumably produce confusion, *i.e.*, that the person could not turn the situation into a play, a joke, an experiment, a deception, and the like, or, in Lewinian terminology, that he could not "leave the field"; that he have insufficient time to work through a redefinition of his real circumstances; and that he be deprived of consensual support for an alternative definition of social reality.

Twenty-eight premedical students were run individually through a three-hour experimental interview. As part of the solicitation of subjects as well as at the beginning of the interview, the experimenter identified himself as a representative of an Eastern medical school who was attempting to learn why the medical school intake interview was such a stressful situation. It was hoped that identifying the experimenter as a person with medical school ties would make it difficult for students to "leave the field" once the expectancy breaching procedure began. How the other two conditions of (a) managing a redefinition in insufficient time and (b) not being able to count on consensual support for an alternative definition of social reality were met will be apparent in the following description.

During the first hour of the interview the student furnished to the "medical school representative" the medical interview facts-of-life by answering for the representative such questions as "what sources of information about a candidate are available to medical schools?"; "What kind of man are the medical schools looking for?"; "What should a good candidate do in the interview?"; and "What should he avoid?" With this much completed the student was told that the representative's research interests had been satisfied. The student was then asked if he would care to hear a recording of an actual interview. All students wanted very much to hear the recording.

The recording was a faked one between a "medical school interviewer" and an "applicant." The applicant was a boor, his language was ungrammatical and filled with colloquialisms, he was evasive, he contradicted the interviewer, he bragged, he ran down other schools and professions, he insisted on knowing how he had done in the interview. Detailed assessments by the student of the recorded applicant were obtained immediately after the recording was finished.

The student was then given information from the applicant's "official record." Performance information, and characterological information was furnished in that order. Performance information dealt with the applicant's activities, grades, family background, courses, charity work, and the like. Characterological information consisted of character assessments by "Dr. Gardner, the medical school interviewer," "six psychiatrically trained members of the admissions committee who had heard only the recorded interview," and "other students."

The information was deliberately contrived to contradict the principal points in the student's assessment. For example, if the student said that the applicant must have come from a lower class family, he was told that the applicant's father was vice president of a firm that manufactured pneumatic doors for trains and buses. Was the applicant ignorant? Then he had excelled in courses like The Poetry of Milton and Dramas of Shakespeare. If the student said the applicant did not know how to get along with people, then the applicant had worked as a voluntary solicitor for Sydenham Hospital in New York City and had raised $32,000 from 30 "big givers." That the applicant was stupid and would not do well in a scientific field was met by citing A's in organic and physical chemistry and graduate level performance in an undergraduate research course.

Students wanted very much to know what "the others" thought of the applicant and had he been admitted? The student was told that the applicant had been admitted and was living up to the promise that the medical school interviewer and the "six psychiatrists" had found and expressed in a strong recommendation of the applicant's characterological fitness which was read to the student. As for the views of other students, the student was told (for example) that thirty other students had been seen, that twenty-eight were in entire agreement with the medical school interviewer's assessment, and the remaining two had been slightly uncertain but at the first bit of information had seen him just as the others had.

Following this the student was invited to listen to the record a second time, after which he was asked to assess the applicant again.

*Results.* Twenty-five of the twenty-eight students were taken in. The following does not apply to the three who were convinced there was a deception. Two of these are discussed at the conclusion of this section.

Students managed incongruities of performance data with vigorous attempts to make it factually compatible with their original and very derogatory assessments. For example, many said that the applicant sounded like or was a lower class person. When they were told that his father was vice president of a national corporation which manufactured pneumatic doors for buses and trains, they replied like this:

> "He should have made the point that he *could* count on money."
>
> "That explains why he said he had to work. Probably his father made him work. That would make a lot of his moans unjustified in the sense that things were really not so bad."
>
> "What does that have to do with values?"

When told he had a straight *A* average in physical science courses, students began to openly acknowledge bewilderment.

> "He took quite a variety of courses . . . I'm baffled. Probably the interview wasn't a very good mirror of his character."
>
> "He did seem to take some odd courses. They seem to be fairly normal. Not normal . . . but . . . it doesn't strike me one way or the other."
>
> "Well! I think you can analyze it this way. In psychological terms. See . . . one possible way . . . now I may be all *wet* but this is the way I look at *that*. He probably suffered from an inferiority complex and that's an overcompensation for his inferiority complex. His *great* marks . . . his *good* marks are a compensation for his failure . . . in social dealings perhaps, I don't know."
>
> "Whoops! And only third alternate at Georgia. (Deep sigh) I can see why he'd feel resentment about not being admitted to Phi Bet.

Attempts to resolve the incongruities produced by the character assessment of "Gardner" and "the other six judges" were much less frequent than normalizing attempts with performance information. Open expressions of bewilderment and anxiety interspersed with silent ruminations were characteristic:

> (Laugh) Golly! (Silence) I'd think it would be the other way around. (Very subdued) Maybe I'm all wrong . . . my orientation is all off. I'm completely baffled.

> Not polite. Self-confident he certainly was. But not polite. I don't know. Either the interviewer was a little crazy or else I am. (Long pause) That's rather shocking. It makes me have doubts about my own thinking. Perhaps my values in life are wrong, I don't know.

> (Whistles) I—I don't think he sounded well bred at all. That whole tone of voice!! I . . . perhaps you noticed though, when he said "You should have said in the first place," *before* he (the recorded medical school examiner) took it with a smile. But even so! No, no I can't see that. "You should have said that before." Maybe he was being funny though. Exercising a . . . No! To me it sounded impertinent!"

> Ugh . . . Well, that certainly puts a different slant on my conception of interviews. Gee . . . that . . . confuses me all the more.

> Well . . . (laugh) . . . Mhh! Ugh! Well, maybe he looked like a nice boy. He did . . . he did get his point across. Perhaps . . . seeing the person would make a big difference. Or perhaps I would never make a good interviewer. (Reflectively and almost inaudibly) They didn't mention any of the things I mentioned. (HG: Eh?) (Louder) They didn't mention any of the things I mentioned and so I feel like a complete failure.

Soon after the performance data produced its consternation, students occasionally asked what the other students made of him. Only after they were given "Dr. Gardner's" assessment, and their responses to it had been made, were the opinions of the "other students" given. In some cases the subject was told "Thirty-four out of thirty-five before you," sometimes forty-three out of forty-five, nineteen out of twenty, fifty-one out of fifty-two. All the numbers were large. For eighteen of the twenty-five students the delivery hardly varied from the following protocols:

> (34 out of 35) I don't know . . . I still stick to my original convictions. I . . . I . . . can you tell *me* what . . . I saw

wrong. Maybe I . . . I . . . had the wrong idea—the wrong attitude all along. (Can you tell me? I'm interested that there should be such a disparity.) Definitely . . . I . . . think . . . it would be definitely the other way. I can't make sense of it. I'm completely baffled, believe me. I . . . I don't understand how I could have been so wrong. Maybe my ideas—my evaluations of people are—just twisted. I mean maybe I had the wrong . . . Maybe my sense of values . . . is . . . off . . . or . . . different . . . from the other thirty-three. But I don't think that's the case . . . because usually . . . in all modesty I say this . . . I . . . I can judge people. I mean in class, in organizations I belong to . . . I usually judge them right. So therefore I don't understand at *all* how I could have been so wrong. I don't think I was under any stress or strain . . . here . . . tonight but . . . I don't understand it.

(43 out of 45) (laugh) I don't know what to say now. I'm troubled by my inability to judge the guy better than that. (Subdued) I shall sleep tonight, certainly (very subdued) but it certainly bothers me. Sorry that I didn't . . . Well! One question that arises . . . I may be wrong . . . (Can you see how they might have seen him?) No. No, I can't see it, no. Sure with all that background material, yes, but I don't see how Gardner did it without it. Well, I guess that makes Gardner, Gardner, and me, me. (The other forty-five students· didn't have the background material) Yeah, yeah, yeah. I mean I'm not denying it at all. I mean for myself, there's no sense saying . . . Of course! With their background they would be accepted, especially the second man, good God! Okay, what else?

(36 out of 37) I would go back on my former opinion but I wouldn't go back too far. I just don't see it. Why should I have these different standards? Were my opinions more or less in agreement? (No.) That leads me to think. That's funny. Unless you got thirty-six unusual people. I can't understand it. Maybe it's my personality. (Does it make any difference?) It does make a difference if I assume they're correct. What I consider is proper, they don't. It's my attitude . . . still in all a man of that sort would alienate me, a wise guy type to be avoided. Of course you can talk like that with other fellows . . . but in an interview? . . . Now I'm more confused than I was at the beginning of the entire inter-

view. I think I ought to go home and look in the mirror and talk to myself. Do you have any ideas? (Why? does it disturb you?) Yes it *does* disturb me! It makes me think my abilities to judge people and values are way off the normal. It's not a healthy situation. (What difference does it make?) If I act the way I act it seems to me that I'm just putting my head in the lion's mouth. I did have preconceptions but they're shattered to hell. It makes me wonder about myself. Why should I have these different standards. It all points to me.

Of the twenty-five subjects that were taken in, seven were unable to resolve the incongruity of having been wrong about such an obvious matter and were unable to "see" the alternative. Their suffering was dramatic and unrelieved. Five more resolved it with the view that the medical school had accepted a good man; five others with the view that it had accepted a boor. Although they changed they nevertheless did not abandon their former views. For them Gardner's view could be seen "in general" but it was a grasp without conviction. When their attention was drawn to particulars the general picture would evaporate. These subjects were willing to entertain and use the "general" picture but they suffered whenever indigestible particulars of the same portrait came into view. Subscription to the "general" picture was accompanied by a recitation of characteristics that were not only the opposite of those in the subject's original assessment but were intensified by superlative adjectives so that where previously the candidate was gauche, he was now "supremely" poised; where he had been boorish, he was "very" natural; where he had been hysterical, he was "very"calm; further, they saw the new features through a new appreciation of the way the medical examiner had been listening. They *saw*, for example, that the examiner *was smiling* when the applicant had forgotten to offer him a cigarette.

Three more subjects were convinced that there was a deception and acted on the conviction through the interview. They showed no disturbance. Two of them showed acute suffering as soon as it appeared that the interview was finished, and they were being dismissed with no acknowledgement of a deception.

Three others, by suffering in silence, confounded the experimenter. Without giving any indication to the experimenter, they regarded the interview as an experimental one in which they were required to solve some problems and thought therefore they were being asked to do as well as possible and to make no changes in their opinions for only then would they be contributing to the study. They were difficult for the experimenter to understand during the interview because they displayed marked anxiety, yet their remarks were bland and were not addressed to the matters that were provoking it.

Finally three more subjects contrasted with the others. One of these insisted that the character assessments were "semantically ambiguous" and because there was insufficient information a "high correlation opinion" was not possible. A second, the only one in the series, according to his account found the second portrait as convincing as the original one. When the deception was revealed he was disturbed that he could have been as convinced as he was. The third one in the face of everything showed only slight disturbance of very short duration. However, he alone among the subjects had already been interviewed for medical school and had excellent medical school contacts. Despite a grade point average of less than $C$, he estimated his chances of admission as fair and had expressed his preference for a career in the diplomatic service over a career in medicine.

As a final observation, twenty-two of the twenty-eight subjects expressed marked relief—ten of them with explosive expressions—when the deception was disclosed. Unanimously they said that the news of the deception permitted them to return to their former views. Seven subjects had to be convinced that there had been a deception. When the deception was revealed they asked what they were to believe. Was the experimenter telling them that there had been a deception in order to make them feel better? No pains were spared and whatever truth or lies that had to be told were told in order to establish the truth that there had been a deception.

Because motivated compliance to the expectancies that make up the attitudes of daily life consists from the person's point of view of his grasp of and subscription to the "natural facts of life," variations in the organizational conditions of motivated compliance for different collectivity members would consist of members' differential grasp of and subscription to the "natural facts of life." Hence the severity of the effects described above should vary directly with the enforceable commitments of members to a grasp of the natural facts of life. Further, because of the *objective* character of the grasped common moral order of the facts of collectivity life, the severity should vary with their committed grasp of the natural facts of life and independently of "personality characteristics." By personality characteristics I mean all characteristics of persons that investigators use methodologically to account for a person's courses of action by referring these actions to more or less systematically conceived motivational and "inner life" variables while disregarding social and cultural system effects. The results of most conventional personality assessment devices and clinical psychiatric procedures satisfy this condition.

Thereby, the following phenomenon should be discoverable. Imagine a procedure whereby a convincing assessment can be made of the extent of a person's committed grasp of the "natural facts of social life." Imagine another procedure whereby the extent of a person's confusion can be assessed ranging through the various degrees and mixtures of the behaviors described before. For a set of unselected persons, and independently of personality determinations, the initial relationship between the committed "grasp of natural facts" and "confusion" should be random. Under the breach of the expectancies of everyday life, given the conditions for the optimal production of disturbance, persons should shift in exhibited confusion in an amount that is coordinate with the original extent of their grasp of the "natural facts of life."

The type of phenomenon that I propose is discoverable is portrayed in Figures 1 and 2 which are based on the study of the twenty-eight premedical students reported above. Prior to the introductions of incongruous material, the extent of students' subscription to a common moral order of facts of premedical school life and the students' anxiety correlated—.026. After the incongruous material had been introduced and unsuccessfully normalized, and before the deception was revealed, the correlation was .751. Because assessment procedures were extremely crude, because of serious errors in design and procedure, and because of the *post hoc* argument, *these results do no more than illustrate what I am talking about. Under no circumstances should they be considered as findings.*

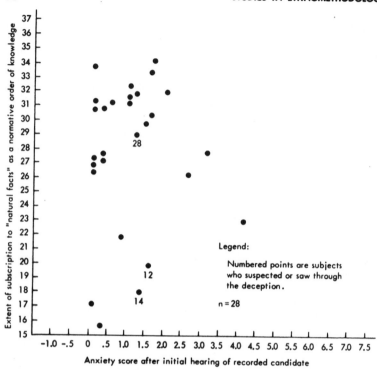

FIGURE 1. Correlation of the extent of subject's subscription to "the natural facts" as an institutionalized order of knowledge about pre-medical circumstances, and initial anxiety score ($r = .026$)

## The relevance of common understandings to the fact that models of man in society portray him as a judgmental dope

Many studies have documented the finding that the social standardization of common understandings, irrespective of what it is that is standardized, orients persons's actions to scenic events, and furnishes persons the grounds upon which departures from perceivedly normal courses of affairs are detectable, restoration is made, and effortful action is mobilized.

Social science theorists—most particularly social psychiatrists, social psychologists, anthropologists, and sociologists—have used the fact of standardization to conceive the character and conse-

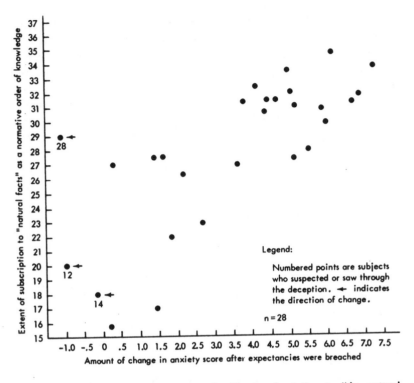

**FIGURE 2.** Correlation of the extent of subject's subscription to "the natural facts" as an institutionalized order of knowledge about pre-medical circumstances, and relative anxiety score (r = .751)

quences of actions that comply with standardized expectancies. Generally they have acknowledged but otherwise neglected the fact that by these same actions persons discover, create, and sustain this standardization. An important and prevalent consequence of this neglect is that of being misled about the nature and conditions of stable actions. This occurs by making out the member of the society to be a judgmental dope of a cultural or psychological sort, or both, with the result that the *unpublished* results of any accomplished study of the relationship between actions and standardized expectations will invariably contain enough incongruous material to invite essential revision.

By "cultural dope" I refer to the man-in-the-sociologist's-society who produces the stable features of the society by acting in compliance with preestablished and legitimate alternatives of action that the common culture provides. The "psychological dope" is the man-in-the-psychologist's-society who produces the stable features of the society by choices among alternative courses of action that are compelled on the grounds of psychiatric biography, conditioning history, and the variables of mental functioning. The common feature in the use of these "models of man" is the fact that courses of common sense rationalities [9] of judgment which involve the person's use of common sense knowledge of social structures over the temporal "succession" of here and now situations are treated as epiphenomenal.

The misleading character of the use of the judgmental dope to portray the relationship between standardized expectancies and courses of action goes to the problem of adequate explanation as the controlling consideration in the investigator's decision to either consider or disregard the common sense rationalities when deciding the necessary relationships between courses of action, given such problematic considerations as perspectival choice, subjectivity, and inner time. A favored solution is to portray what the member's actions will have come to by using the stable structures—i.e., what they *came* to—as a point of theoretical departure from which to portray the necessary character of the pathways whereby the end result is assembled. Hierarchies of need dispositions, and common culture as enforced rules of action, are favored devices for bringing the problem of necessary inference to terms, although at the cost of making out the person-in-society to be a judgmental dope.

How is an investigator *doing* it when he is making out the member of a society to be a judgmental dope? Several examples will furnish some specifics and consequences.

I assigned students the task of bargaining for standard priced

---

[9] Common sense rationalities are discussed at length in Schutz, "Common Sense and Scientific Interpretation of Human Action," in *Collected Papers I: The Problem of Social Reality*, pp. 3-47 and "The Problem of Rationality in the Social World," in *Collected Papers II: Studies in Social Theory*, pp. 64-88, and in Chapter Eight. The common sense rationalities were used by Egon Bittner, *op. cit.*, to recommend a criticism and reconstruction of sociological interest in mental illness.

merchandise. The relevant standardized expectancy is the "institutionalized one price rule," a constituent element, according to Parsons,[10] of the institution of contract. Because of its "internalized" character the student-customers should have been fearful and shamed by the prospective assignment, and shamed by having done it. Reciprocally, anxiety, and anger should have been commonly reported for sales persons.

Sixty-eight students were required to accomplish one trial only for any item costing no more than two dollars, and were to offer much less than the asking price. Another sixty-seven students were required to accomplish a series of six trials: three for items costing two dollars or less, and three for items costing fifty dollars or more.

*Findings*: (a) Sales persons can be dismissed as either having been dopes in different ways than current theories of standardized expectancies provide, or not dopes enough. A few showed some anxiety; occasionally one got angry. (b) Twenty per cent of the single tries refused to try or aborted the effort, as compared with three per cent of those who had been assigned the series of six trials. (c) When the bargaining episode was analyzed as consisting of a series of steps—anticipation of the trial, approaching the sales person, actually making the offer, the ensuing interaction, terminating the episode, and afterwards—it was found that fears occurred with the greatest frequency in both groups in anticipating the assignment and approaching the sales person *for the first try.* Among the single trials the number of persons who reported discomfort declined with each successive step in the sequence. Most of the students who bargained in two or more trials reported that by the third episode they were enjoying the assignment. (d) Most students reported less discomfort in bargaining for high priced than low priced merchandise. (e) Following the six episodes many students reported that they had learned to their "surprise" that one could bargain in standard priced settings with some realistic chance of an advantageous outcome, and planned to do so in the future, particularly for costly merchandise.

Such findings suggest that one can make the member of the society out to be a cultural dope (a) by portraying a member of

[10] Talcott Parsons, "Economy, Polity, Money and Power," dittoed manuscript, 1959.

the society as one who operates by the rules when one is actually talking about the anticipatory anxiety that prevents him from permitting a situation to develop, let alone confronting a situation, in which he has the alternative of acting or not with respect to a rule; or (b) by overlooking the practical and theoretical importance of the mastery of fears. (c) If upon the arousal of troubled feelings persons avoid tinkering with these "standardized" expectancies, the standardization could consist of an *attributed* standardization that is supported by the fact that persons avoid the very situations in which they might learn about them.

Lay as well as professional knowledge of the nature of rule governed actions and the consequences of breaching the rules is prominently based on just such procedure. Indeed, the more important the rule, the greater is the likelihood that knowledge is based on avoided tests. Strange findings must certainly await anyone who examines the expectancies that make up routine backgrounds of common place activities for they have rarely been exposed by investigators even to as much revision as an imaginative rehearsal of their breach would produce.

Another way in which the member of the society can be made a judgmental dope is by using any of the available theories of the formal properties of signs and symbols to portray the way persons construe environmental displays as significant ones. The dope is made out in several ways. I shall mention two.

(a) Characteristically, formal investigations have been concerned either with devising normative theories of symbolic usages or, while seeking descriptive theories, have settled for normative ones. In either case it is necessary to instruct the construing member to act in accordance with the investigator's instructions in order to guarantee that the investigator will be able to study their usages as instances of the usages the investigator has in mind. But, following Wittgenstein,[11] person's actual usages are rational usages in *some* "language game." What is *their* game? As long as this programmatic question is neglected, it is inevitable that person's usages will fall short. The more will this be so the more are subjects' interests in usages dictated by different practical considerations from those of investigators.

[11] Ludwig Wittgenstein, *Philosophical Investigations* (Oxford: Basil Blackwell, 1959).

(b) Available theories have many important things to say about such sign functions as marks and indications, but they are silent on such overwhelmingly more common functions as glosses, synecdoche, documented representation, euphemism, irony, and double entendre. References to common sense knowledge of ordinary affairs may be safely disregarded in detecting and analyzing marks and indications as sign functions *because* users disregard them as well. The analysis of irony, double entendre, glosses, and the like, however, imposes different requirements. Any attempt to consider the related character of utterances, meanings, perspectives, and orders necessarily requires reference to common sense knowledge of ordinary affairs.

Although investigators have neglected these "complex" usages, they have not put their problematic character entirely aside. Instead, they have glossed them by portraying the usages of the member of a language community as either culture bound or need compelled, or by construing the pairing of appearances and intended objects—the pairing of "sign" and "referrent"—as an association. In each case a procedural description of such symbolic usages is precluded by neglecting the judgmental work of the user.

Precisely this judgmental work, along with its reliance upon and its reference to common sense knowledge of social structures, forced itself upon our attention in every case where incongruities were induced. Our attention was forced because our subjects had exactly their judgmental work and common sense knowledge to contend with as matters which the incongruities presented to them as practical problems. Every procedure that involved departures from an anticipated course of ordinary affairs, regardless of whether the departure was gross or slight, aroused recognition in subjects that the experimenter was engaged in double talk, irony, glosses, euphemism, or lies. This occurred repeatedly in departures from ordinary game play.

Students were instructed to play ticktacktoe and to mix their subjects by age, sex, and degree of acquaintance. After drawing the ticktacktoe matrix they invited the subject to move first. After the subject made his move the experimenter erased the subject's mark, moved it to another square and made his own mark but without giving any indications that anything about the play was unusual. In half of 247 trials students reported that subjects treated the move as a gesture with hidden but definite significance. Subjects were convinced that the experimenter was "after something" that he was not saying and whatever he "really" was doing had nothing to do with ticktacktoe. He was making a sexual pass; he was commenting on the subject's stupidity; he was making a slurring or an impudent gesture. Identical effects occurred when students bargained for standard priced merchandise, or asked the other to clarify his commonplace remarks, or joined without invitation a strange group of conversationalists, or used a gaze that during an ordinary conversation wandered "randomly" by time to various objects in the scene.

Still another way of making the person out for a cultural dope is to simplify the communicative texture of his behavioral environment. For example, by giving physical events preferred status one can theorize out of existence the way the person's scene, as a texture of potential and actual events, contains not only appearances and attributions but the person's own lively inner states as well. We encountered this in the following procedure:

Students were instructed to select someone other than a family member and in the course of an ordinary conversation, and without indicating that anything unusual was happening, to bring their faces up to the subject's until their noses were almost touching. According to most of the 79 accounts, regardless of whether the pairs were the same or different sexes, whether they were acquaintances or close friends (strangers were prohibited), and regardless of age differences except where children were involved, the procedure motivated in *both* experimenter and subject attributions of a sexual intent on the part of the other though confirmation of this intent was withheld by the very character of the procedure. Such attributions to the other were accompanied by the person's own impulses which themselves became part of the scene as their not only being desired but their desiring. The unconfirmed invitation to choose had its accompanying conflictful hesitancy about acknowledging the choice and having been chosen. Attempted avoidance, bewilderment, acute embarrassment, furtiveness, and above all uncertainties of these as well as uncertainties of fear, hope, and anger were characteristic. These effects were most pronounced between males. Characteristically, experimenters were unable to restore the situation. Subjects were only partially accepting of the experimenter's explanation that it has been done "as an experiment for a course in Sociology." They often complained, "All right, it was an experiment, but why did you have to choose *me?*" Characteristically, subject and experimenter wanted some further resolution than the explanation furnished but were uncertain about what it could or should consist of.

Finally, the member may be made out to be a judgmental dope by portraying routine actions as those governed by prior agreements, and by making the likelihood that a member will recognize deviance depend upon the existence of prior agreements. That this is a matter of mere theoretical preference whose use theorizes essential phenomena out of existence can be seen by considering the commonplace fact that persons will hold each other to agreements whose terms they never actually stipulated. This neglected property of common understandings has far reaching consequences when it is explicitly brought into the portrayal of the nature of "agreements."

Apparently no matter how specific the terms of common understandings may be—a contract may be considered the prototype— they attain the status of an agreement for persons only insofar as the stipulated conditions carry along an unspoken but understood *et cetera* [12] clause. Specific stipulations are formulated under the rule of an agreement by being brought under the jurisdiction of the *et cetera* clause. This does not occur once and for all, but is essen-

---

[12] The *et cetera* clause, its properties, and the consequences of its use have been prevailing topics of study and discussion among the members of the Conferences on Ethnomethodology that have been in progress at the University of California, Los Angeles, and the University of Colorado since February, 1962, with the aid of a grant from the U. S. Air Force Office of Scientific Research. Conference members are Egon Bittner, Harold Garfinkel, Craig MacAndrew, Edward Rose, and Harvey Sacks. Discussions of *et cetera* by conference participants will be found in Egon Bittner, "Radicalism: A Study of the Sociology of Knowledge," *American Sociological Review*, 28 (December, 1963), 928-940; Harvey Sacks, "On Sociological Description," *Berkeley Journal of Sociology*, 8 (1963), 1-16; Harold Garfinkel, "A Conception and Some Experiments With Trust . . ."; and Chapters One and Three in this volume. Extended studies dealing with coding procedures, methods of interrogation, lawyers' work, translation, model construction, historical reconstruction, "social bookkeeping," counting, and personality diagnosis will be found in unpublished papers by Bittner, Garfinkel, MacAndrew, Rose, and Sacks; in transcribed talks given by Bittner, Garfinkel, and Sacks on "Reasonable Accounts" at the Sixteenth Annual Conference on World Affairs, University of Colorado, April 11-12, 1963; and in Conference transcriptions.

tially bound to both the inner and outer temporal course of activities and thereby to the progressive development of circumstances
and their contingencies. Therefore it is both misleading and incorrect to think of an agreement as an actuarial device whereby persons are enabled as of any Here and Now to predict each other's
future activities. More accurately, common understandings that
have been formulated under the rule of an agreement are used by
persons to normalize whatever their actual activities turn out to
be. Not only can contingencies arise, but persons know as of any
Here and Now that contingencies can materialize or be invented
at any time that it must be decided whether or not what the parties
actually did satisfied the agreement. The *et cetera* clause provides
for the certainty that unknown conditions are at every hand in
terms of which an agreement, as of any particular moment, can
be retrospectively reread to find out in light of present practical
circumstances what the agreement "really" consisted of "in the
first place" and "all along." That the work of bringing present circumstances under the rule of previously agreed activity is sometimes contested should not be permitted to mask its pervasive and
routine use as an ongoing and essential feature of "actions in accord with common understandings."

This process, which I shall call a method of discovering agreements by eliciting or imposing a respect for the rule of practical
circumstances, is a version of practical ethics. Although it has
received little if any attention by social scientists, it is a matter of
the most abiding and commonplace concern in everyday affairs
and common sense theories of these affairs. Adeptness in the deliberate manipulation of *et cetera* considerations for the further-
ance of specific advantages is an occupational talent of lawyers and
is specifically taught to law school students. One should not suppose, however, that because it is a lawyer's skill, that only lawyers
are skilled at it, or that only those who do so deliberately, do so
at all. The method is general to the phenomenon of the society as
a system of rule governed activities.[13] It is available as one of the
mechanisms whereby potential and actual successes and windfalls,

[13] Insofar as this is true, it establishes the programmatic task of reconstructing the problem of social order as it is currently formulated in sociological
theories, and of criticizing currently preferred solutions. At the heart of the
reconstruction is the empirical problem of demonstrating the definitive features of *et cetera* thinking.

on the one hand, and the disappointments, frustrations, and failures, on the other, that persons must inevitably encounter by reason of seeking to comply with agreements, can be managed while retaining the perceived reasonableness of actual socially organized activities.

A small scale but accurate instance of this phenomenon was consistently produced by a procedure in which the experimenter engaged others in conversation while he had a wire recorder hidden under his coat. In the course of the conversation the experimenter opened his jacket to reveal the recorder saying, "See what I have?" An initial pause was almost invariably followed by the question, "What are you going to do with it?" Subjects claimed the breach of the expectancy that the conversation was "between us." The fact that the conversation was revealed to have been recorded motivated new possibilities which the parties then sought to bring under the jurisdiction of an agreement that they had never specifically mentioned and that indeed did not previously exist. The conversation, now seen to have been recorded, thereby acquired fresh and problematic import in view of unknown uses to which it might be turned. An agreed privacy was thereupon treated as though it had operated all along.

## Concluding remarks

I have been arguing that a concern for the nature, production, and recognition of reasonable, realistic, and analyzable actions is not the monopoly of philosophers and professional sociologists. Members of a society are concerned as a matter of course and necessarily with these matters both as features and for the socially managed production of their everyday affairs. The study of common sense knowledge and common sense activities consists of treating as problematic phenomena the actual methods whereby members of a society, doing sociology, lay or professional, make the social structures of everyday activities observable. The "rediscovery" of common sense is possible perhaps because professional sociologists, like members, have had too much to do with common sense knowledge of social structures as both a topic and a resource for their inquiries and not enough to do with it only and exclusively as sociology's programmatic topic.

# THREE

# Common sense knowledge of social structures: the documentary method of interpretation in lay and professional fact finding

Sociologically speaking, "common culture" refers to the socially sanctioned grounds of inference and action that people use in their everyday affairs and which they assume that others use in the same way. Socially-sanctioned-facts-of-life-in-society-that-any-bona-fide-member-of-the-society-knows depict such matters as the conduct of family life, market organization, distributions of honor, competence, responsibility, goodwill, income, motives among members, frequency, causes of, and remedies for trouble, and the presence of good and evil purposes behind the apparent workings of things. Such socially sanctioned, facts of social life consist of descriptions from the point of view of the collectivity member's [1] interests in the management of his practical affairs. Basing our usage upon the work of Alfred Schutz,[2] we shall call such knowledge of socially organized environments of concerted actions "common sense knowledge of social structures."

The discovery of common culture consists of the discovery *from within* the society by social scientists of the existence of common

[1] The term "collectivity membership" is intended in strict accord with Talcott Parsons' usage in *The Social System* and in *Theories of Society*, I, Part Two, pp. 239-240.

[2] Alfred Schutz, *Collected Papers I: The Problem of Social Reality* (1962); *Collected Papers II: Studies in Social Theory* (1964); *Collected Papers III: Studies in Phenomenological Philosophy* (1966).

**76**

sense knowledge of social structures. In that discovery the social scientist treats knowledge, and the procedures that societal members use for its assembly, test, management, and transmission, as objects of theoretical sociological interest.

This paper is concerned with common sense knowledge of social structures as an object of theoretical sociological interest. It is concerned with descriptions of a society that its members, *professional sociologists included,* as a condition of their enforceable rights to manage and communicate decisions of meaning, fact, method, and causal texture without interference—*i.e.*, as a condition of their "competence"—use and treat as known in common with other members, and with other members take for granted. Specifically the paper is directed to a description of the work whereby decisions of meaning and fact are managed, and how a body of factual knowledge of social structures is assembled in common sense situations of choice.

## The documentary method of interpretation

There are innumerable situations of sociological inquiry in which the investigator—whether he be a professional sociologist or a person undertaking an inquiry about social structures in the interests of managing his practical everyday affairs—can assign witnessed actual appearances to the status of an event of conduct only by imputing biography and prospects to the appearances. This he does by embedding the appearances in his presupposed knowledge of social structures. Thus it frequently happens that in order for the investigator to decide what he is now looking at he must wait for future developments, only to find that these futures in turn are informed by *their* history and future. By waiting to see what will have happened he learns what it was that he previously saw. Either that, or he takes imputed history and prospects for granted. Motivated actions, for example, have exactly these troublesome properties.

It therefore occurs that the investigator frequently must elect among alternative courses of interpretation and inquiry to the end of deciding matters of fact, hypothesis, conjecture, fancy, and the rest, despite the fact that in the calculable sense of the term "know," he does not and even cannot "know" what he is doing *prior to or while he is doing it.* Field workers, most particularly those doing ethnographic and linguistic studies in settings where they cannot presuppose a knowledge of social structures, are perhaps best acquainted with such situations, but other types of professional sociological inquiry are not exempt.

Nevertheless, a body of knowledge of social structures is somehow assembled. Somehow, decisions of meaning, facts, method, and causal texture are made. How, in the course of the inquiry during which such decisions must be made, does this occur?

In his concern for the sociologist's problem of achieving an adequate description of cultural events, an important case of which would be Weber's familiar "behaviors with a subjective meaning attached and governed thereby in their course," Karl Mannheim [3] furnished an approximate description of one process. Mannheim called it "the documentary method of interpretation." It contrasts with the methods of literal observation, yet it has a recognizable fit with what many sociological researchers, lay and professional, actually do.

According to Mannheim, the documentary method involves the search for ". . . an identical homologous pattern underlying a vast variety of totally different realizations of meaning." [4]

The method consists of treating an actual appearance as "the document of," as "pointing to," as "standing on behalf of" a presupposed underlying pattern. Not only is the underlying pattern derived from its individual documentary evidences, but the individual documentary evidences, in their turn, are interpreted on the basis of "what is known" about the underlying pattern. Each is used to elaborate the other.

The method is recognizable for the everyday necessities of recognizing what a person is "talking about" given that he does not say exactly what he means, or in recognizing such common occurrences and objects as mailmen, friendly gestures, and promises. It is recognizable as well in deciding such sociologically analyzed occurrence of events as Goffman's strategies for the management of impressions, Erickson's identity crises, Riesman's types of conformity, Parsons' value systems, Malinowski's magical practices,

[3] Karl Mannheim, "On the Interpretation of Weltanschauung," in *Essays on the Sociology of Knowledge*, pp. 53-63.

[4] *Ibid.*, p. 57.

Bale's interaction counts, Merton's types of deviance, Lazarsfeld's latent structure of attitudes, and the U.S. Census' occupational categories.

How is it done by an investigator that from replies to a questionnaire he finds the respondent's "attitude"; that via interviews with office personnel he reports their "bureaucratically organized activities"; that by consulting crimes known to the police, he estimates the parameters of "real crime"? What is the work whereby the investigator sets the observed occurrence and the intended occurrence into a correspondence of meaning, such that the investigator finds it reasonable to treat witnessed actual appearances as evidences of the event he means to be studying?

To answer these questions it is necessary to detail the work of the documentary method. To this end a demonstration of the documentary method was designed to exaggerate the features of this method in use and to catch the work of "fact production" in flight.

### An experiment

Ten undergraduates were solicited by telling them that research was being done in the Department of Psychiatry to explore alternative means to psychotherapy "as a way of giving persons advice about their personal problems" (sic). Each subject was seen individually by an experimenter who was falsely represented as a student counselor in training. The subject was asked to first discuss the background to some serious problem on which he would like advice, and then to address to the "counselor" a series of questions each of which would permit a "yes" or "no" answer. The subject was promised that the "counselor" would attempt to answer to the best of his ability. The experimenter-counselor heard the questions and gave his answers from an adjoining room, via an intercommunication system. After describing his problem and furnishing some background to it, the subject asked his first question. After a standard pause, the experimenter announced his answer, "yes" or "no." According to instructions, the subject then removed a wall plug connecting him with the counselor so that the "counselor will not hear your remarks" and tape-recorded his comments on the exchange. After these were completed, the subject plugged the microphone in and asked his next question. After he received the answer, he again recorded his comments, and thus proceeded through at least ten questions and answers. The subject had been told, "Most people want to ask at least ten questions."

The sequence of answers, evenly divided between yes's and no's, was predecided with a table of random numbers. All subjects asking the same number of questions were administered the same series of yes and no answers. Following the exchange of questions and answers the subject was asked to summarize his impressions of the entire exchange. An interview followed.

The following are illustrative unedited protocols.

### CASE 1

SUBJECT: Ok, this is the situation that I am presented with. I happen to be of the Jewish faith and I have been dating a Gentile girl now for about two months. My dad is not directly opposed to this situation, but I feel at the same time that he is not exactly pleased with it. Mother feels that as long as Dad is not directly opposed to this situation that I should go ahead and continue dating until he makes some direct statement to the contrary. My reason for feeling why he is not too pleased with this is that he has never said don't date her, but at the same time he will come up with digs and sayings that make me feel very ill at ease about dating the girl. My question is, do you feel under the present circumstances that I should continue or stop dating this girl? Let me put that in a positive way. Do you feel that I should continue dating this girl?

EXPERIMENTER: My answer is no.

SUBJECT: No. Well, that is kind of interesting. I kinda feel that there is really no great animosity between Dad and I but, well, perhaps he feels that greater dislike will grow out of this. I suppose or maybe it is easier for an outsider to see certain things that I am blind to at this moment.

I would like to ask my second question now.

EXPERIMENTER: Okay.

SUBJECT: Do you feel that I should have a further discussion with Dad about this situation or not? Should I have further discussion with Dad over this subject about dating the Gentile girl?

EXPERIMENTER: My answer is yes.

SUBJECT: Well I feel that is reasonable but I really don't know what to say to him. I mean he seems to be not really too understanding. In other words he seems to be afraid really to discuss the situation. I mean at least it appears that way to me so far. But I guess if it is worthwhile to me, if I really want to continue to date her that I will go on and have this discussion with Dad. I really don't know what to say because I mean I am dating her. I am not in love with her or anything but I really never know what is going to come out. I guess we should have a discussion based on what the future possibilities might be and how he would feel about that. He may not be too strongly opposed now because we are only dating, but perhaps he sees future complications that he would really like to get off his chest at the moment. I am ready for my third question now.

If after having my conversation with Dad and he says to continue dating her, but at the same time he gives me an impression that he is really not, he really does not want me to date her, but he is only doing it because he wants to be a good Dad, should under these conditions, should I still date the girl?

EXPERIMENTER: My answer is yes.

SUBJECT: Well I am actually surprised at the answer. I expected a no answer on that. Perhaps this is because you are not quite aware of my dad and his reactions and he seems to be the type of person that is sensitive and therefore he is very careful in the way that he will handle things. Even though he might have said go ahead and date her I perhaps would feel guilty in knowing that he really did not want me to continue to date her. Though I don't know that it would actually help the situation any. So, well, perhaps we will look into this further and that is another question. I am ready for the fourth question now.

If after having this discussion with Dad and getting a positive answer from him but at the same time felt that this was not his honest opinion do you think that it would be proper for me to have my mother have a serious talk with him and therefore try and get a truer reaction to Dad's opinion on the situation?

EXPERIMENTER: My answer is yes.

SUBJECT: Well this seems fair to me. I feel perhaps that he would be honester with Mother about the situation. Of course that might present a problem. Would Mother come back and be completely honest with me? She seems to be more liberal than Dad, not to say that Mother would lie about it, but she would be a little more liberal about things like this and perhaps in her course of conversation with Dad she would try and present my side to him and therefore once again I get two answers. If I look at it that way I don't think that I am going to get to first base anyway, but at least I feel that we are moving along some way. I am ready for my fifth question now.

Do you think that I should tell this Gentile girl who I am dating the problem that I am having with my folks at home or should I wait until, well that is another question. Do you feel that I should tell the girl that I am dating the problems that I am having at home over her religion?

EXPERIMENTER: My answer is no.

SUBJECT: Well once again I am surprised. Of course, that might depend on how much you care for the girl and how much longer I feel that I am going to be dating her. But I personally feel that it is only right to tell her for if she is perhaps thinking more serious than I am, she might, it might be best for us to understand the full situation and if she feels that this will be a block then I feel perhaps that would end the situation right there without telling her. I feel that perhaps I am going to show this in different ways and she will be unaware of what the real situation is and perhaps react back to me in a certain way spoiling our dating and everything else like that. I am ready for my sixth question.

If I was to fall in love with this girl and want to make plans for marriage do you feel that it is fair that I should ask her to change her religion over to my belief?

EXPERIMENTER: My answer is no.

SUBJECT: Well, no. Well, this has me stymied. No. Well, I honestly feel that I have been brought up in a certain way and I believe that she has too, and I feel pretty strong about the way that I believe. Not that I am completely orthodox or anything, but of course there is always family pressure and things like that. And I am quite sure that she feels, unfortunately I have never seen a family with a split in religion that really has been able to make a success out of it. So I don't know. I think that perhaps I would be tempted to ask her to change. I don't think that I would be able to really. I am ready for number seven.

Do you feel that it would be a better situation if we were to get married and neither one of us were willing to talk about the religious difference or to give in on either one side, that we bring our children up in a neutral religion other than the two that we believe in?

EXPERIMENTER: My answer is yes.

SUBJECT: Well perhaps this would be a solution. If we could find a religion that would incorporate our two beliefs to a certain extent. I realize that perhaps this might be literally impossible to do. Perhaps in a sense this neutral religion might be something almost made up by ourselves because I honestly feel that religious training no matter which belief it is if not carried to extremes is good, for everyone should have a certain amount of religious training along these lines. Perhaps this might be a solution to the problem. I guess I should follow this along a little bit further and see exactly what happens. I am ready for number eight.

If we were to get married would it be best for us to live in a new community where we will not be in contact with our parents if we were getting a lot of family pressure over religious differences?

EXPERIMENTER: My answer is no.

SUBJECT: Well, I kinda tend to agree with this answer. I feel that you wouldn't be accomplishing too much by running away from the issue and that perhaps it would be one of those things in life that eventually you would just be willing to accept it and that the families and we would get along harmoniously together. At least I hope it would work out if that situation comes about. I think it would be best for both families together that we are not going to work it out if we run away from our problem. So we best remain there and try and work it out. I am ready for number nine.

If we did get married and were to raise our children do you think that we should explain and tell our children that we once had this religious difference or would we just bring them up in this new religion, that is their religion, that we talked about, and let them believe that that is what we originally believed in?

EXPERIMENTER: My answer is no.

SUBJECT: Once again I kinda agree with this. I think they should be told because undoubtedly they will find out. And if they did find out that there was this difference that we once had they would feel that we were sneaking or trying to hide something from them and this would not be the best situation either. So I believe this would be the best situation. I am ready for number ten.

Do you feel that our children, if there were any, would have any religious problems themselves because of us the parents and our difficulties?

EXPERIMENTER: My answer is no.

SUBJECT: Well I really don't know if I agree with that or not. Perhaps they would have trouble if confusion set in and they were to feel that they did not know which is right and which is wrong or what side to pick if they did not want to stick with their religion. But I kinda feel that if their religion was a wholesome one which supplied the needs of a religion and that which a religion does supply that there would not be any problems with them. But I suppose that only time will tell if such problems would come about. I am finished with my comments now.

EXPERIMENTER: Okay, I will be right in.

The experimenter appeared in the room with the subject, handed him a list of points that he might comment on, and left the room. The subject commented as follows.

SUBJECT: Well the conversation seemed to be one-sided because I was doing it all. But, I feel that it was extremely difficult for Mr. McHugh to answer these questions fully without having a complete understanding of the personalities of the different people involved and exactly how involved the situation was itself. The answers I received I must say that the majority of them were answered perhaps in the same way that I would answer them to myself knowing the differences in types of people. One or two of them did come as a surprise to me and I felt that the reason perhaps he answered these questions the way he did is for the reason that he is not aware of the personalities involved and how they are reacting or would react to a certain situation. The answers that I received were most of them I felt that he was for the most part aware of the situation as we moved along in that I was interpreting his answers even though they were yes or no answers as fully meditating over these situations that I presented to him and they had a lot of meaning to me. I felt that his answers as a whole were helpful and that he was looking out for the benefit to the situation for the most part and not to curtail it or cut it short in any means. I heard what I wanted to hear in most of the situations presented at the time. Perhaps I did not hear what I really wanted to hear but perhaps from an objective standpoint they were the best answers because someone involved in a situation is blinded to a certain degree and cannot take this objective viewpoint. And therefore these answers may differ from the person who is involved in the situation and the person who is outside and can take an objective viewpoint. I honestly believe that the answers that he gave me, that he was completely aware of the situation at hand. Perhaps I guess that should be qualified. Perhaps when I said should I talk to Dad for instance he was not positive. When I said should I talk to Dad for instance he was not positive what I was going to talk to Dad about. In a full capacity. He knew the general topic but he is not aware how close I am to Dad or how involved the conversation might get. And if his saying "do talk" in knowing that Dad will not listen, well this perhaps isn't best, or if Dad is very willing to listen he says it may not help. Or don't talk. Well this once again is bringing in personalities which he is not aware of. The conversation and the answers given I believe had a lot of meaning to me. I mean it was perhaps what I would have expected from someone who fully understood the situation. And I feel that it had a lot of sense to me and made a lot of sense. Well I felt that the questions that I asked were very pertinent and did help in understanding the situation on both sides, that is myself and the answerer and my reaction to the answers like I have stated before were mostly in agreement. At times I was surprised but understood that because he is not fully aware of the situation and the personalities involved.

## CASE 2

SUBJECT: I would like to know whether or not I should change my major at the present time. I have a physics major with quite a deficit in grade points to bring up to get my C average in physics. I would like to switch over to mathematics. I have a little difficulty in it, but I think maybe I could handle it. I have failed several math courses here at U.C.L.A., but I have always repeated them and had *C*'s. I have come close to getting a *B* in math in one specific course because I studied a little more than in others but my question is still should I change my major?

EXPERIMENTER: My answer is no.

SUBJECT: Well he says no. And if I don't then I will have to make up my deficit in grade points which will be awfully difficult because I am not doing too well this semester. If I pull through this semester with seven units of *A* then I can count on possibly going on to get my degree in physics in February, but then I have this stigma of nuclear physics facing me. I thoroughly dislike the study of nuclear physics. Nuclear Physics 124 will be one of my required courses to get a degree in physics.

Do you think I could get a degree in physics on the basis of this knowledge that I must take Physics 124?

EXPERIMENTER: My answer is yes.

SUBJECT: He says yes. I don't see how I can. I am not that good of a theorist. My study habits are horrible. My reading speed is bad, and I don't spend enough time in studying.

Do you think that I could successfully improve my study habits?

EXPERIMENTER: My answer is yes.

SUBJECT: He says that I can successfully improve my study habits. I have been preached to all along on how to study properly, but I don't study properly. I don't have sufficient incentive to go through physics or do I?

Do you think I have sufficient incentive to get a degree in physics?

EXPERIMENTER: My answer is yes.

SUBJECT: He says my answer is yes. I think possibly so if I didn't have a bad scholastic record behind me to follow me up. It would be awfully difficult to get that degree.

Do you think I could successfully do my studying while trying to keep happy relations at home with my wife and still get my work done? I don't do my studying well at school and I don't have much incentive to study when I am at home. But when my wife comes home, I like to study. Yet this keeps us from doing things, and whenever she doesn't do things, it gets on my nerves because there is all this work piling up. Do you think I could successfully do my studying at home?

EXPERIMENTER: My answer is no.

SUBJECT: He says no. I don't think so either.

Should I come to school every night after supper and do my studying?

EXPERIMENTER: My answer is no.

SUBJECT: He says I shouldn't come to school and study. Where should I go? Should I go to the library on campus to do my studying?

EXPERIMENTER: My answer is yes.

SUBJECT: He says I should go to the library to do my studying. Which library? They may not have all the references there that I may need but that is not always necessary. I need at least three more questions. Do you think I can develop sufficiently good study habits and incentive to actually achieve developing those habits such that I wouldn't have to stay up late at night and not get the work done in the first place?

EXPERIMENTER: My answer is no.

SUBJECT: He says no. I can't develop the study habits properly to be able to pull myself through. If you don't think that I can develop the proper study habits and carry them through to reach my goal do you on the basis of this still believe that I can get a degree in physics?

EXPERIMENTER: My answer is no.

SUBJECT: According to that I won't get a degree. What should I do? Are you still there?

EXPERIMENTER: Yes, I am.

SUBJECT: If you don't think I will make the . . . achieve the necessary goal of improving my study habits and getting a degree in physics do you recommend that I quit school?

EXPERIMENTER: My answer is yes.

SUBJECT: He says I should quit school. Are you still there?

EXPERIMENTER: Yes.

SUBJECT: I have one more question. I would like to get a commission in the Air Force. I have completed the Air Force R.O.T.C. training program but to get a commission I need a degree. If I don't get the degree the chances are very strong that I may not get the commission although there are in's and out's that there is still some possibility that I may still get a commission without a degree, although this is not desirable. The question is, will I get a commission in the Air Force?

EXPERIMENTER: My answer is yes.

SUBJECT: He says I will get a commission in the Air Force and that is what I am looking forward to, but will I ever get a degree? If I get a commission without a degree will I ever get a degree in anything?

EXPERIMENTER: My answer is no.

SUBJECT: This leaves me somewhat unhappy although I don't really need a degree in the type of work that I desire to do. Are you there? Come back in.

The subject commented as follows.

Well, as far as what I got from the conversation, it is rather foolish for me to pursue my work any further as far as getting a degree in anything. Actually I have felt all along that the type of work I am interested in which is inventing is not something that requires a degree necessarily. It requires a certain knowledge of math and physics but it doesn't require a degree to do inventing. From the conversation I gather that I should just quit school and go ahead and get my commission but how I don't know. But it would be awfully nice to have a degree. That degree would be able to get me into other schools. Otherwise I will have the statement that I went through college but I never got out. I also get the impression that my study habits will never improve as much as I would like them to anyway. I will not get a degree. I will get a commission and it is fruitless for me to study either at home or at school. Especially in the evening. I wonder if I should do any studying at all, or if I should learn to do all my studying at school. What to do? I have the feeling that my parents would be very unhappy and also my wife's parents would be very unhappy if I never did get a degree or at least especially right now. I have the feeling that this past conversation is based on what one should have learned to do years ago, that is, as a growing child. To ask themselves questions and give himself an answer of some type, yes or no, and to think out reasons why either yes or no holds or might hold and upon the validity or the anticipation of the validity of that answer what one should do accomplish his goal or just exist. I personally think I can do better in math than I can in physics. But I won't know until the end of the summer.

## FINDINGS

An examination of the protocols reveals the following:

A. *Getting through the exchange.*

None of the subjects had difficulty in accomplishing the series of ten questions, and in summarizing and evaluating the advice.

B. *Answers were perceived as "answers-to-questions."*

1. Typically the subjects heard the experimenter's answers as answers-to-the-questions. Perceptually, the experimenter's answers were motivated by the questions.

2. Subjects saw directly "what the adviser had in mind." They heard "in a glance" what he was talking about, *i.e.*, what he meant, and not what he had uttered.

3. The typical subject assumed, over the course of the exchange, and during the postexperimental interview, that the answers were advice to the problem, and that this advice as a solution to the problem was to be found via the answers.

4. All reported the "advice that they had been given" and addressed their appreciation and criticism to that "advice."

C. *There were no preprogrammed questions; the next question was motivated by the retrospective-prospective possibilities of the present situation that were altered by each actual exchange.*

1. No subject administered a preprogrammed set of questions.

2. Present answers altered the sense of previous exchanges.

3. Over the course of the exchange the assumption seemed to operate that there was an answer to be obtained, and that if the answer was not obvious, that its meaning could be determined by active search, one part of which involved asking another question so as to find out what the adviser "had in mind."

4. Much effort was devoted to looking for meanings that were intended but were not evident from the immediate answer to the question.

5. The present answer-to-the-question motivated the succeeding set of possibilities from among which the next question was

selected. The next question emerged as a product of reflections upon the previous course of the conversation and the presupposed underlying problem as the topic whose features each actual exchange documented and extended. The underlying "problem" was elaborated in its features as a function of the exchange. The sense of the problem was progressively accommodated to each present answer, while the answer motivated fresh aspects of the underlying problem.

6. The underlying pattern was elaborated and compounded over the series of exchanges and was accommodated to each present "answer" so as to maintain the "course of advice," to elaborate what had "really been advised" previously, and to motivate the new possibilities as emerging features of the problem.

D. *Answers in search of questions.*

1. Over the course of the exchange, subjects sometimes started with the reply as an answer and altered the previous sense of their question to accommodate this to the reply as the answer to the retrospectively revised question.

2. The identical utterance was capable of answering several different questions simultaneously, and of constituting an answer to a compound question that in terms of the strict logic of propositions did not permit either a yes or no or a single yes or no.

3. The same utterance was used to answer several different questions separated in time. Subjects referred to this as "shedding new light" on the past.

4. Present answers provided answers to further questions that were never asked.

E. *Handling incomplete, inappropriate, and contradictory answers.*

1. Where answers were unsatisfying or incomplete, the questioners were willing to wait for later answers in order to decide the sense of the previous ones.

2. Incomplete answers were treated by subjects as incomplete because of the "deficiencies" of this method of giving advice.

3. Answers that were inappropriate were inappropriate for "a reason." If the reason was found, the sense of the answer was thereupon decided. If an answer made "good sense" this was likely to be what the answerer had "advised."

4. When answers were incongruous or contradictory, subjects were able to continue by finding that the "adviser" had learned more in the meantime, or that he had decided to change his mind, or that perhaps he was not sufficiently acquainted with the intricacies of the problem, or the fault was in the question so that another phrasing was required.

5. Incongruous answers were resolved by imputing knowledge and intent to the adviser.

6. Contradictories required that the subject elect the real question that the answer answered which they did by furnishing the question with additional meanings that fit with the meanings "behind" what the adviser was advising.

7. In the case of contradictory answers much effort was devoted to reviewing the possible intent of the answer so as to rid the answer of contradiction or meaninglessness, and to rid the answerer of untrustworthiness.

8. More subjects entertained the possibility of a trick than tested this possibility. All suspicious subjects were reluctant to act under the belief that there was a trick involved. Suspicions were quieted if the adviser's answers made "good sense." Suspicions were most unlikely to continue if the answers accorded with the subject's previous thought about the matter and with his preferred decisions.

9. Suspicions transformed the answer into an event of "mere speech" having the appearance of coincidental occurrence with the occasion of the questioner's question. Subjects found this structure difficult to maintain and manage. Many subjects saw the sense of the answer "anyway."

10. Those who became suspicious, simultaneously, though temporarily, withdrew their willingness to continue.

F. *"Search" for and perception of pattern.*

1. Throughout there was a concern and search for pattern. Pattern, however, was perceived from the very beginning. Pattern was likely to be seen in the first evidence of the "advice."

2. Subjects found it very difficult to grasp the implications of randomness in the utterances. A predetermined utterance was treated as deceit in the answers instead of as an utterance that was decided beforehand and that occurred independently of the subject's questions and interests.

3. When the possibility of deception occurred to the subjects, the adviser's utterance documented the pattern of the deceit instead of the pattern of advice. Thus the relationship of the utterance to the underlying pattern as its document remained unchanged.

G. *Answers were assigned a scenic source.*

1. Subjects assigned to the adviser as his advice the thought formulated in the subject's questions. For example, when a subject asked, "Should I come to school every night after supper to do my studying?" and the experimenter said, "My answer is no," the subject in his comments said, "He said I shouldn't come to school and study." This was very common.

2. All subjects were surprised to find that they contributed so actively and so heavily to the "advice that they had received from the adviser."

3. Upon being told about the deception the subjects were intensely chagrined. In most cases they revised their opinions about the procedure to emphasize its inadequacies for the experimenter's purposes (which they understood still to be an exploration of means of giving advice).

H. *The vagueness of every present situation of further possibilities remained invariant to the clarification furnished by the exchanges of questions and answers.*

1. There was vagueness (a) in the status of the utterance as an answer, (b) in its status as an answer-to-the-question, (c) in its status as a document of advice with respect to the underlying pattern, and (d) in the underlying problem. While, after the course of an exchange, the utterances furnished "advice about the problem," their function of advice also elaborated the entire scheme of problematic possibilities so that the overall effect was that of a transformation of the subject's situation in which the vagueness of its horizons remained unchanged and "problems still remained unanswered."

I. *In their capacity as members, subjects consulted institutionalized features of the collectivity as a scheme of interpretation.*

1. Subjects made specific reference to various social structures in deciding the sensible and warranted character of the adviser's ad-

vice. Such references, however, were not made to any social structures whatever. In the eyes of the subject, if the adviser was to know and demonstrate to the subject that he knew what he was talking about, and if the subject was to consider seriously the adviser's descriptions of his circumstances as grounds of the subject's further thoughts and management of these circumstances, the subject did not permit the adviser, nor was the subject willing to entertain, *any* model of the social structures. References that the subject supplied, were to social structures which he treated as actually or potentially known in common with the adviser. And then, not to *any* social structures known in common, but to *normatively valued social structures* which the subject accepted as *conditions* that his decisions, with respect to his own sensible and realistic grasp of his circumstances and the "good" character of the adviser's advice, had to satisfy. These social structures consisted of normative features of the social system *seen from within* which, for the subject, were definitive of his memberships in the various collectivities that were referred to.

2. Subjects gave little indication, prior to the occasions of use of the rules for deciding fact and nonfact, what the definitive normative structures were to which their interpretations would make reference. The rules for documenting these definitive normative orders seemed to come into play only after a set of normative features had been motivated as relevant to his interpretive tasks, and then as a function of the fact that the activities of interpretation were under way.

3. Subjects presupposed known-in-common features of the collectivity as a body of common sense knowledge subscribed to by both. They drew upon these presupposed patterns in assigning to what they heard the adviser talking about, its status of documentary evidence of the definitive normative features of the collectivity settings of the experiment, family, school, home, occupation, to which the subject's interests were directed. These evidences and the collectivity features were referred back and forth to each other, with each elaborating and being thereby elaborated in its possibilities.

J. *Deciding warrant was identical with assigning the advice its perceivedly normal sense.*

Through a retrospective-prospective review, subjects justified the "reasonable" sense and sanctionable status of the advice as grounds for managing their affairs. Its "reasonable" character consisted of its compatibility with normative orders of social structures presumed to be subscribed to and known between subject and adviser. The subject's task of deciding the warranted character of what was being advised was identical with the task of assigning to what the adviser proposed (1) its status as an instance of a class of events; (2) its likelihood of occurrence; (3) its comparability with past and future events; (4) the conditions of its occurrence; (5) its place in a set of means-ends relationships; and (6) its necessity according to a natural (*i.e.*, moral) order. The subjects assigned these values of typicality, likelihood, comparability, causal texture, technical efficacy, and moral requiredness while using the institutionalized features of the collectivity as a scheme of interpretation. Thus, the subject's task of deciding whether or not what the adviser advised was "true" was identical with the task of assigning to what the adviser proposed its perceivedly normal values.

K. *Perceivedly normal values were not so much "assigned" as managed.*

Through the work of documenting—*i.e.*, by searching for and determining pattern, by treating the adviser's answers as motivated by the intended sense of the question, by waiting for later answers to clarify the sense of previous ones, by finding answers to unasked questions—the perceivedly normal values of what was being advised were established, tested, reviewed, retained, restored; in a word, managed. It is misleading, therefore, to think of the documentary method as a procedure whereby propositions are accorded membership in a scientific corpus.[5] Rather the documentary method developed the advice so as to be continually "membershipping" it.

### Examples in sociological inquiry

Examples of the use of the documentary method can be cited from every area of sociological investigation.[6] Its obvious applica-

---

[5] Cf. Felix Kaufman, *Methodology of the Social Sciences* (New York: Oxford University Press, 1944), especially pp. 33-36.

[6] In his article, "On the Interpretation of 'Weltanschauung,'" Mannheim

tion occurs in community studies where warrant is assigned to statements by the criteria of "comprehensive description" and "ring of truth." Its use is found also on the many occasions of survey research when the researcher, in reviewing his interview notes or in editing the answers to a questionnaire, has to decide "what the respondent had in mind." When a researcher is addressed to the "motivated character" of an action, or a theory, or a person's compliance to a legitimate order and the like, he will use what he has actually observed to "document" an "underlying pattern." The documentary method is used to epitomize the object. For example, just as the lay person may say of something that "Harry" says, "Isn't that just like Harry?" the investigator may use some observed feature of the thing he is referring to as a characterizing indicator of the intended matter. Complex scenes like industrial establishments, communities, or social movements are frequently described with the aid of "excerpts" from protocols and numerical tables which are used to epitomize the intended events. The documentary method is used whenever the investigator constructs a life history or a "natural history." The task of historicizing the person's biography consists of using the documentary method to select and order past occurrences so as to furnish the present state of affairs its relevant past and prospects.

The use of the documentary method is not confined to cases of "soft" procedures and "partial descriptions." It occurs as well in cases of rigorous procedures where descriptions are intended to exhaust a definite field of possible observables. In reading a journal account for the purpose of literal replication, researchers who attempt to reconstruct the relationship between the reported procedures and the results frequently encounter a gap of insufficient information. The gap occurs when the reader asks how the investigator decided the correspondence between what was actually observed and the intended event for which the actual observation is treated as its evidence. The reader's problem consists of having

---

argued that the documentary method is peculiar to the social sciences. There exist in the social sciences many terminological ways of referring to it, viz., "the method of understanding," "sympathetic introspection," "method of insight," "method of intuition," "interpretive method," "clinical method," "emphatic understanding," and so on. Attempts by sociologists to identify something called "interpretive sociology" involve reference to the documentary method as the basis for encountering and warranting its findings.

to decide that the reported observation is a literal instance of the intended occurrence, *i.e.*, that the actual observation and the intended occurrence are identical *in sense*. Since the relationship between the two is a sign relationship, the reader must consult some set of grammatical rules to decide this correspondence. This grammar consists of some theory of the intended events on the basis of which the decisions to code the actual observations as findings are recommended. It is at this point that the reader must engage in interpretive work and an assumption of "underlying" matters "just known in common" about the society in terms of which, what the respondent said, is treated as synonymous with what the observer meant. Correct correspondence is apt to be meant and read on reasonable grounds. Correct correspondence is the product of the work of investigator and reader as members of a community of cobelievers. Thus, even in the case of rigorous methods, if a researcher is to recommend, and the reader is to appreciate, published findings as members of the corpus of sociological fact, the work of the documentary method is employed.

### Sociological situations of inquiry as common sense situations of choice

It is not unusual for professional sociologists to speak of their "fact production" procedures as processes of "seeing through" appearances to an underlying reality; of brushing past actual appearances to "grasp the invariant." Where our subjects are concerned, their processes are not appropriately imagined as "seeing through," but consist instead of coming to terms with a situation in which factual knowledge of social structures—factual in the sense of warranted grounds of further inferences and actions—must be assembled and made available for potential use despite the fact that the situations it purports to describe are, in any calculable sense, unknown; in their actual and intended logical structures are essentially vague; and are modified, elaborated, extended, if not indeed created, by the fact and manner of being addressed.

If many of the features of our subjects' documentary work are recognizable in the work of professional sociological fact production, similarly many situations of professional sociological inquiry have precisely the features that our subjects' situations had. Such features of situations of professional sociological inquiry may be more exactly specified as follows.

1. In the course of an interview an investigator is likely to find himself addressing a series of present situations whose *future states that a contemplated course of treatment will produce* are characteristically vague or even unknown. With overwhelming frequency these as of here-and-now possible future states are only sketchily specifiable prior to undertaking the action that is intended to realize them. There is a necessary distinction between a "possible future state of affairs" and a "how-to-bring-it-about-future-from-a-present-state-of-affairs-as-an-actual-point-of-departure." The "possible future state of affairs" may be very clear indeed. But such a future is not the matter of interest. Instead we are concerned with the "how to bring it about from a here-and-now future." It is this state—for convenience, call it an "operational future"—that is characteristically vague or unknown.

An illustration: A trained survey researcher can describe with remarkable clarity and definiteness what questions he wishes answers to in a questionnaire. How actual replies of actual subjects are to be evaluated as "replies to the questions" are incorporated in a set of procedural decisions known as "coding rules." Any distribution of replies to the questions that is possible under the coding rules is a "possible future state of affairs." After suitable exploratory work such distributions are clearly and definitely imaginable to trained field workers. But with overwhelming frequency it occurs that even late in the *actual* course of the inquiry the questions and answers that will *in effect* have been asked and answered under the various ways of evaluating actual subject's responses as "replies to the question," given the practical exigencies that must be accommodated in accomplishing the actual work of the inquiry, remain sketchy and open to "reasonable decision" even up to the point of composing the results of the inquiry for publication.

2. Given a future, any future, that is known in a definite way, the alternative paths to actualize the future state as a set of stepwise operations upon some beginning present state are characteristically sketchy, incoherent, and unelaborated. Again it is necessary to stress the difference between an inventory of available procedures—investigators can talk about these quite definitely and clearly —and the deliberately programmed stepwise procedures, a set of

predecided "what-to-do-in-case-of" strategies for the manipulation of a succession of actual present states of affairs *in their course*. In actual practices such a program is characteristically an unelaborated one.

For example, one of the tasks involved in "managing rapport" consists of managing the stepwise course of the conversation in such a way as to permit the investigator to commit his questions in profitable sequence while retaining some control over the unknown and undesirable directions in which affairs, as a function of the course of the actual exchange, may actually move.[7] Characteristically the researcher substitutes for a preprogrammed stepwise solution, a set of *ad hoc* tactics for adjusting to present opportunity, with these tactics only generally governed by what the investigator would hope to have finally found out by the end of the conversation. Under these circumstances, it is more accurate to talk of investigators acting in fulfillment of their hopes, or in avoidance of their fears, than of acting in the deliberate and calculated realization of a plan.

3. It frequently occurs that the investigator takes an action, and only upon the actual occurrence of some product of that action do we find him reviewing the accomplished sequences in a retrospective search therein for their decided character. Insofar as the *decision that was taken* is assigned by the work of the retrospective search, the outcome of such situations can be said to occur *before* the decision. Such situations occur with dramatic frequency at the time the journal article is being written.

4. Prior to his actually having to choose among alternative courses of action on the basis of anticipated consequences, the investigator, for various reasons, is frequently unable to anticipate the consequences of his alternative courses of action and may have to rely upon his actual involvement in order to learn what they might be.

5. Frequently, after encountering some actual state of affairs, the investigator may count it as desirable, and thereupon treat it as the goal toward which his previously taken actions, as he reads them retrospectively, were directed "all along" or "after all."

6. It frequently occurs that only in the course of actually manip-

[7] Cf. Robert K. Merton and Patricia L. Kendall, "The Focused Interview," *American Journal of Sociology*, 51 (1946), 541-557.

ulating a present situation, and as a function of his actual manipulation, does the nature of an investigator's future state of affairs become clarified. Thus, the goal of the investigation may be progressively defined as the consequence of the investigator's actually taking action toward a goal whose features as of any present state of his investigative action he does not see clearly.

7. Characteristically such situations are ones of "imperfect information." The result is that the investigator is unable to assess, let alone calculate, the difference that his ignorance in the situation makes upon the accomplishment of his activities. Nor, prior to having to take action, is he able either to evaluate their consequences or to assess the value of alternative courses of action.

8. The information that he possesses, that serves him as the basis for the election of strategies, is rarely codified. Hence, his estimates of the likelihood of success or failure characteristically have little in common with the rational mathematical concept of probability.

In their investigative activities, investigators characteristically must manage situations with the above features, given the following additional conditions: that some action must be taken; that the action must be taken by a time and in pace, duration, and phasing that is coordinate with the actions of others; that the risks of unfavorable outcomes must somehow be managed; that the actions taken and their products will be subject to review by others and must be justified to them; that the elections of courses of action and the resultant outcome must be justified within the procedures of "reasonable" review; and that the entire process must occur within the conditions of, and with his motivated compliance to, corporately organized social activity. In their "shop talk" investigators refer to these features of their actual situations of inquiry and to the necessity for managing them as their "practical circumstances."

Because their features are so easily recognized in the activities of daily life, situations with such features may appropriately be called "common sense situations of choice." The suggestion is recommended that when researchers call upon "reasonableness" in assigning the status of "findings" to their research results, they are inviting the use of such features as these as a context of interpretation for deciding sensibility and warrant. Findings as outcomes of documentary work, decided under circumstances of common sense situations of choice, define the term "reasonable findings."

## The problem

Much of "core sociology" consists of "reasonable findings." Many, if not most, situations of sociological inquiry are common sense situations of choice. Nevertheless, textbook and journal discussions of sociological methods rarely give recognition to the fact that sociological inquiries are carried out under common sense auspices *at the points where decisions about the correspondence between observed appearances and intended events are being made*. Instead, available descriptions and conceptions of investigative decision-making and problem-solving assign to the decision-maker's situation contrasting features as follows.[8]

1. From the decision-maker's point of view there exists as a feature of each of his here-and-now states of affairs a recognizable goal with specifiable features. Where sociological inquiry is concerned, this goal consists of the investigator's present problem for the solution to which the investigation will have been undertaken. The goal's specifiable features consist of the criteria whereby, as of any present state of affairs, he decides the adequacy with which his problem has been formulated. In their terms, too, the event, "adequate solution," is defined as one of the set of possible occurrences.

2. The decision-maker is conceived to have set for himself the task of devising a program of manipulations upon each successive present state of affairs that will alter each present state so that over their succession they are brought into conformity with an anticipated state, *i.e.*, the goal, the solved problem.[9]

[8] I wish to thank Drs. Robert Boguslaw and Myron A. Robinson for many hours of discussion that we had about calculable and noncalculable situations of choice when we were trying together to work through the problem of how consistently successful play in chess is possible.

[9] In some cases, students of decision-making have been interested in those programs that represent fully calculated solutions to the decision-maker's problems. In other cases studies have addressed the fact that the decision-maker may invoke probabilistic rules to decide the differential likelihood that alternative course of action would alter a present state of affairs in the desired direction.

These features may be restated in terms of the rules of evidence. As a calculable state of affairs, an investigator's problem may be regarded as a proposition whose "application" for membership, *i.e.*, whose warranted status, is under review. The rules of procedure whereby its warranted status is decided thereby operationally define what is meant by "adequate solution." In ideal scientific activities an investigator is required to decide the steps that define an adequate solution prior to his taking the decided steps. He is required to make this decision before he carries out the operations whereby the possibilities that the proposition proposes will be decided as to their having actually occurred or not. The task of deciding an adequate solution thereby has logical precedence over the actual observation. The observation is said thereby to be "programmed," or, alternatively, the intended event is given an "operational definition," or, alternatively, the conditions for the occurrence of an intended event are furnished, or, alternatively, a "prediction" is made.

A prominent argument on behalf of this emphasis is that the documentary method is a scientifically erroneous procedure; that its use distorts the objective world in a mirror of subjective prejudice; and that where common sense situations of choice exist they do so as historical nuisances. Protagonists for methods such as those used in survey research and laboratory experimentation, for example, assert their increasing exemption from situations with common sense characteristics and documentary dealings with them. After World War II a flood of textbooks on methods was written to provide remedies for such situations. These methods are intended to depict the ways of transforming common sense situations into calculable ones. Most particularly, the use of mathematical models and statistical schemes of inference are invoked as calculable solutions to the problems of deciding sensibility, objectivity, and warrant in a rigorous way. Immense sums of foundation money, criteria defining adequate research designs, and many careers rest on the conviction that this is so.

Yet it is common knowledge that in the overwhelming number of researches that are methodologically acceptable, and, paradoxically, precisely to the extent that rigorous methods are used, dramatical discrepancies are visible between the theoretical properties of the intended *sociological* findings of inquirers and the mathematical assumptions that must be satisfied if the statistical measures are to be used for the literal description of the intended events. The result is that statistical measurements are most frequently used as indicators, as signs of, as representing or standing on behalf of the intended findings, rather than as literal descriptions of them. Thus, at the point where sociological findings must be decided from statistical results,[10] rigorous methods are being asserted as solutions to the tasks of literal description on the grounds of "reasonable" considerations.

Even if it is demonstrable that these features are present, let alone prominent, in sociological inquiries, is it not nevertheless true that a situation of inquiry might receive documentary treatment and still the factual status of its products would be decided differently? For example, is it not the case that there are strictures against *ex post facto* analysis? And is it not so that a field worker who learned after he consulted his notes what problems he had "in the final analysis" obtained answers to, might reapply for a grant to perform a "confirmatory study" of the "hypotheses" that his reflections had yielded? Is there, therefore, any *necessary* connection between the features of common sense situations of choice, the use of documentary method, and the *corpus of sociological fact?* Must the documentary method necessarily be used by the professional sociologist to decide sensibility, objectivity, and warrant? Is there a necessary connection between the theoretical subject matter of sociology, as this is constituted by the attitude and procedures for "seeing sociologically" on the one hand, and the canons of adequate description, *i.e.*, evidence, on the other?

Between the methods of literal observation and the work of documentary interpretation the investigator can choose the former and achieve rigorous literal description of physical and biological properties of sociological events. This has been demonstrated on many occasions. Thus far the choice has been made at the cost of

---

[10] The term "results" is used to refer to the set of *mathematical* events that are possible when the procedures of a statistical test, like chi square, for example, are treated as grammatical rules for conceiving, comparing, producing, etc., events in the mathematical domain. The term "findings" is used to refer to the set of *sociological* events that are possible when, under the assumption that the sociological and mathematical domains correspond in their logical structures, sociological events are interpreted in terms of the rules of statistical inference.

either neglecting the properties that make events sociological ones, or by using documentary work to deal with the "soft" parts.

The choice has to do with the question of the conditions under which literal observation and documentary work necessarily occur. This involves the formulation of, and solution to, the problem of sociological evidence in terms that permit a descriptive solution. Undoubtedly, scientific sociology is a "fact," but in Felix Kaufmann's sense of fact, *i.e.*, in terms of a set of procedural rules that *actually* govern the use of sociologists' recommended methods and asserted findings as grounds of further inference and inquiries. The problem of evidence consists of the tasks of making this fact intelligible.

# FOUR

# Some rules of correct decision making that jurors respect*

Jurors make their decisions while maintaining a healthy respect for the routine features of the social order. This paper is concerned to show some consequent features of that decision making. Several features of jurors' activities, conceived as a *method of social inquiry,* will first be described. We shall then describe some rules of decision making that are used in daily life that jurors respect, and following this we shall describe the rules of decision making that make up the "official line" that jurors also respect. It will then be suggested that (1) jurors feel called upon to modify the rules used in daily life; (2) the modifications they make are slight and produce an ambiguous situation of choice for them; and (3) it is the management of this ambiguity and not his "judiciousness," that commonly characterizes the activity of being a juror.

## Jurors' activities as a method of social inquiry

Several features characterize jury activities as a method of social inquiry. As a decision-making body, the jury has the task of deciding the legally enforceable situation that exists between contenders. Such a legally enforceable situation is known as a "verdict." As phases of this task, the jurors (a) decide the harm and its extent;

* *In collaboration with Saul Mendlovitz, The Law School, Rutgers University.*

(b) decide an allocation of blame; and (c) decide a remedy. The question of deciding the harm is that of deciding what socially defined types of persons are legitimately entitled to have what kinds of trouble.[1] By allocating the blame is meant that jurors decide socially acceptable causal orderings of agents and outcomes. In recommending remedies, the jurors decide what measures are required to make matters right.[2] In short, jurors are engaged in deciding "reasonable causes and remedies."[3]

In the course of their deliberations, jurors sort alternative depictions made by lawyers, witnesses, and jurors of what happened and why between the statuses of relevant or irrelevant, justifiable or unjustifiable, correct or incorrect grounds for the choice of the verdict. When jurors address such matters as dates, speeds, the plaintiff's injury and the like, what do the jurors' decisions specifically decide?

In something like the jurors' own terms, and trying to capture the jurors' dialectic,[4] jurors decide between what is fact and what is fancy; between what actually happened and what "merely appeared" to happen; between what is put on and what is truth, regardless of detracting appearances; between what is credible and, very frequently for jurors, the opposite of credible, what is calculated and said by design; between what is an issue and what was decided; between what is *still* an issue compared with what

---

[1] Weber's definition of misfortune as the discrepancy between "destiny and merit" is the type of phenomenon that the term "trouble" is intended to refer to. "The Social Psychology of the World Religions," in *From Max Weber, Essays in Sociology*, ed. H. H. Gerth and C. Wright Mills, pp. 267-301.

[2] Should the plaintiff's circumstances be adjusted to what they would have been had there not occurred the "aberrancy" to the "normal" course of events? Should the plaintiff be compensated for an irreversible change of circumstances?

[3] By "reasonable" is meant those rational properties of action exhibited to a member by actions governed by the system of relevances of the attitude of daily life. "Reasonable" as contrasted with "rational" properties of action are discussed in Alfred Schutz, "The Problem of Rationality in the Social World," in *Collected Papers II: Studies in Social Theory*, pp. 64-88. See also Chapter Eight.

[4] These are formal categories, although not in the sense of conventional logic. The-amount-that-is-sufficient is a general category of juror discourse. It does not yet say anything about an amount that is, as a matter of bookkeeping, "sufficient." It does not say anything about whether, for example, $11,000 will cover doctor bills. It only says whatsoever is an amount that is an instance of an amount-that-is-sufficient. The term refers therefore to an intended general object, the amount-that-is-sufficient.

is irrelevant and will not be brought up again except by a person who has an axe to grind; between what is mere personal opinion and what any right-thinking person would have to agree to; between what-may-be-so-but-only-for-an-expert-and-we-aren't-experts on the one hand, and what-we-know-that-you-don't-learn-out-of-books on the other; between what-you-say-may-be-right-and-we-may-be-wrong, and what-eleven-of-us-say-may-be-wrong-but-I-doubt-it; between an amount that is sufficient and an amount that won't begin to cover the needs; between an amount-that-is-an-average-of-several-unstated-and-unknown-sums, and the amount-that-is-best-for-her-that-twelve-people-can-agree-on-if-you-want-to-get-any-thing-at-all.

Jurors come to an agreement amongst themselves as to what actually happened. They decide "the facts," [5] *i.e.*, among alternative claims about speeds of travel or extent of injury, jurors decide which may be correctly used as the basis for further inferences and action. They do this by consulting the consistency of alternative claims with common sense models.[6] Those common sense models are models jurors use to depict, for example, what culturally known types of persons drive in what culturally known types of ways at what typical speeds at what types of intersections for what typical motives. The test runs that the matter that is meaningfully consistent may be correctly treated as the thing that actually occurred. If the interpretation makes good sense, then that's what happened.[7]

The sorting of claims between the statuses of correct and incorrect grounds of inference produces a set of accepted points of fact and accepted schemes for relating these points. The sorting

[5] Felix Kaufmann's conception of fact is used throughout this paper. He proposes that the factual character of a statement is found in a rule that governs its use and is not found in the ontological characteristics of the events that the statement depicts. See *Methodology of the Social Sciences* (New York: Oxford University Press, 1944).

[6] The use of "common sense models" as culturally presupposed standards, and the logical properties of these models in everyday activities are illuminatingly discussed in Alfred Schutz, "Part I, On the Methodology of the Social Sciences," in *Collected Papers I: The Problem of Social Reality*, pp. 3-96; and in his remarkable study, "Symbol, Reality, and Society," pp. 287-356.

[7] Cf. Felix Kaufmann's discussion of the "rule of dogmatics" as a definition of fact compared with the "rule of observation" as a definition of fact in *Methodology of the Social Sciences*. These rules are definitions of fact for they state the conditions that must be met to warrant a statement, i.e., to sanction its use as grounds for further inference and action.

produces a "corpus of knowledge"[8] that has in part the form of a chronological story, and in part the form of a set of general empirical relationships.[9] This "corpus" is treated by the jurors at any given time as "the case." By "the case" is meant the logical mode of "actual" and is contrasted by jurors with the logical modes of "supposed," "possible," "fanciful," "hypothetical," and the like.

The decisions to treat, say, claims of speed, directions of travel, and so on as parts of "the case" are, in the jurors' eyes, critical decisions. The decisions as to what "actually happened" provide jurors the grounds that they use in inferring the social support that they feel they are entitled to receive for the verdict they choose. The "corpus" permits them to infer the legitimacy of their expectation that they will be socially supported for their choice of verdict.

### Jurors' decision rules

The jurors methodology consists of those rules that govern what depictions jurors permit each other to treat as "the case." Of several sets of variables that governed what went into "the case," only one set will concern us: the features of the actual and potential social structuring of court and outside scenes that were treated by jurors as ethically and morally required uniformities, *i.e.*, the normative orders of interaction outside of as well as within the court.[10]

Several such normative orders can be cited as rules that governed what jurors could correctly treat as "the case." Conformity with these orders served thereby to determine jurors' satisfaction or dissatisfaction with the verdict. Stated as rules of correct decision-making procedure, they run as follows.

[8] The term "corpus of knowledge" and its meaning is borrowed from Felix Kaufmann, *op. cit.*, pp. 33-66.

[9] The sorting produces the set of statements that can correctly be used as the basis for further inferences and action. The set is constituted by the members' use, as procedural rules, of the attitude of daily life. The set, termed the "corpus" of fact, or "the case," has properties that are relevant to the problems of this paper but which cannot be treated here. For example, it is retained in unrecorded fashion, successive reproductions are subject to operations of successive recall, it is uncodified, etc. See Chapter Three.

[10] Other important sources of variables were (1) the present state of the case at any moment of the trial and deliberations, and (2) the actual organizational and operational features of the trial and deliberations.

Those decisions [11] on the facts are correct:

1. That are made within a respect for the time that it takes to arrive at them.

2. That do not require of the juror as a condition for making them that adequate exercise of doubt requires that he act as if he knows nothing, *i.e.*, that do not require that he make no use of What Any Competent Member of the Society Knows That Anyone Knows.

3. That do not require of the juror, as a condition for making them, that he adopt a neutral attitude toward the everyday relationships that exist among the persons on the jury.

4. That do not require that the juror call into doubt "What Anyone Knows" about the ways in which competence, authority, responsibility, and knowledge are usually distributed among and evidenced by social types of persons.

5. If the number of variables defining the problem (and thereby the adequacy of a solution) can be reduced to a minimum by trusting that the other persons on the jury subscribe to the same common sense models.

6. If the opportunity and the necessity for looking behind the appearance of things is held to a minimum.

7. If only as much of the situation is called into question as is required for a socially supportable solution to the immediate problem in hand.

8. If the jurors emerge from the inquiry with their reputations intact.

Somehow, in the course of his career in court, the juror is "asked" to modify the decision-making rules that he uses in the conduct of his daily affairs. The juror comes to appreciate an additional set of these culturally defined uniformities of social life, those that we shall call the "official juror line."

The following is a list of the rules making up the official line that the juror feels called upon to use:

[11] The rules that follow are to be compared with the rules that serve as definitions of correct decisions of scientific inquiry (i.e., scientific methodology).

1. Between what is legal and what is fair, the good juror does what is legal.

2. For a good juror, choices vary independently of sympathy.

3. For a good juror, the "law" and the "evidence" are the only legitimate grounds for a decision.

4. The good juror does not innovate upon the judge's instructions.

5. The good juror delays judgment until the important matters of trial have been completed. This includes paying particular inattention to the final arguments of lawyers, and not keeping score as the trial goes along.

6. For the good juror, personal preferences, interests, social preconceptions, *i.e.*, his perspectival view, are suspended in favor of a position that is interchangeable with all positions found in the entire social structure. His point of view is interchangeable with that of "Any Man." [12]

7. As a social type, the good juror is anonymous with reference to the social types of contending parties and their legal representatives. The good juror is without an identifiable position in their eyes. What he is going to decide cannot be told by any social evidences he gives in the course of trial by way of appearance, manner, questions, personal data, and so on.

8. The good juror suspends the applicability of the formulas that he habitually employs in coming to terms with the problems of his own everyday affairs. The formulas that are particular to the occasions of his everyday life on the outside are treated by the good juror as merely theoretically. applicable to the situation in court. Those formulas are correct for the good juror that apply irrespective of considerations of particular biography, special knowledge, structurally specific time, place, and persons.

9. Judgments are formed by the good juror independently of other persons but without suspending his respect for the possibility that other persons may form contrary judgments and are entitled to form contrary judgments.

[12] Any Man is the person universalistically defined within the terminology of types employed by the in-group.

10. For a good juror the expression of a position that involves an irrevocable commitment is withheld. A good juror will not take a position at a time that will require him to defend it "out of pride" instead of "on the merit of the argument and the regard for truth."

What we have listed are the rules that the *jurors talked about*. They depict not only some attributes of the good juror, but they depict what the actual jurors came to call and to accept for themselves as their relationships to the court. By and large, actual jurors did not want these relationships to be less than what the judge, by his treatment of the jurors, implied them to be.

Jurors learned the official line from various places: from the juror's handbook; from the instructions they received from the court; from the procedures of the *voire dire* when jurors were invited by the court to disqualify themselves if they could find for themselves reasons why they could not act in this fashion. They learned it from court personnel; they learned it from what jurors told each other, from TV, and from the movies. Several jurors got a quick tutoring by their high school children who had taken courses in civics. Finally, there is the fact that in the course of their ordinary outside affairs, jurors had built up a stock of information about procedures that were in their view merely theoretic, impractical, playful, make-believe, "high-class," "low-class" and so on.

### Deciding in a juror's fashion

As a person underwent the process of "becoming a juror" the rules of daily life were modified. It is our impression, however, that the person who changed a great deal, changed as much as 5 per cent in the manner of making his decisions. A person is 95 per cent juror before he comes near the court. What did the change consist of, and how does the change characterize a person acting as a juror?

Jurors' decisions that sort fact from fancy do not differ substantially from the decisions that he makes in this respect in his ordinary affairs. Nevertheless, there is a difference. The difference bears on the work of assembling the "corpus" which serves as grounds for inferring the correctness of a verdict.

Decisions in daily life that sort fact from fancy are not confined by an exclusive concern for achieving a definition of a situation for the sake of that definition.[13] But in the jury room, jurors must decide only what the situation is as a matter of fact, *e.g.*, who caused whom what troubles. It is the clarification as such of the grounds of a᾿choice of verdict that is the specific purpose of the jurors' inquiry. That the clarification is a step in a program of active manipulation of the situations of the contenders is known to the jurors, of course, but they put aside its relevance to the choice of verdict. In a word, the juror treats the situation as an object of theoretic interest.

Now it is by contrast to uniformities of events of daily life that are so well known as to serve as unproblematic grounds for ordinary social judgments, that the juror appreciates the "mere theoretic" character of social structures that contrast with them. The modification of these rules consists in the fact that the juror can treat them in Huizinga's sense of the "spirit of play," [14] that is, as matters that the juror is willing to "just go along with to see where it leads." Service as a juror invites the juror to honor the conceits that the judge expresses when, for example, during the *voire dire* the judge asks the juror if he can himself think of any reason why he cannot render a perfectly fair and legal judgment. In various ways the judge and others in the court invite the juror to see himself as a person who can act in accordance with the official line. Jurors were typically avid to accept this invitation. In effect the juror is invited to restructure his everyday conceptions of "fundamental" and "derivative" events. But having accepted such an invitation to treat the contenders' situations as a matter of theoretic interest, he undergoes an unsettling surprise. He comes to understand that what he feels called upon to so treat is, contrastively, treated with utmost seriousness by the contenders. Actions which on the grounds of the socially defined uniformities of daily life appear straightforward and plain in their meanings and consequences, are made equivocal by the contending advocates. The contenders insistently depict the sense of actions in clearly incompatible ways. Under these conditions, it is of interest that among

[13] Schutz, *On Multiple Realities*. See citation on p. 272.
[14] Johan Huizinga, *Homo Ludens, A Study of the Play Element in Culture* (New York: Roy Publishers, 1950), especially Chapter 1.

the alternative interpretations that someone is mistaken, that someone is lying, or that each could seriously believe what he contends, jurors typically believe the last.

Clearly the juror is asked to change his habitual rules of social judgments. Does then the change of the decision-making rules of daily life consist in the fact that jurors substitute for them the rules making up the official juror line? We think not. Becoming a juror does not mean becoming judicious. Instead, it seems to mean something like the following:

1. The rules of everyday life, as well as the rules of the official line, are simultaneously entertained. That is to say that the conditions of correct choice are ambiguously defined. Typically there were complaints from jurors that the situation they sought to make legally intelligible lacked clarity *after* the verdict.

2. Describing their deliberations in retrospect, jurors typically singled out evidences of normative integration in the deliberations and avoided evidences of anomie.

3. Such selective "redeliberations," as "solutions" to the ambiguities in their situations of "choice," were uneasily held and were productive of incongruity. But such discrepancies were privately entertained. Publically, jurors either described their decisions as having been arrived at in conformity with the official line or they preferred to withhold comment.

4. During the deliberations small failure in the use of the official line quickly sent the jurors back to the formulas of daily life, and when, afterwards, even small failures were called to their attention by the interviewers, the response was one of intense chagrin. If we make the plausible assumption that the structural conditions of chagrin are largely the same as those for shame,[15] the uneasy disparity between the public and private self-conceptions leads to the conjecture that becoming a juror may involve placing a person in a position of being easily if not actually personally compromised.

5. In interviews jurors masked, through the devices of myth, the actual extent to which ambiguities were part of the situation. Thus,

[15] See Richard Hays Williams, "Scheler's Contribution to the Sociology of Affective Actions with Special Reference to the Problem of Shame," *Philosophy and Phenomenological Research*, Vol. 2, No. 3, March, 1942 for Scheler's description of the structural conditions of shame.

(a) regardless of the procedures that were actually followed, as these were learned by the interviewer from other sources, jurors identified them with procedures depicted in the official line; (b) in their ideal accounts of how jurors arrived at their decisions, jurors told how the *right* decision was arrived at; (c) in their idealized accounts, jurors talked as if they knew the rules of decision making before they went into the deliberations; jurors did not say, nor did they care to discuss the fact, that it was in the course of the deliberations that they learned how the decisions were made; (d) as we noticed, their accounts of how the decisions were arrived at stressed integrative features of the deliberations and neglected anomic ones; (e) jurors were most unwilling to say that they learned in the course of the deliberations or afterwards in retrospect what had been expected of them. Their accounts stressed instead that from the beginning they knew what was expected of them and used this knowledge.

6. When, during the interviews, their attention was drawn by interviewers to the discrepancies between their ideal accounts and their "actual practices" [16] jurors became anxious. They looked to the interviewer for assurance that the verdict nevertheless had been correct in the judge's opinion. It is noteworthy too that such references rapidly used up interview rapport.

### Decision making in common sense situations of choice

The usual emphasis in studies of decision making is that persons know beforehand the conditions under which they will elect any one of a set of alternative courses of action, and that they correct their previous elections on the way through the action as additional information turns up.

We are proposing that perhaps for decisions made in common sense situations of choice whose features are largely taken for granted, *i.e.*, in everyday situations, it does not actually happen that way. In place of the view that decisions are made as the occasions require, an alternative formulation needs to be entertained.

---

[16] The "actual practices" that a juror was confronted with consisted of the picture of the deliberations that the investigators reconstructed from their previous interviews with a member or members of the jury on which the subject served.

It consists of the possibility that the person defines retrospectively the decisions that have been made. *The outcome comes before the decision.*

In the material reported here, jurors did not actually have an understanding of the conditions that defined a correct decision until after the decision had been made. Only in retrospect did they decide what they did that made their decisions correct ones. When the outcome was in hand they went back to find the "why," the things that led up to the outcome, and then in order to give their decisions some order, which namely, is the "officialness" of the decision.

If the above description is accurate, decision making in daily life would thereby have, as a critical feature, the *decision maker's task of justifying a course of action.* The rules of decision making in daily life, *i.e.,* rules of decision making for more or less socially routinized and respected situations, may be much more preoccupied with the problem of assigning outcomes their legitimate history than with the question of deciding before the actual occasion of choice the conditions under which one, among a set of alternative possible courses of action, will be elected.

Several fugitive remarks are thereby in order:

1. The procedure of deciding, before the actual occasion of choice the conditions under which one, among a set of alternative possible courses of action will be elected, is one definition of a rational strategy.[17] It is worth noting that this rational property of the decision-making process in managing everyday affairs is conspicuous by its absence.[18]

2. It is suggested that students of decision making may find it profitable to reconsult Cassirer's laws [19] that describe the ways that human situations are progressively clarified. Cassirer's "law of continuity" states that each outcome is a fulfillment of the preceding definition of the situation. His "law of new emphasis" states

[17] John Von Neumann and Oskar Morgenstern, *Theory of Games and Economic Behavior* (Princeton, N.J.: Princeton University Press, 1947).

[18] Cf. Alfred Schutz, "The Problem of Rationality in the Social World," *Economica,* 10 (May, 1943), 130-149.

[19] Robert S. Hartman, "Cassirer's Philosophy of Symbolic Forms," in *The Philosophy of Ernst Cassirer,* ed. Paul Arthur Schilpp (Evanston, Ill.: The Library of Living Philosophers, Inc., 1949), pp. 297 ff.

that each outcome develops the past definition of the situation. These "laws" remind us that persons, *in the course of a career of actions,* discover the nature of the situations in which they are acting, and that the actor's own actions are first order determinants of the sense that situations have, in which, literally speaking, actors *find* themselves.

3. We suggest, in conclusion and conjecturally, that instead of conceiving the sophisticated juror as a lay replica of the judge, that he be conceived as a lay person who, when changes occur in the jury's structure and operations, can alter the grounds of his decisions without becoming confused in his expectations of social support for what he will have done.

# FIVE

# Passing and the managed achievement of sex status in an "intersexed" person part 1*

Every society exerts close controls over the transfers of persons from one status to another. Where transfers of sexual statuses are concerned, these controls are particularly restrictive and rigorously enforced. Only upon highly ceremonialized occasions are changes permitted and then such transfers are characteristically regarded as "temporary" and "playful" variations on what the person "after all," and "really" is. Thereby societies exercise close controls over the ways in which the sex composition of their own populations are constituted and changed.

From the standpoint of persons who regard themselves as normally sexed, their environment has a perceivedly normal sex composition. This composition is rigorously dichotomized into the "natural," i.e., moral, entities of male and female. The dichotomy provides for persons who are "naturally," "originally," "in the first place," "in the beginning," "all along," and "forever" one or the other. Changes in the frequency of these moral entities can occur only through three legitimate paths: birth, death, and migration.

* In collaboration with Robert J. Stoller, M.D., The Neuropsychiatric Institute, University of California, Los Angeles. An appendix to this chapter is on p. 285.

Except for a legal change in birth certificate no legitimate path exists between the statuses of male and female. Even the legal change is regarded with considerable reservation by societal members who take their *bona fide* sex status for granted.

The normative, *i.e.*, legitimate sexual composition of the population as seen from the point of view of members who count themselves part of the perceivedly normally sexed population, can be described with the following table of transition probabilities:

At time$_2$

|  | | Male | Female |
|---|---|---|---|
| | Male | 1.0 | 0.0 |
| At time$_1$ | Female | 0.0 | 1.0 |

This study reports one of a series of cases that fall into the normatively prohibited lower left and upper right cells. These persons are being studied in the Departments of Psychiatry, Urology, and Endocrinology in the Medical Center of the University of California, Los Angeles. These persons have severe anatomical irregularities. In each case the transfer occurred late in the developmental life cycle and was accomplished as a more or less clear matter of personal election. Severe anatomical anomalies—for example, the case to be reported here is that of a nineteen-year-old girl raised as a boy whose female measurements of 38-25-38 were accompanied by a fully developed penis and scrotum—were contradictory of the appearances that were otherwise appropriate to their claimed rights to live in culturally provided sexual statuses. The transfers were accompanied by the subscription, by each of these persons, to the cultural conception of a dichotomized sex composition in which, with vehement insistence, they included themselves. Such insistence was not accompanied by clinically interesting ego defects. These persons contrast in many interesting ways with transvestites, trans-sexualists, and homosexuals.

In each case the persons managed the achievement of their rights to live in the chosen sexual status while operating with the realistic conviction that disclosure of their secrets would bring swift and certain ruin in the form of status degradation, psychological trauma, and loss of material advantages. Each had as an enduring practical task to achieve rights to be treated and to treat others according to the obligated prerogatives of the elected sex status. They had as resources their remarkable awareness and uncommon sense knowledge of the organization and operation of social structures that were for those that are able to take their sexual status for granted routinized, "seen but unnoticed" backgrounds of their everyday affairs. They had, too, great skills in interpersonal manipulations. While their knowledge and interpersonal skills were markedly instrumental in character, by no means were they exclusively so.

*The work of achieving and making secure their rights to live in the elected sex status while providing for the possibility of detection and ruin carried out within the socially structured conditions in which this work occurred I shall call "passing."*

In the lives of these persons the work and the socially structured occasions of sexual passing were obstinately unyielding to their attempts to routinize the rounds of daily activities. This obstinacy points to the omnirelevance of sexual statuses to affairs of daily life as an invariant but unnoticed background in the texture of relevances that comprise the changing actual scenes of everyday life. The experiences of these intersexed persons permits an appreciation of these background relevances that are otherwise easily overlooked or difficult to grasp because of their routinized character and because they are so embedded in a background of relevances that are simply "there" and taken for granted.

I shall confine my attention in this paper to a discussion of one case. I should like to tell what this person had specifically to hide, the structural relevance of her secrets, the socially structured situations of crisis, the management strategies and justifications that she employed, and the relevance of these considerations for the task of treating practical circumstances as a sociological phenomenon.

### Agnes

Agnes appeared at the Department of Psychiatry at U.C.L.A. in October, 1958 where she had been referred to Dr. Robert J. Stoller by a private physician in Los Angeles to whom Agnes had in turn been referred by her physician in her home town, Northwestern

City. Agnes was a nineteen-year-old, white, single girl, who was at the time self-supporting and working as a typist for a local insurance company. Her father was a machinist who died when Agnes was a child. Her mother supported a family of four children, of whom Agnes was the youngest, with occasional and semi-skilled work in an aircraft plant. Agnes said that she was raised as a Catholic but has not taken Communion for the past three years. She said of herself that she no longer believed in God.

Agnes' appearance was convincingly female. She was tall, slim, with a very female shape. Her measurements were 38-25-38. She had long, fine dark-blonde hair, a young face with pretty features, a peaches-and-cream complexion, no facial hair, subtly plucked eyebrows, and no makeup except for lipstick. At the time of her first appearance she was dressed in a tight sweater which marked off her thin shoulders, ample breasts, and narrow waist. Her feet and hands, though somewhat larger than usual for a woman, were in no way remarkable in this respect. Her usual manner of dress did not distinguish her from a typical girl of her age and class. There was nothing garish or exhibitionistic in her attire, nor was there any hint of poor taste or that she was ill at ease in her clothing, as is seen so frequently in transvestites and in women with disturbances in sexual identification. Her voice, pitched at an alto level, was soft, and her delivery had the occasional lisp similar to that affected by feminine appearing male homosexuals. Her manner was appropriately feminine with a slight awkwardness that is typical of middle adolescence.

Details of her medical, physical, and endocrinological characteristics have been reported elsewhere.[1] To summarize her medical, physical, and endocrinological characteristics, prior to any surgical procedures she appeared as a person with feminine body contours and hair pattern. She had large, well-developed breasts coexisting with the normal external genitalia of a male. An abdominal laparotomy and pelvic and adrenal exploration, performed two years before she was first seen at U.C.L.A., revealed no uterus or ovaries, no evidence of any vestigial female apparatus nor any

---

[1] A. D. Schwabe, David H. Solomon, Robert J. Stoller, and John P. Burnham, "Pubertal Feminization in a Genetic Male with Testicular Atrophy and Normal Urinary Gonadotropin," *Journal of Clinical Endocrinology and Metabolism*, 22, No. 8 (August, 1962), 839-845.

abnormal tissue mass in the abdomen, retroperitoneal area, or pelvis. Bilateral testicular biopsy showed some atrophy of the testes. A large number of laboratory tests on blood and urine as well as X-ray examinations of the chest and skull were all within normal limits. A buccal smear and skin biopsy revealed a negative (male) chromatin pattern. There was some evidence of a urethral smear showing cellular cornification suggestive of moderately high estrogenic (female hormone) activity.

Agnes was born a boy with normal-appearing male genitals. A birth certificate was issued for a male and she was appropriately named. Until the age of seventeen she was recognized by everyone to be a boy. In the biography furnished to us over many hours of conversations, the male role was both consistently and insistently described as a difficult one and poorly managed. Her accounts exaggerated the evidences of her natural femininity and suppressed evidences of masculinity. Secondary feminine sex characteristics developed at puberty. According to her account, grammar school years were at least tolerable whereas the three years of high school were stressful in the extreme. At the age of seventeen, at the end of her junior year of high school, she refused to return to complete the senior year. This was in June, 1956. After considerable planning, rehearsals, dieting to "make myself pretty," and similar preparations, she left her home town in August, 1956 for a month's visit with a grandmother in Midwest City. At the end of the month's visit, according to plan, she left her grandmother's house without leaving word of her whereabouts, and in a downtown hotel changed to feminine attire with the hope of finding a job in that city. For various reasons she felt unable to carry through with the plan of remaining in Midwest City and after phoning her mother returned home on the evening of the change. In the fall of 1956, she entered a hospital in her home town for examinations and the exploratory laparotomy which was done under the supervision of her private physician. During the fall of 1956 and following her hospitalization, she continued her schooling with the help of a tutor that had been provided under her mother's arrangement with the Public School system. She chafed under this as a resented confinement. In December, 1956 the tutor was dismissed and Agnes got a job as a typist in a small factory on the outskirts of town. She continued with this job until August, 1957 when, accompanied by girlfriends, she came to Los Angeles. She lived in Long Beach with a girlfriend and worked in downtown Los Angeles in a small insurance office. In December, 1957 she and her roommate moved into downtown Los Angeles "to be close to our work." In February 1958 she met her boyfriend Bill, and in April, 1958, to be closer to him, moved to the San Fernando Valley. She quit her job in March 1958 and was out of work at the time that she moved to the Valley. After a succession of crises with her boyfriend she returned to her home town in April, 1958 to see her previous physician for the purpose of obtaining a letter from him "explaining" Agnes' condition to her boyfriend. This letter was deliberately written by her physician in a general manner so as to mask the actual character of the difficulty. The boyfriend found this only temporarily satisfactory. His increasing insistence upon intercourse and plans for marriage, which Agnes frustrated, produced a series of increasingly severe quarrels. In June, 1958 Agnes disclosed her actual condition to her boyfriend and the affair continued on this basis. In November, 1958 Agnes was seen for the first time at U.C.L.A. Regular conversations at weekly intervals were held until August, 1959. In March, 1959 a castration operation was performed at U.C.L.A. in which the penis and scrotum were skinned, the penis and testes amputated, and the skin of the amputated penis used for a vagina while labia were constructed from the skin of the scrotum.

During this period Agnes was seen regularly by Dr. Robert J. Stoller, psychiatrist and psychoanalyst, Dr. Alexander Rosen, a psychologist, and by me. Approximately thirty-five hours of conversations that I had with her were tape recorded. My remarks in this paper are based upon transcriptions of these materials and upon materials collected by Stoller and Rosen with whom the work was done collaboratively.

### Agnes, the natural, normal female

Agnes had an abiding practical preoccupation with competent female sexuality. The nature of her concerns, as well as the incongruity that such an abiding concern presents to "common sense," permits us to describe, preliminarily at least, the strange features that the population of legitimately sexed persons exhibit as *objec-*

*tive* features from the point of view of persons who are able to take their own normally sexed status for granted. For such members perceived environments of sexed persons are populated with natural males, natural females, and persons who stand in moral contrast with them, *i.e.*, incompetent, criminal, sick, and sinful. *Agnes agreed with normals in her subscription to this definition of a real world of sexed persons, and treated it, as do they, as a matter of objective, institutionalized facts, i.e., moral facts.*

Agnes vehemently insisted that she was, and was to be treated as, a natural, normal female. The following is a preliminary list of properties of "natural, normally sexed persons" as cultural objects. Intended as an anthropological paraphrasing of members' beliefs, these properties are to be read with the use of the invariable prefix, "From the standpoint of an adult member of our society, . . ." Examples are furnished in the first two properties.

1. From the standpoint of an adult member of our society, the perceived environment of "normally sexed persons" is populated by two sexes and only two sexes, "male" and "female."

2. From the standpoint of an adult member of our society, the population of normal persons is a morally dichotomized population. The question of its existence is decided as a matter of motivated compliance with this population as a legitimate order. It is not decided as a matter of biological, medical, urological, sociological, psychiatric, or psychological fact. The question of its existence is instead decided by consulting both the likelihood that compliance to this legitimate order can be enforced and the conditions that determine this likelihood.

3. The adult member includes himself in this environment and counts himself as one or the other not only as a condition of his self-respect, but as a condition whereby the exercise of his rights to live without excessive risks and interference from others are routinely enforceable.

4. The members of the normal population, for him the *bona fide* members of that population, are essentially, originally, in the first place, always have been, and always will be, once and for all, in the final analysis, either "male" or "female."

5. Certain insignia are regarded by normals as essential in their

identifying function,[2] whereas other qualities, actions, relationships, and the like are treated as transient, temporary, accidental, circumstantial, and the rest. For normals the possession of a penis by a male and a vagina by a female are essential insignia. Appropriate feelings, activities, membership obligations, and the like are attributed to persons who possess penises and vaginas. (However the possession of a penis or a vagina as a biological event is to be distinguished from the possession of one or the other or both as a cultural event. The differences between biological and cultural penises and vaginas as socially employed evidences of "natural sexuality" will be commented on at greater length below.)

6. The recognition of either male or female is made by normals for new members not only at the point of their first appearance, *e.g.*, the neonate, but even before. It extends as well to the entire ancestry and to posterity. The recognition is not changed by the death of the member.[3]

7. For normals, the presence in the environment of sexed objects has the feature of "a natural matter of fact." This naturalness carries along with it, as a constituent part of its meaning, the sense of its being right and correct, *i.e.*, morally proper that it be that way. Because it is a natural matter of fact, for the members of our society there are only *natural* males and *natural* females. The good society for the member is composed only of persons who are either one sex or the other. Hence the *bona fide* member of the society, within what he subscribes to as well as what he expects others to subscribe to as committed beliefs about "natural matters of fact" regarding distributions of sexed persons in the society, finds the claims of the sciences like zoology, biology, and psychiatry strange. These sciences argue that decisions about sexuality are problematic matters. The normal finds it strange and difficult to lend credence to "scientific" distributions of *both* male and female characteristics among persons, or a procedure for deciding

[2] For example, the Board of Health officer in Midwest City where Agnes was born, when he refused to approve Agnes' application for a change of birth certificate, was supposed to have agreed that "in the final analysis" the capacity to perform the male reproductive function settled Agnes' sex.

[3] These properties need to be reviewed by considering actual cases that vary them along one or another "parameter" of recognition: deities, for one example; and war combatants whose genitals were destroyed as part of heroic mortal wounds, etc.

sexuality which adds up lists of male and female characteristics and takes the excess as the criterion of the member's sex, or the practice of using the first three years of training to decide sexuality, or the provision for the presence in the familiar society of males who have vaginas and females who have penises.

This "common sense" characterization is in no way limited to nonprofessional opinion. For example, a leading member of a prominent Department of Psychiatry in this country commented after hearing about the case, "I don't see why one needs to pay that much interest to such cases. She is after all a very rare occurrence. These persons are after all freaks of nature." We could not have solicited a more common sense formula. A measure of the extent of the member's commitment to the moral order of sexual types would consist of the reluctance to lend credence to a characterization that departed from the "natural facts of life." As we shall see below, in many different ways Agnes taught us as well, though unwittingly, the institutionally motivated character of this reluctance.

I have stressed several times that for the *bona fide* member "normal" means "in accordance with the mores." Sexuality as a natural fact of life means therefore sexuality as a natural and *moral* fact of life. The member's willingness, therefore, to treat normal sexuality as an object of theoretical interest requires, in deciding for himself the real nature of sexed persons, that he suspend the relevance of his institutionally routinized practical circumstances. We find, however, that the normal member does *not* treat sexuality, his own or others', as a matter of mere theoretic interest, whereas this is in principle the limit of our investigative interest in the phenomenon of normal sexuality as it is in other sciences as well. The normal also treats the sexed character of persons populating his everyday environment as a quality that is "decided by *nature*." This quality, once the member's "nature" decides it, holds thereafter irrespective of time, occasion, circumstance, or considerations of practical advantage. The person's membership as a normally sexed member, male or female, has the characteristic of, and is treated by the normal as remaining invariant throughout that person's biography and throughout his future lifetime and beyond. His sexual membership remains unchanged through any imputed actual and potential lifetime. To use Parsons' phrasing, it is "invariant to all exigencies."

8. From the standpoint of the normal member, if one examines the population of sexed persons at one time counting the presence of males and females, and at a later time examines the population again, no transfers will have occurred from one sex status to the other except for those transfers that are ceremonially permitted.

Our society prohibits willful or random movements from one sex status to the other. It insists that such transfers be accompanied by the well-known controls that accompany masquerading, play-acting, party behavior, convention behavior, spying, and the like. Such changes are treated both by those making the changes as well as those observing them in others as limited both by the clock as well as by occasions and practical circumstances. The person is expected "after the play" to "stop acting." On the way home from the party the person may be reminded that the party "is over," and that he should conduct himself like the person he "really is." Such admonitions as a "first line of social control" make up commonly encountered sanctions whereby persons are reminded to act in accordance with expected attitudes, appearances, affiliations, dress, style of life, round of life, and the like that are assigned by the major institutions. In our society these consist prominently of occupational and kinship arrangements with their intended obligatory statuses. Their importance is this: that persons are held to compliance with them regardless of their desires, i.e., "whether they like it or not." From the standpoint of the normal, changes of the population's composition can be accomplished by the paths only of birth, death, and migration.

Agnes was all too aware that an alternative path had been traveled, that it was traveled with negligible frequency, and that the transfer was harshly punishable. Like Agnes, the normal knows that there are persons who make the change but he, as did she, counts such persons as freaks, unusual, or bizarre. Characteristically he finds the change itself difficult to "understand" and urges either punishment or medical remedy. Agnes did not depart from this point of view [4] even though her sex was for her a matter of willful election between available alternatives. This knowledge

[4] Nevertheless, further information is needed comparing Agnes with normals with respect to the possibility that normals are more accepting of willful election than she was. For example, several lay persons who were told about her case expressed considerable sympathy. They found as the thing to be sympathetic about that she should have had to have been confronted with the election in the first place.

was accompanied by a burdensome necessity for justifying the election. The election consisted of choosing to live as the normally sexed person that she had always been.

Agnes subscribed to this description of a real world even though there were for her in that world persons, among whom she included herself, who had made the change from one sex to the other. Her early history stood in contrast for her to what she was nevertheless convinced about as to her normal sexuality. In seeking a change of birth certificate Agnes treated the change as the correction of an original error committed by persons who were ignorant of the "true facts."

Agnes held the conviction that there are not many people who could be told what she had done and who "will really understand." Hence, for Agnes an otherwise important common understanding with others had the troublesome feature that does not occur for normals, particularly where the dichotomy of sex types is concerned, namely, Agnes was unable to exercise the assumption that her circumstances, as they appeared to her would appear in a more or less identical way to her interactional partners, were they to exchange places. We might refer to this as the existence of a problematic "community of understandings" by and about sexed persons treating each other's sex as known in common and taken for granted by them.

9. In the cultural environments of normally sexed persons males have penises and females have vaginas. From the point of view of a normal member, wherever there are cases of males with vaginas and females with penises there are persons who, though they may be difficult to classify, must nevertheless be in principle classifiable and must be counted as members of one camp or the other. Agnes subscribed to this view too as a natural fact of life, even though this same population included at least one female with a penis, *i.e.*, herself, and following the operation included a female with a man-made vagina. It included others as well that she had learned of through her readings and contacts with physicians both in her home town and in Los Angeles. According to her account all others besides herself were personally unknown to her.

10. That Agnes could insist on her membership in the natural population of sexed persons even though she was, prior to the operation, a female with a penis and, following the operation, a

female with a man-made vagina, suggests another important property of a naturally sexed person. When we compare Agnes' beliefs not only with those of normals but with what normals believe about persons whose genitals for one reason or another change in appearance, or suffer damage or loss, through aging, disease, injuries, or surgery we observe that it is not that normals and Agnes insist upon the possession of a vagina by females (we consider now only the case of the normal female; the identical argument holds for males). They insist upon the possession of *either* a vagina that nature made *or* a vagina that *should have been there all along*, i.e., the *legitimate* possession. The legitimately possessed vagina is the object of interest. *It is the vagina the person is entitled to.* Although "nature" is a preferred and *bona-fide* source of entitlement, surgeons are as well if they repair a natural error, *i.e.*, if they serve as nature's agents to provide "what nature meant to be there." Not *just this* vagina but *just this* vagina as the case of the *real thing*. In the identical way that for a member of a language community a linguistic utterance is a case of a-word-in-the-language, or for a game player a move is a move-in-the-game, the genitals that serve the normal member as insignia of normally sexed membership consists of penises-and-vaginas-in-the-moral-order-of-sexed-persons. (I am speaking descriptively. I propose these "essences" as attributions that members find in their environments. To avoid any misunderstandings, I would like to stress that I am talking data. I am not arguing platonic realism as a philosophy of social science.)

Agnes' experiences with a female cousin, sister-in-law, and aunt may illuminate this property. In the course of commenting on what she characterized as her cousin's "jealousy" when a male visitor to her brother's home who had not met either one clearly preferred Agnes to her cousin who was approximately the same age, Agnes commented on her cousin's change in attitude from one in which she was favorable to Agnes before the trip to Midwest City but showed strong disapproval afterwards. According to Agnes' comments, Agnes felt that her cousin thought of Agnes as a fake, not a real woman. Agnes said of her cousin that the cousin felt that Agnes was a rival. (The portrayed rivalry was reciprocally felt, for Agnes said that she found it hard to "get her out of my mind.") Similarly for Agnes' sister-in-law, a mild disapproval on the sister-in-law's part prior to the Midwest City trip changed to open hostility upon Agnes' return. Agnes attributed this to the sister-in-law's resentment that Agnes was hardly the person to compare herself to the sister-in-law in affairs of proper domestic and marital conduct. By comparison with these rivals, Agnes commented on the dramatic change on the part of the elderly aunt who accompanied her mother to Los Angeles to care for Agnes during her convalescence from the castration operation. Agnes characterized the aunt as a natural female with no questions about it. The aunt, said Agnes, reflected the attitude of other family members. This attitude, said Agnes, was one of general acceptance prior to the trip to Midwest City, consternation and severe disapproval after the return, and relieved acceptance and treatment of her as a "real female after all" (Agnes' quotation of the aunt's remark) following the operation and during our conversations while the aunt was in Los Angeles. The point: in each case the object of interest was not the possession of the penis or of the man-made vagina, but, in the case of the cousin and sister-in-law, Agnes' penis was *prima facie* contradictory of Agnes' claims, by her other appearances, to possess the real thing. In the case of the aunt, although the vagina was man-made it *was* a case of the real thing since it was what she was now seen to have been entitled to all along. Both the aunt and the mother were strongly impressed by the fact that the operation had been done at all "in this country." That the physicians at the U.C.L.A. Medical Center by their actions reconstructed and validated Agnes' claim to her status as a natural female needs, of course, to be stressed.

Some additional features of Agnes as the natural female require mention.

Not only did Agnes directly express the claim "I have always been a girl," but it was advanced by the device of a remarkably idealized biography in which evidences of her original femininity were exaggerated while evidences of a mixture of characteristics, let alone clear-cut evidences of a male upbringing, were rigorously suppressed. The child Agnes of Agnes' accounts did not like to play rough games like baseball; her *"biggest"* problem was having to play boys' games; Agnes was more or less considered a sissy; Agnes was always the littlest one; Agnes played with dolls and cooked mud patty cakes for her brother; Agnes helped her mother with the household duties; Agnes doesn't remember what kinds of gifts she received from her father when she was a child. I once asked Agnes if she had lined up with the boys in public school. Her startled and angry reply was, "Lining up with the boys for what!" When I told her I was thinking of lining up in dancing class or lining up for physical examinations at school Agnes said, "Lining up never came up." I asked her if medical examinations with boys never happened. She agreed "That's right, they never happened." We came to refer to her presentation of the 120 per cent female. Not only in her accounts, but at times in her conversations with me, Agnes was the coy, sexually innocent, fun-loving, passive, receptive, "young thing." As a kind of dialectical counterpart to the 120 per cent female Agnes portrayed her boyfriend as a 120 per cent male who, she said, when we first started to talk, and repeated through eight stressful weeks following the operation when post-operative complications had subsided and the recalcitrant vagina was finally turning out to be the thing the physicians had promised, "wouldn't have been interested in me at all if I was abnormal." The penis that was possessed by the natural female was, repeatedly and under recurrent questioning, an accidental appendage used for the sole purpose of passing urine. The penis of Agnes' accounts had never been erect; she was never curious about it; it was never scrutinized by her or by others; it never entered into games with other children; it never moved "voluntarily"; it was never a source of pleasurable feelings; it had always been an accidental appendage stuck on by a cruel trick of fate. When it was amputated and Agnes was asked now that her penis and scrotum were gone what did she think of the penis and scrotum that were gone, her answer was that she did not feel it was necessary to give it any more thought than one would give to having had a painful wart that had been removed.

Agnes frequently called my attention to her lack of a biography that was appropriate to the fact that she was accepted by others and most particularly by her boyfriend as a girl. Agnes talked of the seventeen year gap in her life and indicated that her present female character was assigned by others a continuous history as a female that extended to the time of her birth. She pointed out that only since the time that she made the change had she been able to establish a female biography of experiences which she and others could draw on as a precedent in managing present appearances and circumstances. She lacked a proper biography to serve as a historico-prospective context for managing current situations. For others, and most particularly with her boyfriend, an all-along female corresponded to the anticipations that she encouraged with her boyfriend. Two years of accumulating memories presented her a chronic source for a series of crises about which more will be spoken below when I discuss her passing occasions and her management devices.

Another feature of the normal natural female was found in Agnes' portrayal of and insistence upon her life-long desire to be the thing that she had always known she was. Within her portrayals, her desires came essentially from mysterious and unknown sources, and withstood all vicissitudes posed by an ignorant environment that attempted to force, though unsuccessfully, an arbitrary line of departure from a normal course of development. Agnes stressed repeatedly, "I've always wanted to be a girl; I have always felt like a girl; and I have always been a girl but a mistaken environment forced the other thing on me." On many occasions of our conversations she was asked how she accounted for the desire that withstood environmental exigencies. Her replies invariably elaborated the theme, "There's no explaining it."

Given Agnes' subscription to the normal's distinction between the normal natural male and the normal natural female, there was less ambiguity for Agnes in distinguishing between herself as either a male or a female than there was in distinguishing between herself as a natural female and a male homosexual. The very extensiveness of the exaggerations of her feminine biography, of the masculinity of her boyfriend, of her anaesthetized penis, and the like, furnish the feature continually insisted upon: an identification which is consistently feminine. Much of the instrumental realism that she directed to the management of her chosen sexual status was concerned with so managing her circumstances as to avoid what she treated as a mistaken and degrading identity. Confounding the two were matters of objectively assessable error, ignorance, and injustice on the parts of others. Those of her defenses which cost her dearly in effectiveness and reality orientation were directed to keeping the distances between her natural normal femininity and male homosexuals in repair. Time after time in the course of our meetings when I directed the conversation to homosexuals and transvestites Agnes had a great deal of difficulty, simultaneously managing her fascination for the topic and the great anxiety that the conversation seemed to generate. The picture she would present then was that of a mild depression. Her answers would become impoverished. Occasionally her voice would break as she denied knowledge of this or that. There was a repeated insistence that she was in no way comparable. "I'm not like them," she would continually insist. "In high school I steered clear of boys that acted like sissies . . . anyone with an abnormal problem . . . I would completely shy away from them and go to the point of being insulting just enough to get around them . . . I didn't want to feel noticed talking to them because somebody might relate them to me. I didn't want to be classified with them."

Just as normals frequently will be at a loss to understand "why a person would do that," *i.e.*, engage in homosexual activities or dress as a member of the opposite sex, so did Agnes display the same lack of "understanding" for such behavior, although her accounts characteristically were delivered with flattened affect and never with indignation. When she was invited by me to compare herself with homosexuals and transvestites she found the comparison repulsive. Although she wanted to know more, when I proposed that a transvestite who was being seen by another researcher was interested in talking with her she refused to have any contact with him. Nor would she consider talking with any of the other patients that I mentioned to her who we were seeing who had experiences similar to hers. When I told her that a group of about seventeen persons in San Francisco who had either received or were planning to have a castration operation were interested in meeting and exchanging experiences with persons with similar problems, Agnes said that she could not imagine what they would have to talk with her about and insisted that she was in no way any concern of theirs.

As we have seen, she insisted that her male genitals were a trick of fate, a personal misfortune, an accident, above all "it was beyond my control" whose presence she never accepted. She treated her genitals as an abnormal growth. Ocassionally she would speak of them as a tumor. With genitals ruled out as essential signs of her femininity, and needing essential and natural signs of female sexuality, she counted instead the life-long desire to be a female and her prominent breasts. Her self-described feminine feelings, behavior, choices of companions, and the like were never portrayed as matters of decision or choice but were treated as *given* as a natural fact. As they were displayed in her accounts, their natural exercise would have been displayed from the beginning, she insisted, were it not for a misdirecting, frustrating, misunderstanding environment.

Before all she counted her breasts as essential insignia. On several occasions in our conversations she expressed the relief and joy she felt when she noticed at the age of twelve that her breasts were starting to develop. She said that she kept this discovery from her mother and siblings because "it was none of their business." It was clear from her later remarks that she meant by this that she feared that they would regard the development of the breasts as a medical abnormality and because of her age and incompetence might decide, regardless of and contrary to her wishes and to what she felt that she could have enforced upon them, that she receive medical attention and thereby risk their loss. She took particular pride in the size of her breasts, as she did in her measurements. Prior to the operation she was fearful that "the doctors at U.C.L.A." would decide among themselves, and without consulting her, and at the time of the operation, that the remedy for her condition consisted in amputating her breasts instead of her penis and scrotum. Following the operation, because of endocrinological changes and for other reasons, she lost weight. Her breasts became smaller; her chest measurement dropped from 38 to 35. The distress that she showed was sufficiently apparent to have been considered by us as one of the factors making up a short-lived but severe postoperative depression. When the Departments of Endocrinology and Urology had finished their medical work, but before the operation, she permitted herself a mild optimism which she kept under heavy check by the continual reminder that the decision was no longer in her hands, and by reminding herself, me, Stoller and Rosen that on prior occasions, most particularly after examinations in her home town, after permitting herself great optimism, she had been left with "nothing but encouragement. Just words." When she was told to report to the U.C.L.A.

Medical Center and that the decision had been made to amputate the penis and make an artificial vagina for her, she spoke of the decision with great relief. She spoke of the medical decision as an authoritative vindication of her claims to her natural femininity. Even the complications following the operation furnished episodes of pleasurable vindication. For example, following the operation she developed a mild urethral drip for which she had been advised by the physician to wear a Kotex pad. When I observed rather pleasantly that this was certainly a new experience for her, she laughed and was obviously pleased and flattered.

There were many occasions when my attentions flattered her with respect to her femininity; for example, holding her arm while I guided her across the street; having lunch with her at the Medical Center; offering to hang up her coat; relieving her of her handbag; holding the automobile door for her while she entered; being solicitous for her comfort before I closed the auto door and took my own seat behind the wheel. At times like this her behavior reminded me that being female for her was like having been given a wonderful gift. It was on such occasions that she most clearly displayed the characteristics of the "120 per cent female." At such times she acted like a recent and enthusiastic initiate into the sorority of her heart's desire.

### Achieving the ascribed properties
### of the natural, normal female

The natural, normal female was for Agnes an ascribed object.[5] In common with normals, she treated her femininity as independent of the conditions of its occurrence and invariant to the vicissitudes of desires, agreements, random or willful election, accident, considerations of advantage, available resources, and opportunities. It remained for her the temporally identical thing over all historical and prospective circumstances and possible experiences. It remained the self-same thing in essence under all

[5] Parsons treats "ascription" as a "relation concept." *Any* feature of an object may be treated by the actor according to the rule of its invariance to considerations of adaptation and goal attainment. This property of any feature's treatment Parsons speaks of as "ascription." A person's sex is a common illustration, but not because of the properties of a person's sex but because and only because a person's sex is frequently treated this way.

imaginable transformations of actual appearances, time, and circumstances. It withstood all exigencies.

The ascribed, normal natural female was the object that Agnes sought to achieve for herself.

Two meanings of "achievement" are meant in speaking of Agnes' having achieved her status as a female. (1) Having become female represented for her a status up-grading from that of a male which was for her of lesser value than the status of a female. For her to be female made her a more desirable object by far in her own eyes and, as she was realistically convinced, in the eyes of others as well. Prior to the change and afterwards as well, the change to female not only represented an elevation of herself as a worthwhile person, but was a status to which she literally aspired. (2) The second sense of achievement refers to the tasks of securing and guaranteeing for herself the ascribed rights and obligations of an adult female by the acquisition and use of skills and capacities, the efficacious display of female appearances and performances, and the mobilizing of appropriate feelings and purposes. As in the normal case, the tests of such management work occurred under the gaze of and in the presence of normal male and female others.

While her claims to her natural femininity could be advanced they could not be taken for granted. Many matters served as obstinate reminders that her femininity, though claimed, could be claimed only at the cost of vigilance and work. Prior to the operation she was a female with a penis. The operation itself substituted one set of difficulties for another. Thus, after the operation she was a female with a "man-made" vagina. In her anxious words, "Nothing that is made by man can ever be as good as something that nature makes.". She and her boyfriend were agreed on this. In fact, her boyfriend who, in her accounts of him, prided himself as a harsh realist, insisted on this and taught it to her to her dismayed agreement. In addition, her brand new vagina proved to be recalcitrant and tricky. Shortly after the operation an infection developed from the mold. When the mold was removed adhesions formed and the canal would no longer receive a penis-sized mold. Manual manipulations to keep the canal open had to be done out of the sight of others and with care that the nature of this private work remain concealed. These manipulations caused pain. For many weeks after the operation she suffered discomfort and was exasperated and humiliated by fecal and urethral dripping. This was followed by further hospitalization. There were mood changes and feelings that she had lost the sharpness, alertness, and definiteness of her thoughts. Unpredictable mood changes produced severe quarrels with her boyfriend who threatened to leave her if she showed any further anger with him. In addition there was the reminder that while she now had the vagina that she had with it a male biography. She would say, "There is a big gap in my life." In addition there was the fact that the change to a public feminine appearance had been made only three years before. Most of her prior rehearsals had been those in imagination. Thus she was still learning to act and feel like a woman. She was learning this new role only as a function of actually playing it out. There were risks and uncertainties involved. The job of securing and guaranteeing the rights of female by coming to deserve such attributions through her accomplishments—through her success in acting out the female role—thereby involved her in circumstances whose omnirelevant feature was that she knew something vitally relevant to the accepted terms of the interaction that the others did not know and that she was in fact engaged in the uncertain tasks of passing.

What were some matters that after and/or before the operation Agnes was required to hide?

1. Prior to the operation the contradictory insignia of her feminine appearance; the masked male genitals.

2. That she was raised as a boy and thus did not have a history to correspond to her appearance as an attractive female.

3. That she made the change only three years before and was still learning to act like the thing that she wanted to be taken for.

4. That she was unable and would be unable to fulfill the things expected of her by males who were attracted to her precisely to the extent that she succeeded in putting herself over as a sexually attractive female.

5. There was a man-made vagina.

6. That she wanted the penis and scrotum removed and a vagina constructed in its place. After the operation that she had a vagina that had been constructed from the skin of an amputated penis, and labia from the skin of the lost scrotum.

7. There were the matters to mask about the sexual services that her boyfriend demanded that she somehow satisfied.

8. There was what she did, and with whose help, to alter her appearance.

9. There were the activities of active management of persons around her in order to achieve the operation, most particularly the physicians and research personnel at U.C.L.A., and of course the medical personnel during the years when she sought medical help.

Agnes sought to be treated and to treat others according to a legitimate sexual status, while there accompanied this a deep dark secret which was concerned not with the skills and adequacy with which she acted out the status but with the legitimacy of her occupancy. For Agnes, acting out the new status was accompanied by the feelings that she knew something that the other person did not know, the disclosure of which, she was convinced and feared, would ruin her. The sex status transfer involved the assumption of a legitimate status the disclosure of which involved great risks, status degradation, psychological trauma, and loss of material advantages. This kind of passing is entirely comparable to passing found in political undergrounds, secret societies, refugees from political persecution, or Negroes who become whites. In Agnes' case it is of particular interest because the change of sexual status was accompanied by her paying marked and deliberate attention to making the new identity secure against some known and many unknown contingencies. This was done via active and deliberate management of her appearances before others as an object. She placed great stress on manners and proprieties and manipulation of personal relationships. The work had to be done in situations known with the most faltering knowledge, having marked uncertainty about its rules of practice, with severe risks and important prizes simultaneously involved, one not being available without the other. Punishment, degradation, loss of reputation, and loss of material advantages were the matters at risk should the change be detected. In almost every situation of interaction the relevance of the secret operated as background knowledge. Her concern to escape detection had a value of highest priority. Almost every situation had the feature therefore of an actual or potential "character and fitness" test. It would be less accurate to say of her that she has passed than that she was continually engaged in the work of passing.

### Passing

*The work of achieving and making secure her rights to live as a normal, natural female while having continually to provide for the possibility of detection and ruin carried on within socially structured conditions I call Agnes'* "passing." Her situations of activity—a very large number of them—were chronically ones of "structured strain." We may think of them as socially structured situations of potential and actual crisis. Sociologically speaking, the stress is a "normal stress" in the sense that the stress occurred precisely because of her active attempts to comply with a *legitimate order* of sex roles. Each of a great variety of structurally different instances required vigilance, resourcefulness, stamina, sustained motivation, preplanning that was accompanied continually by improvisation, and, continually, sharpness, wit, knowledge, and very importantly her willingness to deal in "good reasons"—*i.e.*, to either furnish or be ready to furnish reasonable justifications (explanations) or to avoid situations where explanations would be required.

Passing was not a matter of Agnes' desire. It was necessary for her. Agnes had to be a female. Whether she liked it or not she had to pass. She enjoyed her successes and feared and hated her failures. When I asked her to tell me the "real good things" that had happened to her she talked about her first job after her return to her home town; fun on group dates in her home town after the change; living with her roommate in Los Angeles; her skill as a stenographer; a succession of increasingly better jobs; the operation eight weeks afterwards when the new vagina looked good, was finally healing without pain, and to the surprise of the surgeons was responding to her efforts to achieve five inches of depth. "Of course the best thing that ever happened to me was Bill."

When I asked Agnes if there were any "real bad things" that had happened to her, the strain in her attempt to reply was so evident that I found it necessary to modify the question and asked instead for some things that were "bad things but not such bad things." To this she replied, "Being noticed (in grammar and especially high school) and being noticed that I didn't have any friends or companions or anything." (After pausing). "I didn't have friends because I didn't react normally under any kind of a relationship like that. I couldn't have a boyfriend. I didn't *want* a boyfriend. Because of the way I was I couldn't have girlfriends either, so there I was . . . I didn't have friends because I couldn't react normally under any kind of a relationship like that." I asked why she couldn't have friends. "How *could* I have girlfriends? How *could* I have pals?" My question: why not? "I probably felt it would be impossible. At school I didn't joke around with the girls or pal around or do anything like that because then I was being very conspicuous." From her other descriptions, particularly diffi- cult times can be briefly, but of course not exhaustively, enu- merated as follows: growing up; the three years of high school; life at home immediately after the change; the attitudes of family, neighbors, and former friends after she returned from Midwest City; the acute disappointment when she was told that no action could be taken after her examinations and exploratory laparatomy in her home town; managing her boyfriend Bill's demands for intercourse; the episode with Bill when she finally disclosed to him that she had a penis between her legs; managing her conversa- tions with us at U.C.L.A. in the hope that the decision would be favorable and that the operation would be done soon; her fear that the doctors would decide to amputate her breasts instead of her penis and that she was committed to an operation the decision being no longer within her control; following the operation her convalescence which lasted approximately six weeks and which was marked by a moderate depression, quickly changing moods which she was unable either to control or to justify to herself or to her boyfriend, and a succession of severe quarrels with her boy- friend; a recalcitrant vagina that would not heal properly and had a fraction of the depth she had hoped for; a severe bladder infec- tion that required rehospitalization; the reduction in the size of her breasts from 38 inches to 35 and her attendant fear that the penis was after all necessary to keep her feminine appearance; her changed relationship with Bill for three months following the operation; and finally, anticipatorily, Los Angeles, if her marriage plans did not materialize.

The "real good situations" were those in which the work of

passing permitted her the feelings of, and permitted her to treat others and to be treated by others as, a "normal, natural girl." The "real bad things" were the situations in which the management work, for various reasons, failed or promised to fail. Only in retrospect did they acquire the dramatic features of successes or failures. For our interests the critical cases were those that had to be handled *in their course.* What kinds of situations were they? How did she manage over their course to come to terms with them? In many of these situations and somehow, despite the socially structured character of the crises, she achieved some approximation to routinized management and "life as usual."

An illustrative instance may be used to introduce our discussion of these questions.

Before reporting for a physical examination for a job that she later obtained with a large insurance company, and because she had had similar previous physical examinations, Agnes decided that she would allow the physician's examination to proceed as far as her lower abdomen. If the physician then proceeded or gave any indication of examining the genital area she had decided to protest modesty and if this wasn't enough to put the physician off she would simply leave, perhaps feigning modesty, or if necessary giving no excuse. It was much to be preferred to forego the job than to risk disclosure, with one condition being dependent of course upon the other.

In instance after instance the situation to be managed can be described in general as one in which the attainment of commonplace goals and attendant satisfactions involved with it a risk of exposure. She employed a strategy by which she was prepared to get out from under if exposure seemed likely though at the cost of sacrificing these advantages. Her characteristic situation in passing was one in which she had to be prepared to choose, and frequently chose, between securing the feminine identity and accomplishing *ordinary* goals. Her chronic situation was one in which both conditions had to be simultaneously satisfied by her active deliberate management. The thing that she knew that others did not know was that the two conditions—managing to obtain opportunities for institutionalized and commonplace satisfaction, while minimizing the risk of disclosure—were ranked in a fixed priority: security was to be protected first. The common satisfactions were to be obtained only if the prior conditions of the secured identity could be satisfied. Risks in this direction entailed the sacrifice of the other satisfactions.

A variety of situations furnish us with the variations on this essential theme.

### Passing occasions

To help collect my thoughts about the various occasions on which Agnes had to pass, I tried to think of these situations as a game. When I did so only a comparatively small amount of the material that was collected from Agnes can be handled without encountering severe structural incongruities. In addition the materials that *can* be conceived under the auspices of a game, while they facilitate comparisons between the passing occasions, also seem not to be particular to Agnes' experiences in sexual passing. The materials that *are* particular to sexual passing are difficult to clarify with the notion of a game because of the structural incongruities that are motivated by applying the model.

The following formal properties of games facilitate the analysis of one set of these materials but interfere with it for the other set.

(1) There is the peculiar time structure of games and events in games. For the players, as of any present state of the game, there is potentially available to each the knowledge that by a time the game will have been completed. (2) If things go badly it is possible for a player to "leave" the game or to change it to another one and the like. (3) To be "in the game" involves, by definition, the suspension of the presuppositions and procedures of "serious" life. Many commentators on games have taken notice of this feature by speaking of the game as an "artificial world in microcosm." (4) The mutual biographies that are established for players as a function of their actual play together, furnish precedents that are particular to that game's interactions. (5) An accomplished play of a game consists of an encapsulated episode. The rules and actual accomplished course of play furnish the episode its entire character as a texture of relevances. (6) Characteristically, success and failure are clearly decidable and one or the other outcome is ordinarily very little subject to reinterpretation. Players need not await developments outside of the play of the game in order to permit

decisions as to what the episode was all about. (7) Insofar as the players are committed to compliance with the basic rules that define the game, the basic rules provide for players the definitions of consistency, effectiveness, efficiency, *i.e.*, of rational, realistic action in that setting. Indeed, actions in compliance with these basic rules define in games "fair play" and "justice." (8) Although strategies may be highly improvised and although the conditions of success and failure may, over the course of play, be unclear to the players, the basic rules of play are known and are independent of the changing present states of the game and of the selection of strategies. The basic rules are available for use by players and presumed by players to be available as required knowledge that players have prior to the occasions under which these rules might be consulted to decide among legal alternatives. (9) Within the basic rules, procedures of strict instrumental efficacy are, in principle, adoptable by either player, and each player can assume this for himself or for his opponent or insist upon them for himself and his opponent without impoverishing his grasp of the game.

The game illuminates several of Agnes' passing occasions both as a texture of relevant environmental possibilities and in its operational structure. The game applies, for example, to her management of beach attire. The problematic situation was one of simultaneously accompanying friends, males and females, to the local Santa Monica beach without risking disclosure. Instrumental devices provided adequate solutions to the problem. Agnes wore tight-fitting underpants and a bathing suit with a skirt. In her words "I don't know why, it's a miracle, but it doesn't show." She would go along with the crowd, reciprocating their enthusiasm for bathing, if or until it was clear that a bathroom or the bedroom of a private home would be available in which to change to her bathing suit. Public baths and automobiles were to be avoided. If the necessary facilities were not available excuses were easy to make. As she pointed out, one is permitted not to be "in the mood" to go bathing, though to like very much to sit on the beach.

Similarly, Agnes talked about the desirability of having a job that was comparatively close and preferably within walking distance of her residence, and in any case one that permitted the use of public transportation. Although Agnes drove an automobile she did not own one. She feared an accident, being rendered unconscious, and thereby risking exposure.

Another example. After she arrived in Los Angeles she roomed with a girlfriend. The situation was managed by a general understanding with her roommate to respect each other's privacy and to avoid nudity in each other's presence. On one occasion a problem arose for Agnes. While taking off her dress she exposed the scar from the exploratory laparotomy. A friendly question from her roommate was met by the explanation that it was an operation for appendicitis. Agnes told me that it occurred to her when she told this to her roommate that the question might remain for the roommate of why an appendicitis operation should leave such a long and ugly scar. She offered, therefore, the uninvited explanation that "there had been complications" and counted on the fact that the roommate did not have enough medical knowledge to know the difference.

A more complicated game but nevertheless one in which game resources were employed, occurred on the occasion that her brother's boyfriend visited his home after the brother was married. Agnes, her brother, her sister-in-law, and her cousin Alice, for whom Agnes had intense feelings of rivalry, were in the living room when the brother's boyfriend entered. Later the brother left the room with the boyfriend to see him to his car. When the brother re-entered the room he said that the boyfriend has asked him, "Who is that good-looking chick?" Agnes said that her cousin Alice assumed that the boyfriend meant Alice. When the brother pointed out ironically that Agnes had been meant, Alice became angry. Agnes here depended upon family discipline to protect her against humiliation. But this very family discipline, while it permitted the victory, soured the victory as well. Agnes described a structurally similar incident when she was shopping with her brother and was taken by the clerk as his wife. Agnes was flattered and amused. Her brother was not amused at all. She could rely on her brother to respect the family secret but she could rely upon him as well to remind her later of how disapproving he was of the change.

Dating, both in her home town and in Los Angeles before she started going with Bill, furnishes other occasions that exhibited the game properties of episodic character, preplanning, and a reliance upon instrumental knowledge of rules that she could assume were known and binding upon the various parties in a more or less similar way. Despite an interest in pickups she refused any pick-ups. Prior introductions were the order of the day, most particu-larly because they permitted her to postpone the date until she and her girlfriends had consulted with each other on a character checkup for the new prospect. Necking was handled according to the rule: no necking on the first date; maybe on the second. As Agnes said, "If you neck with a boy on the first date and say no on the second date, then you have trouble." Some petting was permitted but under no circumstances below the waist. She de-lighted in the thought that some boy was a "wolf" but would not go out with a wolf. In any case there was safety in numbers so multiple dating and house and church parties were preferred. Agnes did not drink. She said she had never been drunk and said she would never permit herself to be drunk.

One of the more intricately worked out game-structured epi-sodes occurred when Agnes had to furnish a urine specimen when she was examined as part of a physical examination for a job with an insurance company. On the day she applied for the job and at the time of the personal interview, a physical examination was scheduled for the same day. She had little time to prepare. To manage the risks involved in having to expose her body she found it necessary to improvise. She was asked to furnish a urine speci-men and was invited by the physician to use a urinal in his office. She had expected a toilet with a door. A threat resided in the fact that the nurse, because she was entitled to enter the office, would come in while Agnes was manipulating her genitals. Agnes made the excuse to the physician after sitting on the urinal but delib-erately doing nothing that she was unable to urinate but that she would be happy to return the specimen later in the day. When he agreed she returned to her apartment where she had a female roommate. It then occurred to her that it might be possible from an examination of the urine to determine the sex of the person. Not knowing whether or not this was so and not knowing how thorough the urinalysis would be, but being unwilling to run any risks on either score, she told her roommate that she had a mild kidney infection and was afraid that if the infection showed up in the urine she would be turned down for the job. The roommate did her the favor of furnishing her the bottle of urine which Agnes submitted as her own.

On another occasion she had just obtained a job as a legal secretary as the only girl in the office for a small firm of two lawyers who had just started their practice. Agnes was delighted with the job, most particularly because she was unqualified for it at the time that she was hired. Her employers, not being able to afford more, were willing to buy a lesser skilled employee for less pay. This arrangement couldn't have suited Agnes more since it was both an opportunity for more interesting work and a chance to upgrade her stenographic skills. Several months after the work began, the castration operation was scheduled at U.C.L.A. It was necessary then to arrange time out from the job in order to have the operation, but to arrange it as well so as to ensure that her employers would hire only a temporary replacement. It was her secondary goal that she be given a letter of recommendation by them in the event that she was not able to return in time, and that the letter say that she had worked there for six months instead of the actual two months in order that she not be required later to explain her absence to another employer given that she already had a work history with several short intervals, and of course in order to continue working as a legal secretary. This was managed by having the urological surgeons at U.C.L.A. call her employers and tell them, in league with Agnes, that she would be temporarily hospitalized for a severe bladder infection.

One of the most dramatic game-like passing occasions consisted in the series of events that terminated in the trip to Midwest City, her change, and her return home. Agnes made the trip in August, 1956. For several months prior to the trip she prepared for the change. She said that in about two month's time she lost twenty-five pounds. This produced the attractive shape that she later turned up with at U.C.L.A. The diet was self-imposed. None of the family, said Agnes, had any knowledge of her intent and of the place that the developing attractive female shape had in her plans. She managed the inquiries from various family members by protesting, "All kinds of people go on diets, don't they?" She spent considerable time in her room rehearsing the actions that would be appropriate to the new appearance. Her family understood that the trip to Midwest City would consist of a month's vacation which she was to spend with her grandmother. Agnes had many relatives in Midwest City who had not seen her for many years. She planned minimum contacts with them during her stay by staying with her grandmother. While she had relatives in many other cities, Midwest City was chosen because it was a large city. According to plan, at the end of August she left her grandmother's home early one morning leaving no note or any other indication as to her reason for leaving or her whereabouts. Taking a room in a downtown hotel she changed into female clothes and went to a local beauty shop where her hair, which was short, was cropped and rearranged in the Italian cut that Sophia Loren had made popular. She had planned to remain in Midwest City and to obtain work having picked the city, she said, because it was large enough to provide work opportunities and necessary anonymity, but was also large enough to permit her to avoid relatives. If they did meet, she reasoned, the relatives would not recognize her because they had not seen her for many years. Further, if she did meet them, and they asked, she would deny who she was. She counted for a fact, "Most people wouldn't insist that they knew you anyway." As it turned out, "I had not planned carefully enough." Confronted with the necessity of having to earn her own way, having no prior job experience to speak of, not knowing how to proceed to find the job that she needed, having only low-grade skills as a typist, and still being uncertain about her skills as a female, she became frightened of the risks of failure. When I asked why she was unable to go back to her grandmother she replied, "How could I? She wouldn't even know who I was. She was seventy-two. How could I ever tell her something like *that?*" Finally, she had very little money; as she said, "just enough to get home." On the evening of the day that she made the change she telephoned her mother, told her what she had done, and, according to Agnes' story, upon her mother's urging returned home that evening by bus in her new female attire. The trip was made pleasant, she said, by the attentions of several soldiers.

### Passing occasions that the game model does not analyze properly

There are many occasions which fail to satisfy various game properties. When the game is used to analyze them, the analysis contains structural incongruities.

One type of such an occasion occurred very frequently: Agnes, by acting in the manner of a "secret apprentice" would learn, as she told it, "to act like a lady." Its feature was something like this: Agnes and her interaction partners would be directed to a valuable mutually understood goal while at the same time another goal of equivalent value, to which the other person contributed, remained known to Agnes alone and was carefully concealed. In contrast to the episodic character of the occasions that were described previously, such an occasion was characterized by its continuing and developmental character. Further, its "rules" are learned only over the course of the actual interaction, as a function of actual participation, and by accepting the risks involved.

Several persons were prominent in her accounts with whom she not only acted like a lady but learned, from them, how to act like a lady. An important partner-instructor was Bill's mother in whose home she spent a great deal of time as a prospective daughter-in-law. Bill's mother was of Dutch-Indonesian ancestry and supported herself as a dressmaker. While teaching Agnes how to cook Dutch dishes to please Bill, she also taught Agnes how to cook in the first place. Agnes said that Bill's mother taught her dressmaking and materials; she taught her which clothes she should wear; they discussed dress shops, shopping, styles that were appropriate for Agnes, and the skills of home management.

Agnes spoke of the "long lectures" that she would receive from Bill upon occasions that she did something which he disapproved. One evening he returned from work at around five in the afternoon to find her sunbathing on the lawn in front of her apartment. She learned a great deal from his detailed and angry arguments of the ways in which this "display in front of all those men coming home from work" was offensive to him, but attractive to other men.

On another occasion she received a lecture from Bill on how a lady should conduct herself on a picnic. This he did by angrily analyzing the failings of a companion's date who had insisted, in his angry account, on wanting things her own way, of offering her opinions when she should have been retiring, of being sharp in her manner when she should have been sweet, of complaining instead of taking things as they were, of professing her sophistication instead of being innocent, of acting bawdy instead of abjuring any claims of equality with men, of demanding services instead of looking to give the man she was with pleasure and comfort. Agnes quoted Bill with approval: "Don't think the others are taking your part when you act like that. They're feeling sorry for the guy who has to be with her. They're thinking, where did he ever pick her up!"

With her roommates and wider circles of girlfriends Agnes exchanged gossip, and analyses of men, parties, and dating post-mortems. Not only did she adopt the pose of passive acceptance of instructions, but she learned as well the value of passive acceptance as a desirable feminine character trait. The rivalry with her female cousin, for all its hurtfulness, furnished her instruction by forcing a reflection upon the things that were wrong with her cousin, while claiming for herself qualities that contrasted with those that she found to criticize in the cousin.

On these occasions Agnes was required to live up to the standards of conduct, appearance, skills, feelings, motives, and aspirations while simultaneously learning what these standards were. To learn them was for her a continuous project of self-improvement. They had to be learned in situations in which she was treated by others as knowing them in the first place as a matter of course. They had to be learned in situations in which she was not able to indicate that she was learning them. They had to be learned by participating in situations where she was expected to know the very things that she was simultaneously being taught.

An occasion that was very much like that of the secret apprenticeship was one in which she permitted the environment to furnish her the answers to its own questions. I came to think of it as the practice of "anticipatory following." This occurred, I regret to say, with disconcerting frequency in my conversations with her. When I read over the transcripts, and listened again to the taped interviews while preparing this paper, I was appalled by the number of occasions on which I was unable to decide whether Agnes was answering my questions or whether she had learned from my questions, and more importantly from more subtle cues both prior to and after the questions, what answers would do. For another example, on the occasion of the physical examination for the insurance company job the examining physician palpated her abdomen. Agnes was uncertain as to what he was "feeling for." "Maybe he was feeling for my 'female organs'" (of course she has none),

"or for something hard." To all his questions about pain or discomfort she answered that there was none. "When he didn't say anything I figured he hadn't found anything unusual."

Another common set of occasions arose when she engaged in
friendly conversation without having biographical and group affiliation data to swap off with her conversational partner. As Agnes
said, "Can you imagine all the blank years I have to fill in? Sixteen
or seventeen years of my life that I have to make up for. I have
to be careful of the things that I say, just natural things that could
slip out . . . I just never say anything at all about my past that
in any way would make a person ask what my past life was like.
I say general things. I don't say anything that could be miscon-
strued." Agnes said that with men she was able to pass as an interesting conversationalist by encouraging her male partners to talk
about themselves. Women partners, she said, explained the general
and indefinite character of her biographical remarks, which she
delivered with a friendly manner, by a combination of her niceness
and modesty. "They probably figure that I just don't like to talk
about myself."

There were many occasions whose structure was such as not to
contain any criteria whereby a goal could be said to have been
achieved, a feature intrinsic to game activities. Instead, success in
managing the present interaction consisted in having established or
sustained a valuable and attractive character, of acting in a present
situation that was consistent with the precedents and prospects
that the presented character formulated, and for which present
appearances were documentary evidences. For example, Agnes said
that it was soon clear to her after she started working for the
insurance company that she would have to quit the job. The duties
were dull and unskilled and there was little chance for advancement. The little innovations that she made in order to make the
job more interesting gave only temporary relief. She wished very
much to up-grade her skills and to establish a more impressive job
history. For these reasons she wished to quit the job for a better
one but would have had to quit in the face of Bill's opposition. She
was convinced that he would credit none of these reasons but
would instead use the reasons she gave as evidences of deficiencies
in her attitude toward work. He had admonished her that for him,
quitting for such reasons was not acceptable and that if she quit
it would only reflect again on her immaturity and irresponsibility.

When she quit nevertheless she justified it by saying that it was entirely out of her hands. She had been fired because of a work lay-off. This was not true.

A further set of passing occasions are particularly resistant to analysis as games. These occasions have the features of being continuous and developmental; of a retrospective-prospective significance of present appearances; of every present state of the action being identical in meaning with the-situation-as-it-has-developed-thus-far; in which commonplace goals could neither be abandoned, postponed, or redefined; in which Agnes' commitment to compliance with the natural, normal female was under chronic threat or open contradiction; and in which remedies were not only out of her hands but were beyond the control of those with whom she had to deal. All of these situations, both by her reports as well as by our observations, were stressful in the extreme.

One such "occasion" consisted of the continuing tasks that Agnes referred to as "remaining inconspicuous." Agnes said that this was very much a problem in high school. She insisted, "to set you right," that this was no longer her concern, and that it had been replaced by a fear of being exposed. The fact is, nonetheless, that it remained very much a matter of concern. My impression is that Agnes said this because of the way in which the problem had been brought up in our conversation. I had introduced it to her by relating to her comments by E.P., a male patient, about his preoccupation with remaining inconspicuous. I described E.P. to her as a person who was much older than she, had been raised as a female and at eighteen had had a castration operation which removed a vestigial penis. I told her that E.P. had continued to dress as a female but wanted to be treated as a male; and that the change for E.P. had occurred only several years before. I described E.P.'s appearance and illustrated his preoccupation with remaining inconspicuous with E.P.'s account of "this kind of nasty thing is always happening to me:" *i.e.*, of being approached in a bar by a man who would say, "Excuse me, my friend and I over there have a bet. Are you a man or a woman?" Agnes immediately detected E.P.'s "abnormality" and denied flatly that she and E.P. were in any way comparable. In this context she said that she did not recognize that the problem of remaining inconspicuous was any longer a problem for her.

Agnes described the problem of remaining inconspicuous in

high school by talking about the way she avoided being conspicuous: by never eating in the high school lunch room; by joining
no clubs; by restricting her physical movements; by generally
avoiding conversations; by avoiding at any cost "those boys who
had something queer about them"; by wearing a loose shirt somewhat larger than her size and sitting with her arms folded in front
of her, leaning forward on the desk so that her breasts did not
show; by avoiding choices of either male or female companions;
by sitting in the far rear corner of every classroom and not responding to classroom discussions so that, as Agnes said, "whole days
would pass and I wouldn't say a word"; and by following a rigid
schedule of time and movements around the high school building
so that, as her account of it runs, she always entered the same gate
to the schoolyard entering the same door to the schoolroom, following the same path to her room, arriving at the same time, leaving by the same exit, following the same path home, and the like.
This account had come up in reply to my question, "Was there
any particular bad situation that occurred?" to which she replied,
"I don't know about any particular bad situation but just that these
things that were so obvious that you couldn't hide. . . . My general appearance . . . it was very obvious that it wasn't masculine,
too masculine." Despite all this, Agnes compromised her dress.
She said that she dressed "pretty much the same way" in grade
school as in high school. Her typical outfit consisted of white cordu-
roy pants and a shirt worn open at the neck which she arranged
in the manner of a loose blouse. It turned out that the loose blouse
as a management device was taught to her by her brother. Even
with the developing breasts she had preferred to wear her blouse
tightly tucked in. She changed only upon the disapproval of her
brother who was a few years older than she and attended the same
school, who was embarrassed by her appearance because of its
feminine overtones and berated her for dressing like a girl. Her
brother urged that she loosen the shirt. It was her brother, too,
who complained that she carried her books like a girl and who
demonstrated to her and insisted that she carry them like a boy.

Another example of an "occasion of continuous development"
consisted of having to manage the opinions of friends, neighbors,
and family after her return from Midwest City. These were circles
that Agnes complained "knew all about her from before." In the

first part of her remarks when this topic came up she had asserted flatly that the problem of remaining inconspicuous was not a problem "even when I got home from Midwest City." A few moments later in that conversation when I questioned her rather closely about what her mother, her brother and sisters, previous friends, her mother's friends, and neighbors had to say, and how they treated her after her return, Agnes said, "It was so different that nobody in town knew how to treat it." Then after saying, "Everyone treated me nice; nicer than they ever treated me before, and they accepted me. They just wanted to find out," she changed her story. From the time of her return from Midwest City until she left for Los Angeles life was described by her as "terrible." She excepted her work experiences on her first job in her home town. In a later interview she said that she would never return to her home town. After the castration operation was performed at U.C.L.A. she talked of how much she wished to leave Los Angeles because she felt that so much was known about her and so many people knew about her, "All these doctors, nurses, and interns, and everybody."

A part of this situation was the rivalry with her cousin Alice and the combination of rivalry and mutual disapproval that went on between Agnes and her sister-in-law. After her return from Midwest City there was open disapproval and overt expressions of anger from her sister-in-law, her aunt, and most particularly her brother, who continually wanted to know "when she was going to stop this thing." Agnes said that those memories were painful and that she hated to remember them. To obtain her comments on them required considerable effort with questionable results because of the prominence of her denials and idealizations. She would repeat, "They accepted me" or she would deny that she could be expected to know *what* the others were thinking.

Another such "occasion" focused on the unsuccessful management by all parties concerned of the impugned self-esteem that Agnes suffered by the fact that an arrangement had been made after she dropped out of high school to continue her high school education with the use of a tutor that was provided by the public schools. Agnes did not return to high school in September, 1957 which would have been her senior year. Instead, according to Agnes' report, her mother arranged with the vice principal of the high school for the services of a teacher furnished by the public school system who came each day to her house. Agnes was very evasive in saying what she and her mother had talked about in this respect and what kind of arrangement the two might have agreed or disagreed on about her schooling and tutor. Agnes professed to have no information on this agreement and claimed not to know what her mother thought about the arrangement, or what the mother had discussed specifically with the vice principal. Agnes claimed further to be unable to recall how long each one of the tutorial sessions lasted or how long the home visits continued. The vagueness and apparent amnesia led us to feel that these were memories about which Agnes had said that she hated to "remember." Agnes did describe, though briefly, the period during which she was tutored as one of great discontent and chronic conflict with her mother. From my first inquiries about this discontent she insisted that though she had had a great deal of time, and that retrospectively she saw that she could have done more with it than she did, "I felt like a recluse . . . I wanted to go out and meet people and have a good time. Before I went to Midwest City I could hardly bear to leave the house. After I came back I wanted to start going out and having a social life and mix in public and there I was, cooped up in the house with nothing to do." Along with this Agnes furnished the brief comment that the special teacher was also one who taught other pupils who, as Agnes described them, were "abnormal in some way." Given Agnes' general refusal to consider her condition as that of an abnormal person, it was my feeling that she might have refused to comment further because of a general refusal to acknowledge in any way that she was "abnormal" as well as her insistence that except for a misunderstanding and hostile environment she would have been able to act and feel "naturally and normally."

One of the most dramatic "nongame-analyzable occasions" started with the castration operation and lasted for approximately six weeks afterwards.[6] Starting with the convalescence in the hospi-

[6] NOTE: *The following alternative description of the two week period immediately following the operation was written by Robert J. Stoller. Reasons for including it are made clear at the conclusion of the study.*

"One of the most dramatic 'non-game analyzable occasions' started with the castration operation and lasted for approximately two months. Starting imtal immediately following the operation Agnes tried to sustain the privacy in the management of the care of her vagina by arranging for her own sitz-bath, and herself changing the dressing for the wound. This she insisted on doing out of the sight of the nurses and interns whom she resented. From her accounts, apparently, the nurses resented her as well. The vagina did not heal properly. An infection developed shortly after the operation. A large penis sized plastic mold had to be removed in order to facilitate healing with the result that adhesions developed and the canal closed down over its entire length, including the opening. The promised depth was lost and attempts to restore it by manual manipulation were made by both the attending surgeon, and under his advice, by

mediately postoperatively, Agnes tried to sustain privacy in managing the care of her vagina by arranging to give herself the prescribed sitz baths and changing her own surgical dressings. She insisted on doing this out of sight of the nurses and house officers, which may have added to the resentment the nurses felt toward her. Immediately postoperatively, she developed bilateral thrombophlebitis of the legs, cystitis, contracture of the urethral meatus, and despite the plastic mold which was inserted into the vagina at the time of surgery, a tendency for the vagina outlet to contract. She also required postoperatively several minor surgical procedures for modification of these complications and also to trim the former scrotal tissue to make the external labia appear more normal. Despite the plastic mold, the newly-made vagina canal had a tendency to close and heal, which required intermittent manipulations of the mold and daily dilatations. Not only were all of these conditions painful or otherwise uncomfortable but also, although minor, since they were frequent, they produced increasing worry that the surgical procedure would not end up with the desired result of a normal functioning and appearing set of female genitalia. Although these distressing conditions were carefully (and ultimately successfully) treated, at the time that she was well enough to go home these complications were still not fully resolved. During her first week home, there was difficulty with occasional uncontrolled seepage of urine and feces. In addition, her physical activities had to be restricted because of pain. The cystitis did not immediately clear with treatment but persisted for a couple of weeks, producing unpleasant symptoms ranging from urinary frequency, urgency, burning on urination, to bouts of considerable pelvic pain.

"About two weeks after surgery, another set of very unpleasant symptoms developed. She gradually became increasingly weak and tired, was listless, lost her appetite, lost a great deal of weight so that her breasts and hips became noticeably smaller, her skin lost its fresh and smooth appearance, and became waxy; she lost interest in sex; and she rather rapidly became increasingly depressed, being subject to sudden uncontrollable spells of crying. The first time she was seen by us following her return home, she presented this picture. It sounded like a rather typical and moderately severe depression. It seemed to be rather strong evidence that a mistake had been made. The operation had been performed primarily for psychological reasons; it had been

Agnes. The efforts of both produced severe pain. For almost a
week after her release from the hospital there was a combined
urethral and fecal dripping with occasional loss of fecal control.
Movements were painful and restricted. The new vagina required
almost continual attention and care. The vagina had been anchored
to the bladder and this together with its bearing on the lower
intestine set up mixed signals so that as the bladder expanded
under the flow of urine Agnes would experience the desire to
defecate. A bladder infection developed. It was accompanied by
continual pain and occasional severe abdominal spasms. The ampu-
tation of the testes upset the androgen-estrogen balance which pre-
cipitated unpredictable changes of moods. Arguments ensued with

---

the judgment of the medical staff that her identity was so strongly fixed in a
female direction that no forms of treatment could ever make her masculine.
In addition, it was felt that she was unequivocally sincere in her expressions
of desperateness about her anomalous anatomical situation and her feelings
that if anybody attempted to make her a male, not only would the attempts
be of no use but that they would drive her to despair if not suicide. There is
always the possibility when a patient makes such claims about something they
want in reality that there is more ambivalence present than is observable, and
it is the responsibility of the experts making the evaluation to determine that
such a degree of ambivalence does not exist. We had felt without doubt that
our evaluation was extensive and adequate and that it revealed that this patient was as well fixed in her femininity as are many anatomically normal
females and that whatever latent or vestigial masculinity was present was not
greater in degree or quality than that found in anatomically normal women.
If this judgment was wrong, then it would be expected that the absoluteness
of the castrating operation, the uncontrovertible and unalterable fact of the
loss of male genitalia would, when the patient was faced with its actuality,
produce a severe psychological reaction only if the hidden masculinity and
unconscious desires to be a man were strong enough and had been missed
by us.

"Therefore, on being confronted with a rather severely depressed patient,
we had presumptive evidence that an error in judgment had been made and
that the patient was now depressed from having lost her insignia of masculinity. Thus, the clear listing of all of these classical symptoms of depression
was scarcely a happy occasion for the investigators. However, towards the end
of her recital, an additional symptom was mentioned. She reported that she
had been having increasingly frequent episodes of sudden sweating accompanied by a very peculiar sensation which started in her toes and swept up
her legs through her trunk and into her face, a rushing sensation of heat. She
was having hot flashes on the basis of a surgical menopause. When the operation was performed and her testes removed, the source of the estrogens which
had produced the whole complicated anatomical picture of secondary sex characteristics of a woman was removed. Thus, she had acutely developed a menopausal syndrome no different from what is frequently seen in young women

Bill who was quickly out of patience and threatened to leave her. Despite a campaign to discourage her mother from coming to Los Angeles, it became increasingly apparent to Agnes that the situation was beyond her control and that she could not hope to manage her convalescence by herself. This motivated the additional anxiety that if her mother were to appear, Agnes would hardly be in a position to keep Bill and Bill's family from learning the terrible last thing that her mother and she knew about Agnes that Bill and his family did not know, *i.e.*, that Agnes had been raised as a boy. Until she was rehospitalized for the bladder spasms she managed the care of the vagina and her general illness by spending her days in bed in Bill's home, returning in the evening

---

who have their ovaries removed. Every one of the symptoms named above can be accounted for by the acute loss of estrogen (though this is not to say that the menopausal syndrome in anatomically normal women is usually to be explained simply on the basis of decrease of estrogen). At this point, hormone assays revealed an increase in urinary FSH and the absence of urinary estrogen. She was immediately placed on estrogen replacement therapy and *all* of the above signs and symptoms disappeared. She lost her depression, regained her interest in life and sexual drive; her breasts and hips returned to their normal ampleness; her skin took on its more usual feminine appearance, and so on.

"It may be of value to mention briefly the pathological findings of the testes. They were severely changed from the normal male as a result of the chronic presence of estrogens in their milieu so that, in brief, the normal pathological evidence for production of fertile sperm was absent. Various degenerative and abortive forms of spermatogenesis were found in the abnormal cells. However, there was no tumor found, and there was no evidence of an ovotestis (that is, a hermaphroditic condition in which ovarian and testicular tissue are found in the same organ). The conclusion of the endocrinologist was that Agnes 'presented a clinical picture that seemed to suggest a superimposition of an excess of estrogen upon the substratum of a normal male.' What could not be explained, and what therefore made her unique in the endocrinologic literature is that even in the presence of large enough production of estrogen to produce completely feminine secondary sex characteristics, the development of the normal sized penis in puberty was not interrupted. There is at this time no adequate explanation for this anomaly.

"It is safe to assume that the findings of depression were due simply to the acute loss of estrogen following castration. Agnes had never had such an episode before; the episode was abruptly ended by the administration of estrogen and no such episode has occurred again. She has been on daily estrogen since that time.

"Agnes subsequently had to return to the hospital for further treatment of cystitis and for the minor surgical procedure of completely opening up the vaginal canal. Her subsequent course surgically and endocrinologically was uneventful."

to her own apartment. Thus it was necessary to manage the secrecy with Bill's mother who had been told only that she had had an operation for "female troubles." In addition, she suffered a moderately severe depression with bouts of unexplained and uncontrollable weeping, restlessness, deep feelings of nostalgia which were both strange to her and unpredictable in onset. Bill berated her for feeling sorry for herself and insisted on knowing, though she could give no reply, whether her condition was physical or whether she was "really like that all along." She complained to me that her thoughts and feelings had lost their sharpness, that she found it difficult to concentrate, that she was easily distracted, and that her memory failed her. As a further complication she became fearful of her depression and would ruminate about "going crazy."

After a particularly severe attack of bladder spasms she was readmitted to the hospital and remedies were administered. The spasms were quieted; testosterone injections were started; the bladder infection was brought under control; the vaginal canal was reopened and a regime first of manual manipulations of the canal and later of manipulations with the use of a plastic penis were started. At the end of approximately six weeks the depression had cleared entirely. The vagina was healing, only tenderness remained, and under Agnes' conscientious use of the mold she had achieved a depth of five inches and was able to insert a penis of an inch and a half in diameter. Quarrels with Bill had subsided and were replaced by an anticipatory waiting on the part of both Agnes and Bill for the time when the vagina would be ready for intercourse. Agnes described their relationship as, "It's not the way it was at the beginning. We're just like an old married couple now."

The full variety of game-analyzable and nongame-analyzable occasions were involved at one time or another or in one way or another when Agnes described her relationship with Bill. If for Agnes all roads led to Rome, they did so by coming together at the boyfriend as a common junction point. For passing illustration, in the course of one of our conversations, at my request, Agnes recited in detailed succession the events of a usual day, and considered for each the possibility of acting differently than she had acted. The recited chain of consequences led to Bill, and from him to her secrets and "problem." This occurred regardless of the commonplace events with which the "chain of relevances" began. Then

I asked Agnes to start with something that she felt was extremely worthwhile, to imagine something that could alter it for the worse and to tell me what would happen then, and after that, and so on. She said, "The best thing that ever happened to me was Bill." Then the two of us laughed at the ineffectiveness of the trial.

Bill was discussed in every conversation we had. If she was discussing her confidence in herself as a female, the image of Bill was nearby as someone with whom she could feel "natural and normal." When she discussed her feelings of failure, of being a degraded, inferior female, Bill furnished the occasion when these feelings were most acutely encountered, for he was the only other one besides the physicians to whom she had voluntarily disclosed her condition. After the disclosure, her feelings of being an inferior female were in part assuaged by Bill's assurance that she need not feel inferior because the penis was nothing that she could have helped, and in any case it was not a sexual penis, it was a tumor or "like an abnormal growth." He was implicated in her accounts of her job aspirations, work attitude, work discipline, earnings, chances of advancement, occupational attainments. I mentioned before his "lectures" on how a lady should conduct herself whereby without knowing how he was teaching her he was nevertheless doing just that. On the occasions following the performance of household duties, their domestic relations, her conduct with strange companions, her conduct in Las Vegas, in his urging the operation and insisting that if she could not "get action out of those doctors at U.C.L.A. who only want to do research on you" that she drop the U.C.L.A. physicians and get a physician who would do her some good, in love-making, companionship, and the rehearsals for marriage, in all this Bill was either directly or indirectly relevant.

I proposed earlier that the occasions of passing involved Agnes in the work of achieving the ascribed status of the natural normal female. Bill's relevance to this work attenuated considerations of strict utility and instrumental effectiveness in her choice of strategies and in her assessments of the legitimacy of her procedures and their results. Among all her accounts, those that implicate Bill are invariably the most resistant to game analysis. One of the most obstinate structural incongruities that results when game analysis is used consists of the historico-prospective character of the mutual biography that their intimate interactions assembled, and the diffuse use to which this mutual biography could be and was put by each. It is the diffuse relevance of this biography that helped to make understandable how frantic Agnes' fears were of the disclosure to Bill and how particularly resistant she was to tell me how the disclosure had occurred. Only toward the end of our conversations and then only upon the only occasion in which I insisted that she tell me, did she tell the story, and then it was delivered in the manner of defeat, and piecemeal. The mutual biography aided us, as well, in understanding how the possibility of disclosure became increasingly unavoidable for her, and how the disclosure increasingly assumed the proportions of a major agony.

I shall confine my attention to two occasions, each of which was represented by a question that Bill had, which Agnes, while she stayed in the situation and precisely because there was no choice but to stay, found agonizingly difficult to answer. Prior to the operation and before Bill knew Agnes' condition his question was: "Why no intercourse?" After he knew, his reported question was, "What is all the talking at U.C.L.A. all about? If the doctors at U.C.L.A. wouldn't promise her anything why didn't she drop them and go to a physician who would do something as they would for any other person?"

Agnes met Bill in February, 1958. She had her own apartment. Bill would go there after work and spend the remainder of the evening. There was a great deal of necking and petting. While Agnes permitted fondling and stroking she would not permit Bill to put his hand between her legs. At first he berated her for teasing. Agnes met his first demands for fondling and intercourse by claiming her virginity. This did not satisfy him because, according to her story, she entered willingly "and passionately" into the lovemaking. (She denied that the love-making stimulated an erection at any time.) As a condition for continuing the affair Bill demanded a satisfactory explanation. She told him that she had a medical condition that prohibited intercourse; that the condition could not be repaired immediately; that she required an operation; that after the operation they could have intercourse. She talked only generally and vaguely about the "condition" which motivated Bill's curiosity to the point where he once again insisted upon knowing the condition in detail. She told him that she was not expert enough to furnish this information but would get it from her physician in Northwest City who was taking care of her. Fearful that Bill would leave her, Agnes returned to Northwest City where she asked the physician who had been taking care of her to write Bill a letter about her condition. The physician's letter, written deliberately in aid of Agnes, talked only generally about "a condition" that could not be repaired until she was 21 because an operation performed before that would endanger her life, which of course was not true. Although Bill did not know this, the answer nonetheless failed to satisfy him. He insisted that she tell him exactly what was wrong, and after a severe quarrel following frustrated intercourse made this a condition of any further courtship or marriage. Once more she tried to placate him by telling Bill that what was there was repulsive to her and would be repulsive to him, to which he replied, "What can be so repulsive? Are there bumps there?" She was convinced that she had the choice of either not telling him and losing him, or of telling him with the hope that he would understand, or if he did not, of losing him. She finally told him. On the many occasions when I asked her to tell me how he had convinced himself—for example had he made an inspection—she refused any further comment. She would insist that she was entitled to a private life and under no circumstances would she reveal how he had been convinced. To my question, "What does he know?" her answer invariably was, "He knows what you know," or "He knows everything that the doctors know." She would say nothing more. Agnes said that prior to the disclosure "I was like on a pedestal." Afterwards and since then she said that she was no longer able to feel, as she had felt prior to it, that she was "his queen." Agnes said that window shopping expeditions for home furnishings and discussion of wedding plans occurred prior to the disclosure. "Since April," when she returned home for the physician's letter, there had been no conversation about the wedding "because of the doubt for everyone concerned." Her account was not to be taken at face value. Later conversations occurred precisely because of the doubt. Some part, therefore, of what Agnes was talking about in saying "there had been no further conversations" referred to the degradation that she suffered upon finally having to tell Bill that she had a penis and scrotum between her legs and that this was behind all his frustrated attempts to pursue their love-making.

The feelings that persisted following this disclosure, that she was an inferior female, were accompanied at first by the repelling thought that perhaps Bill was "abnormal." She dismissed this by recalling that Bill had fallen in love with her before he knew about her condition; by recalling the stories he had told her of his love affairs and sexual successes; and by reviewing the fact that he regarded it as "more or less a tumor or something like that" and that he began to urge an operation to remedy the condition. At different times in the course of our conversations she insisted that there was nothing in his manner, appearance, character, treatments of her and other women, and treatments of men that "resembled homosexuals." By homosexuals she meant effeminate appearing men who dressed like women. She found the possibility of his "abnormality" repulsive saying that she could not bear to see him again if she thought "at all" that he was "abnormal." Following the operation we obtained an account of Bill's appearance and manner from the urological intern and resident who had attended her case. The resident had encountered Bill one day when Bill was leaving her hospital room. He visited her regularly while she was in the hospital. The resident reported that he was struck by Bill's small stature, fine dark features, and swishy manner. In leaving the room Bill batted his eyes at the resident from which the resident took the message, "You and I know what's in there." We were reluctant to credit the resident's account since his dislike for Agnes was evident on other scores. He was firmly opposed to the decision to operate, stating that the operation was neither necessary nor ethical. It was his conviction that there had been anal intercourse, a conviction that he held because of the flabbiness of the anal sphincter. With respect to the unknown source of estrogens he preferred the hypothesis that Agnes, either alone or in league with others, had for many years obtained them from an exogenous source. Despite our attempts to talk with Bill, he refused all contact.

With respect to the second question, Agnes' passing occasions consisted of justifying to Bill her "choice" of "the doctors at U.C.L.A." The task of justifying to Bill her visits to U.C.L.A. arose as a topic in almost all our conversations not only prior to the operation but after it as well, though of course for different reasons. Bill urged that she should get the doctors at U.C.L.A. to treat her "without all this funny business. They're taking you for a ride. They're not going to do anything. They just want to do research. You're just a guinea pig for them." In response to this Agnes, at her Saturday morning conversations with us, would press for a definite commitment as soon as possible. She said repeatedly that she was unable to argue with him because "in the sense that he's thinking, he's perfectly right. But I know something that he doesn't know." (That she had been raised as a boy and that the specific way in which she was of interest to us had to remain concealed in her arguments with Bill.) Agnes had to manage Bill's impatience by somehow convincing him that she was in the right hands at U.C.L.A., given Bill's impatience with the slowness of the procedure, and the mysteriousness of the Saturday morning talks which she portrayed to him as our insistence on research. She had to allow his insistence that she need not put up with all this "monkey business" and she could not argue his claim that, because she had something wrong, she should insist with us that we either do something about it or release her. Yet along with this, Agnes had the additional aim of getting an operation done by competent hands at minimum or no cost, but to get this she had to engage in the research, not only because of the anatomical condition that Bill was preoccupied with, but which was only a small part of our research interests. Additional research interests were directed to the fact that she was raised until she was seventeen as a male. So Agnes was unable to answer Bill because in her own words "this is something I know that he doesn't know. So he thinks of me as I suppose more or less of someone coming in here and being baffled or fooled or messed around with by doctors that think, oh here's a young girl that doesn't think too much and we can you know just do some research on her. . . . That's my big problem because I can't argue the point with him and I can't show him that he's wrong in that sense, because in the sense he's thinking he's perfectly right. But actually if I felt that way I'd be perfectly wrong. That's why I have to wait. It's because I know something he doesn't know. That's why I have to wait."

Following the operation Agnes needed arguments again, because she was afraid of her depression and of the swarm of difficulties during the first few weeks of convalescence. As she said, she swapped one set of troubles for another. She was frightened of what was happening. Among other things she wanted assurance that she was not "crazy" and confided that she got considerable relief from talking with us, but was entirely unable to explain this to Bill. When she discussed it with Bill he either took the line or wanted her assurance that her psychological problems were due entirely to physical changes after the operations, and that she was not *that* kind of a person *i.e.*, moody, irritable, self-pitying, weepy, selfish, and that this was not her *"real"* character. Even after the vagina had started to heal properly and the depression had lifted, she was still willing, and in fact desired, to continue the weekly conversations. A part of her uneasiness concerned the functional character of her vagina and the question for her as to whether or not Bill would promise marriage before or after they had had intercourse. She took as a matter of course that she had to permit Bill intercourse with the new vagina before marriage. As she said, "That's what it's for; it's for intercourse." Another part of her concern consisted of the uncertainty which she felt in sensing a changed relationship to Bill as she compared present arrangements with what they had been many months before. She sensed as well that the relationship would change even more in the ensuing months. "Now," she said, "we are like an old married couple." At this time she expressed, too, the conviction that we knew more about Bill than she did and knew more than we were saying. In one of the last interviews she asked, for the first time in all our conversations, if I would give her my opinion of Bill and did I think that Bill was "abnormal." I replied that I knew of Bill only from what she had told me about him, that I had never seen or talked with him, and that it would be unfair to give her such an opinion.

That Agnes was passing with us is a feature of the way in which our research was conducted with her, her problem being to obtain a competent, guaranteed, and low-cost operation without "submitting to research," by which she meant protecting her privacy. Thus, although she showed her willingness to take "all those tests" and to sort the Q-deck in accordance with various instructions, she herself furnished evidences of dissembling. Agnes had been given the Q-deck to take home with her and to sort and return the sorted deck to the psychologist the following week. Agnes said that Bill was forever wanting to see how she arranged the cards, "but I had the cards all mixed up so he couldn't find out anything." (Agnes laughed.) Another measure of her passing with us is found in the "secrets" that Agnes managed nevertheless to protect. Despite a total of approximately seventy hours of talks arranged with the three of us and additional talks with various members of the staff of the Urology and Endocrinology Departments, and despite the fact that direct and indirect questioning had been attempted to obtain information, there were at least seven critical areas in which we obtained nothing: (1) the possibility of an exogenous source of hormones; (2) the nature and extent of collaboration that occurred between Agnes and her mother and other persons; (3) any usable evidence let alone any detailed findings dealing with her male feelings and her male biography; (4) what her penis had been used for besides urination; (5) how she sexually satisfied herself and others and most particularly her boyfriend both before and after the disclosure; (6) the nature of any homosexual feelings, fears, thoughts, and activities; (7) her feelings about herself as a "phony female." Some details as to the way in which this passing with *us* was managed may become clear in the following section where specific features of her management devices are discussed.

If Agnes was passing with us, it must be stated in all fairness that there were many times, indeed, when I was passing with her. There were many occasions in the exchanges between Agnes and me when it was necessary for me to side-step her requests for information in order to avoid any display of incompetence and so as to maintain the relationship with Agnes. For example, I was unable to tell her whether or not there was a difference between male and female urine. There were several legal angles to the case, about which she asked questions which were obvious enough as questions when they were asked, but had not occurred to me nor did I have the faintest idea as to what their proper answers were. When she was suffering with the bladder and bowel impairment she asked if I could tell her how long this would go on and what she could expect to happen next. On several occasions prior to the operation she wanted to know if I could tell her what I knew about the likely decision. Several times she asked me details about the operation and the nature of postoperative care. She asked anatomical questions. One of these concerned a mysterious "hard thing" that she had encountered in the roof of the new vaginal canal. She assumed I would be able to tell her what it was. My wife had done graduate work with the hormone relaxin and its effects on the symphasis pubis in guinea pigs. I identified the hard thing as the symphasis pubis and told her what relaxin does by way of the spectacular relaxation of this cartilage prior to the passage of the neonate guinea pigs down the vaginal canal. I had to hope with a secret fervor that in transferring the story to humans that I was not telling her altogether a cock-and-bull story, partly because I would have liked to tell the truth, but perhaps even more importantly to preserve the friendship, the conspiracy, and the sense that we were in league with each other, that there were no secrets between us because I already knew many private things about her and nothing she might tell me would in any way change our sympathy for her or our desire to do what we could to see her happy and doing well. My typical reply therefore was to find out as much as I could about what she wanted to know, and why, and to reassure her that I could answer her questions but that it was to her best interest that she should have Stoller, the physician, give her the answers because answers to such questions were recognizedly of great importance to her and therefore she required authoritative answers. I must confess that this was an improvised answer that occurred on the first occasion that Agnes caught me short. Once it worked, however, I had it as a strategy to use on later occasions. It is of additional interest that despite such assurances Agnes could not ask me, apparently *knew* she could not ask me, nor would I have been prepared to tell her truthfully whether or how the decision to operate would be changed if she disclosed the answers to the seven points that we wanted her to tell us about but on which we could get no information from her.

### Review of management devices

In contrast to homosexuals and transvestites, it was Agnes' conviction that she was naturally, originally, really, after all female.

No mockery or masquerading accompanied this claim that we were able to observe. In this respect Agnes shared, point for point, the outlook of "normals."

But important differences nevertheless existed between Agnes and "normals" in that normals are able to advance such claims without a second thought whereas for her such claims involved her in uncertainties of responses from others. Her claims had to be bolstered and managed by shrewdness, deliberateness, skill, learning, rehearsal, reflectiveness, test, review, feedback, and the like. Her achieved rights to treat others and be treated herself as a natural female were achieved as the result of the successful management of situations of risk and uncertainty. Let me review some of the measures whereby she was able to secure and guarantee her claims.

Her devices were carried out within the conditions of, and were motivated by a knowledge of herself that was, for almost every occasion of contact with others, none of somebody's business who was nevertheless important to her. As I have noted, the concealed knowledge of herself was regarded by her as a potentially degrading and damaging disclosure. She was realistically convinced that there would be little by way of an available remedy by which other persons might be "set right" if the disclosure occurred. In this respect, the phenomena of Agnes' passing are amenable to Goffman's descriptions of the work of managing impressions in social establishments.[7] This amenability however is only superficial for reasons that will be apparent over the course of the discussion.

When I say that Agnes achieved her claims to the ascribed status of a natural female by the successful management of situations of risk and uncertainty, I do not mean thereby that Agnes was involved in a game, or that it was for her an intellectual matter, or that ego control for her extended to the point where she was able to switch with any success, let alone with any ease, from one sex role to the other. I have already mentioned several evidences of this. Other evidences can be cited. Even in imagination Agnes found it not only difficult to contemplate herself performing in the "male" way but found it repugnant. Some memories were so excep-

[7] Erving Goffman, *The Presentation of Self in Everyday Life*, University of Edinburgh, Social Sciences Research Centre, 1956.

tionally painful to her as to be lost as grounds of deliberate action. When she learned that the decision had been made to operate, the knowledge that she was committed to the operation as a decision was accompanied by a fear that when she was on the table, because the decision would then be entirely out of her hands, the doctors without consulting her would decide to amputate her breasts rather than her penis. The thought provoked a mild depression until she was assured that nothing of the sort was the case. The natural female was a condition that her various strategies had to satisfy. Agnes was not a game player. The "natural female" was one among many institutional constraints, "irrational givens," a *thing* that she *insisted upon* in the face of all contrary indications and the seductions of alternative advantages and goals. It attenuated the deliberateness of her efforts, the actual availability, let alone exercise of choices, and the consistency of her compliance with norms of strict utility and effectiveness in her choices of means. It furnished "constraints" upon the exercise of certain rational properties of conduct, particularly of those rational properties that are provided for when certain games are used as procedural models to formulate formal properties of practical activities.

Not only is it necessary to stress the shortcomings of strategy analysis in discussing her "management devices," but the very phrase "management device" is only temporarily helpful. It is useful because it permits an enumerated account of these devices. For the same reason that it facilitates the enumeration it also clouds the phenomena that it is necessary to come to terms with. *These phenomena consist of Agnes in on-going courses of action directed to the mastery of her practical circumstances by the manipulation of these circumstances as a texture of relevances.* The troublesome feature encountered over and over again is the cloudy and little-known role that time plays in structuring the biography and prospects of present situations over the course of action as a function of the action itself. It is not sufficient to say that Agnes' situations are played out over time, nor is it at all sufficient to regard this time as clock time. There is as well the "inner time" of recollection, remembrance, anticipation, expectancy. Every attempt to handle Agnes' "management devices" while disregarding this time, does well enough as long as the occasions are episodic in their formal structure; and all of Goffman's analyses either take episodes for illustration, or turn the situations that his scheme analyzes into episodic ones. But strategic analyses fail whenever these events are not episodic. Then to keep the analysis in good repair, there is required the exercise of theoretical ingenuity, and a succession of theoretical elections, one compounded on the other, with the frantic use of metaphor in the hope of bringing these events to faithful representation. This caveat can be summarized, although poorly, by pointing out that it would be incorrect to say of Agnes that she has passed. The active mode is needed: she is passing. Inadequate though this phrasing is, it summarizes Agnes' troubles. It stands as well for *our* troubles in describing accurately and adequately what her troubles were.

After enumerating some of her management devices I shall discuss her practical circumstances, to the end of treating her devices as manipulations of her practical circumstances conceived as a texture of relevances.

### Passing devices

Agnes used a number of devices, all of them familiar enough, in managing to give us no information. Prominently, she employed euphemism—making the thing she was talking about out to be a vastly better, more valuable, nicer, more pleasant thing than it could realistically have been. Some examples: Agnes' description of the first job she had, following her return from Midwest City, was little better than a "blah" response. "Oh, everything was just so wonderful"; "It was the best job I *ever* had"; "Everyone was so nice; the arrangements were so harmonious"; "I still correspond with *all* the girls there"; "It was just a ball"; "Everyone was just bubbling over with friendship and cheer." Her specific duties were slighted in her account. When she was pressed, she did not find them "at all" interesting to discuss. Also, as we have seen, the female character of her early history was exaggerated while evidences that she had been raised as a boy were suppressed.

Another way of withholding information was to speak in generalities, or to use allusion or guarded and impersonal references, or to speak in the impersonal case. We came to mean that this was what she was doing when we would say of Agnes that she was "evasive." Another favorite device was to pretend that she did not know what was being talked about, or to deny that something that had previously been talked about had ever really been mentioned.

When we made it unavoidable that she discuss with us something that she did not want to talk about she would use what we came to call "legalisms." She would respond and insist that she was responding correctly to the literal sense of the words and the question. Or, if I proposed to have recalled something that Agnes had said on a previous occasion she would hold me to the literally accurate recollection of what exactly had been said. A favorite device was to permit other persons, and, in many of our conversations, me, to take the lead so as to see which way the wind was blowing before offering a reply. She had a way of permitting the environment to teach her the answers that it expected to its own questions. Occasionally Agnes would give this device away by asking me, after an exchange, whether I thought she had given a normal answer.

For the many situations where she knew enough, she would have mapped out possible alternative developments beforehand and would have decided the conditions of her choice of one course or another prior to her having to exercise those choices. For example in providing for the possibility of backing out of the physical examination should the physician have proceeded to examine her genitals, Agnes considered well beforehand the variety of ways that the physician might respond when she refused to permit the examination to proceed. She said, "I have never been examined by a doctor and I don't intend to." I asked Agnes what she thought the physician's response would have been if she did not permit the genital examination. She said, "I thought he would mark it under, oh, idiosyncrasy or something."

Where it was possible to do so and particularly where there were important gains and important risks involved, Agnes would secretly "case" the situation beforehand. She tried to make herself knowledgeable about critical situations before she had to encounter them. For example, she wanted very much to apply for a civil service examination but she was afraid that the civil service physical examination would be very thorough. She remembered that her landlord, a fireman, would have had to take a civil service examination and so arranged to talk with him. She wished to avoid having to explain to him her reluctance to risk an examination that she might not pass: "He didn't realize anything about what I was really asking him in regard to my problem. It was—I posed the questions in a casual way. I said, well, like—you do have to take a physical exam, don't you? He says, oh yeah. I said Oh? What kind? Is it a real thorough one? Do they judge how happy you are or something? No, he said, it isn't that thorough, it's a real light one."

She was particularly adept at furnishing information that would lead the other person away from entertaining the possibility that she was raised as a male. "Frankly, I don't want anyone checking up. By checking up I mean more or less looking into my past life. . . . I don't *think* it would be *too* possible unless they ran across something to find out anything about me when I was younger, but. . . ." Therefore she avoided giving information on job application forms that would motivate employers to "check up." She described her procedure in filling out job applications: "When the question is asked, 'Have you had any major operations?' I always say no. 'Do you have any physical defects?' I always say no. 'Would you resent too thorough a physical examination?' I always say no. I say I wouldn't protest because if I say yes they would probably notice that on the application and want it explained. So I more or less let it pass over so it won't become noticeable. If I started doing anything like that I would probably wind up in a lot worse situation. I mean it's harder to find a job or anything like that. Anyway, I don't think I have to be truthful about things like that." Agnes summarized the case for herself: "It is necessary for me to tell little white lies a lot of the time and I think there are those that . . . those are necessary and they have to be necessary to accomplish results."

Some of these little white lies were prefigured, many were improvised. With regard to employment questionnaires her characteristic answers showed several features: (1) She selected those answers that as she assessed them would appear not to require a later explanation. (2) The answers, while they were false about her biography, were likely to be answers for the *type* of female typist that she presented herself as, answers that set up anticipations that she was hopeful to be able to satisfy once she was on the job. (3) She depended upon her ability to improvise satisfactory explanations for any discordancies that might be detected. Agnes was highly attuned to, and knew in detail, conventional expectancies in an extremely wide range of everyday situations that she had to meet: "I'm always aware" of contingencies. Her awareness of routine, otherwise unnoticed, workings of social structures, and her interest in and willingness to address them as grounds of her own actions lends to Agnes' actions their "manipulative" flavor. To use Parsons' phrasing, in Agnes knowledge of the exigencies of a stable order she assigned clear priority of relevance to the "adaptation" cell.

It was necessary for Agnes to continue to be alert to the tasks of keeping attributions of the natural female from being confounded with alternative attributions of male, male homosexual, and the like. An inevitable sense of double entendre occurred particularly in her discussions with physicians and with me. She was subject to the impulse to "check out," to "set right" companions whose remarks might have been innocent enough, but whose imputations, as she detected them, intended or not, were very uncomfortable for her—imputations of the fake female, the freak, the male homosexual, the abnormal female, and the like. The natural female was of course the single choice. On many occasions with me Agnes insisted that I "get things right." On many occasions she insisted that I was not saying something correctly the reason being that the priority of relevance was clouded by the wrong imputations. For example, once I reviewed some materials that she had presented about her feelings at the time that she was living with her roommate in Los Angeles and of the first parties that they had. She said, "I felt that *they* felt me to be completely normal and natural and it more or less gave me a satisfied natural feeling, you know, to be felt that way." I recapitulated: "You mean to be treated as a female, is that what you're saying?" Agnes answered, "Not as a *female*, not to be treated as a *female*—to be treated completely normally, without any regard to my problem at all." On the occasions with her on which I employed the usage that she had been "acting like a female" I would get one variation or another on the essential theme: I *am* a female but the others would misunderstand if they knew how I was raised or what I have between my legs. The conversational demand that I talk of Agnes as the natural female was accompanied by the demand, "I want you to get it exactly right." For example, "I didn't feel assured because I expected to act normally. I didn't expect to act in any other way." Or, it wasn't that the occasion of the first party with her roommates was "particularly delightful." I had characterized that occasion as particularly delightful, to which her sharp and irritated retort was, "What do you mean by that? It wasn't particularly delightful. I said it was the first time in my life I was having fun, going out with people, and doing different things. . . . Nothing particularly delightful. Everything was, I would say, *natural!*"

Another concern of hers for my getting things right had to do with my taking notes. On one occasion she questioned what I was writing down and seemed a little uncomfortable with the fact that the sessions were being recorded, though the discomfort disappeared after about the fourth or fifth session. After a moment's reflection she seemed reconciled to the recording, saying "Of course you can always go back to the recording and correct your notes. A person no matter how smart can misunderstand what someone else is saying if it is said without the proper explanations—something that's said might have a bearing on—I'm sure the other doctors would probably want to listen to the conversations and where there's something like they might . . . use it to have a bearing on the case."

Finally, Agnes literally forbade me from "misunderstanding" the "reasons" and "explanations" that she furnished me for her actions. She was also much concerned to maintain the contrast between her biography and prospects, and the way in which they would appear in fiction, games, play, pretending, mockery, masquerading, supposition, mere theorizing, and the like. It is possible that Agnes had herself sensed the intimate tie between the way in which later interpretations may be bound by the precedents established in the mutually known histories of her interactions with one person or another and, of course, particularly in her histories with physicians and with Bill. With us, the possibility of a "misunderstanding" not only motivated the further possibility of an unfavorable decision with respect to the operation but, because of the confidence that had been built up, raised a nasty prospect of betrayal.

Several times in our talks Agnes emphasized the rehearsed character of something that she called "carelessness," by which she meant the presentation of a casual appearance. She talked several times about rehearsed "carelessness." "It sounds like you're being *very* careless but—when you notice the circumstances, then you can tell it's not being careless at all." Agnes stressed the importance of the appearance of casualness which was accompanied by an inner vigilance. When I remarked to her, "So while it may look as if you're being casual, you're really not, you don't feel casual. Is that what you're saying?" To this she replied, "Not quite. I just feel casual in the sense that I feel normal and natural and everything, but I'm *aware* . . . that I . . . must be careful that way." To which she then added, "But remember I'm still a normal girl." As a companion tactic to the rehearsed casualness Agnes said that she preferred to avoid any tests, and that she attempted where possible to assess beforehand the severity and her chances of successfully completing a test to which she might be put. She clearly preferred to avoid any tests that she thought she might fail.

### Management devices as manipulations
#### of a texture of relevances:
#### Coming to terms with "practical circumstances"

Sociologists have long been concerned with the task of describing the conditions of organized social life under which the phenomena of rationality in conduct occur. One such condition is continually documented in sociological writings: *routine as a necessary condition of rational action.* The rational properties of action that are of concern in this respect are those which are particular to the conduct of everyday affairs. Max Weber, in his neglected distinction between substantive rationality and formal rationality, and almost alone among sociological theorists, used this distinction between the two sets of rationalities throughout his work.

The relationships between routine and rationality are incongruous ones only when they are viewed according to everyday common sense or according to most philosophical teachings. But sociological inquiry accepts almost as a truism that the ability of a person to act "rationally"—that is, the ability of a person in *conducting his everyday affairs* to calculate; to act deliberately; to project alternative plans of action; to select before the actual fall of events the conditions under which he will follow one plan or

another; to give priority in the selection of means to their technical efficacy; to be much concerned with predictability and desirous
of "surprise in small amounts"; to prefer the analysis of alternatives
and consequences prior to action in preference to improvisation;
to be much concerned with questions of what is to be done and
how it is to be done; to be aware of, to wish to, and to exercise
choice; to be insistent upon "fine" as contrasted with "gross" structure in characterizations in the knowledge of situations that one
considers valuable and realistic knowledge; and the rest—that this
ability depends upon the person being able to take for granted,
to take under trust, a vast array of features of the social order.
In the conduct of his everyday affairs in order for the person to
treat rationally the one-tenth of this situation that, like an iceberg
appears above the water, he must be able to treat the nine-tenths
that lies below as an unquestioned and, perhaps even more interestingly, as an unquestionable background of matters that are
demonstrably relevant to his calculation, but which appear without
even being noticed. In his famous discussion of the normative
backgrounds of activity, Emil Durkheim made much of the point
that the validity and understandability of the stated terms of a
contract depended upon unstated and *essentially unstatable* terms
that the contracting parties took for granted as binding upon their
transactions.

These trusted, taken for granted, background features of a person's situation, that is, the routine aspects of the situation that
permit "rational action," are commonly referred to in sociological
discourse as the mores and folkways. In this usage the mores depict the ways in which routine is a condition for the appearance
of rational action or, in psychiatric terms, for the operativeness of
the reality principle. The mores have been used thereby to show
how the stability of social routine is a condition which enables
persons in the course of mastering and managing their everyday
affairs to recognize each other's actions, beliefs, aspirations, feelings, and the like as reasonable, normal, legitimate understandable,
and realistic.

Agnes' passing occasions and her management devices throw
into relief the troubled relationship in her case between routine,
trust, and rationality. By considering these passing occasions and
management devices with respect to this troubled relationship we

may be able to break free of mere "diagnosis" or Goffman's epi-sodic emphasis. One may allow, in agreement with Goffman, the accuracy of Goffman's "naughty" view that members of a society generally, and Agnes in a particularly dramatic way, are much con-cerned with the management of impressions. We may allow, as well, the accuracy and acuteness of his descriptions of this con-cern. Nevertheless if one tries to reproduce the features of the real society by populating it with Goffman-type members we are left with structural incongruities of the sort that were discussed in previous sections of this paper.

A review of Agnes' passing occasions and management devices may be used to argue how practiced and effective Agnes was in dissembling. We would have to agree with Goffman that, like his persons who are engaged in the management of impressions, she was a highly accomplished liar, and that as it is in the society produced by Goffman's dissembling members, lying provided for Agnes and her partners conservative effects for the stable features of their socially structured interaction.

But a troublesome point in Goffman's interpretive procedure emerges with full clarity when his views are used to analyze other aspects of Agnes' case. The trouble revolves around the general absence with which deliberateness, calculation, or what Agnes calls her "awareness" enters as a property of the work of managing im-pressions for Goffman's members. In the empirical applications of Goffman's notions one is continually tempted to press the in-formant with exasperation, "Oh come on now, you must know better than that. Why don't you confess?" Agnes' case helps us to see what this trouble might be due to.

Agnes treated with deliberateness, calculation, and express man-agement (*i.e.*, in the manner that Goffman would like every one of his informants to confess, if his mode of analysis is to be counted correct) matters that members (a) not only take under trust, but (b) require of each other, for their mutual judgments of normality, reasonableness, understandability, rationality, and legitimacy, that they treat in a trusting and trusted manner, and (c) require of each other that evidences of trust be furnished wherever deliber-ateness, calculation, and express management are used in manag-ing problems of daily life. Agnes would have wanted to act in this trusting fashion *but routine as a condition for the effective, calculated, and deliberate management of practical circumstances was, for Agnes, specifically and chronically problematic.* To have disregarded its problematic character, she was convinced, was to risk disclosure and ruin. A review therefore of her case permits the re-examination of the nature of practical circumstances. It leads us also to think of the work of impression management—in Agnes' case, these consist of her passing "management devices"— as attempts to come to terms with practical circumstances as a texture of relevances over the continuing occasions of interpersonal transactions. Finally, it permits us to ask what this "preoccupation" for impression managements is about by seeing how a concern for "appearances" is related to this texture of relevances.

In the course of one of our conversations Agnes had been questioning the necessity for any more research. She wanted to know how it bore on her chances of the operation. She wanted to know as well whether it would help "the doctors" to get the "true facts." I asked Agnes, "What do you figure the facts are?" She answered, "What do *I* figure the facts are, or what do I think everyone else thinks the facts are?" This remark may serve as a theme in elaborating Agnes' practical circumstances as a texture of relevances. The theme for her of the nature of her practical circumstances was furnished in yet another remark. Prior to the operation I had asked her about the discussions and activities that she and Bill might have engaged in by way of preparation for their marriage. In her answer she portrayed her discussions with Bill as overwhelmingly concerned with the necessity for the operation. She firmly dismissed my question with the remark: "You don't talk about how much fun you're going to have in New York when you're sinking on a ship in the middle of the ocean. . . . You're worried about the problem that's present."

### Practical circumstances

Agnes' circumstances were striking in the stringency with which past and future events were related and regulated as an arena by the clock and the calendar. Her futures were dated futures, most particularly as present actions and circumstances were informed by the assumption of a potential remedy for "her problem" that had to have occurred by some definite time. That there were many years during which no such date had been set did not detract in the slightest from the definiteness of this future even though its specific calendar date was entirely unknown. Agnes was required by specific performances not only to establish mastery over this arena, but by her performances to establish her moral worth as well. For her the morally worthwhile person and the "natural, normal female" were identical. In the pursuit of jobs, in the management of the love affair, in her aspirations to marriage, in her choice of companions, in the management of Northwest City friends and family, the tasks of achieving the status of the normal natural female had to be accomplished at, within, and by a time. Perhaps nowhere does this come out more dramatically than in the quarrels that anticipated the disclosure to Bill, and in the terrible recalcitrance of the new vagina that made up such a central feature of the postoperative depression. Her constant recourse to self-reassessment consisted of continual comparison of anticipated and actual outcomes, of continual monitoring of expectancies and pay-offs, with strong efforts to accommodate and to normalize the differences. Agnes expended a great deal of effort upon bringing ever more areas of her life under conceptual representation and control. Expectations in areas of life that to persons better able than she to take their normal sexuality for granted would appear to be far removed from the concerns of criticism and review of "common sense knowledge" of the society were, for her, matters of active and critical deliberation, and the results of these deliberations were tied to uppermost levels in her hierarchy of plans. The contents of biographies and futures were highly organized with respect to their relevance to the achieved natural female status. It was indeed difficult for her to find any area that she could not in a few short steps make relevant to the prize.

There was very little of a "take it or leave it" attitude on Agnes' part toward past, present, or future fall of events. Agnes reasoned as follows: I have had this terrible time in high school, I was without companions as a child, I was raised as a boy, I have this face and these breasts, I've had dates and fun with girlfriends in the normal natural way that girls do, I lost seventeen years because a misunderstanding environment did not recognize the accidental character of the penis and refused to take action, hence I *deserve* the status that unfortunately I find myself in the position of having to ask for. For Agnes the likelihood of being accorded treatment as a natural, normal female was a moral likelihood. She reckoned her chances in terms of deservingness and blame. She found it repugnant to consider that an enumeration of such factors would or should serve in probability fashion merely to fix the likelihood that she was "female." With respect to that past as well as to her anticipated validation of her claims, the occurrence of a remedy for her condition had a moral requiredness. For her there must be and should be a plan and a reason for the way things had transpired as well as how they would have finally occurred. Very few things could occur for Agnes, bearing in their relevance on "her problem," in an accidental or coincidental manner. Agnes was motivated to search for patterns and for the "good reasons" that things occurred as they did. The events of Agnes' environment carried along for her, as their invariant features, that they could actually and potentially affect her and could be affected by her. To refer to this as Agnes' egocentricity, if it is left at that, may be seriously misleading. For Agnes her conviction that she had grasped the order of events arranged around her in an accurate and realistic fashion consisted in the conviction that her assessments were to be tested and were testable without ever suspending the relevance of what she knew, what she took to be fact, supposition, conjecture, and fantasy by reason of her bodily features and social positions in the real world. Everyday events, their relationships, and their causal texture were in no way matters of theoretic interest for Agnes. The possibility of considering the world otherwise "just to see where it leads"—a peculiar suspension and reordering of relevances that scientific theorists habitually employ—was for Agnes a matter of inconsequential play; as she would talk about it, "just words." When she was invited to consider it otherwise, the invitation amounted to a bid to engage in a threatening and repugnant exercise. It was no part of Agnes' concern to act in active alteration of "the social system." Instead she sought her remedy as an adjustment to it. One could never consider Agnes a revolutionary or a utopian. She had no "cause" and avoided such ·"causes" as one frequently finds among homosexuals who may seek to re-educate a hostile environment, or who might scrutinize that environment for evidences that it was not what it appeared to be but instead contained, in masked fashion, the identical types that it was hostile to and punishing of. Challenges to the system were for Agnes not even so much as hopeless risks. She wanted "in." The "credentials committee" was at fault.

Time played a peculiar role in constituting for Agnes the significance of her present situation. With regard to the past, we have seen the prominence with which she historicised, making for herself and presenting us with a socially acceptable biography. We have already remarked on the fact that the work of selecting, codifying, making consistent various elements in a biography, yielded a biography that was so consistently female as to leave us without information on many important points. Two years of arduous female activities furnished for her a fascinating input of new experiences upon which this historicizing process operated. Her attitude toward her own history required ever new rereadings of the trail that wound off behind her as she sought in reading and rereading the past for evidences to bolster and unify her present worth and aspirations. Before all, Agnes was a person with a history. Or, more pointedly perhaps, she was engaged in historicizing practices that were skilled, unrelieved, and biased.

On the side of future events, one is struck by the prevalence with which her expectations were expectations of the timing in the fall of events. There was little tolerable "slack" in this respect. It was to their timing that Agnes looked to inform her of their character. Events did not "just occur." They occurred in pace, duration, and phasing, and she looked to these as parameters of their meaning and to recognize them for "what they really are." She had only a thin interest in events characterized for their own sake and without regard for temporal determinations such as pace, duration, phasing. It was a prominent characteristic of Agnes' "realism" that she addressed her environment with an expectation of the scheduled fall of events. We were struck by the sharpness and extensiveness of her recall. An important part of this impression stemmed from the ease with which she dated events and arranged recalled sequences in strict chronology. The effect of such an orientation was to assimilate events both past and prospective to the status of means to ends and lent to the stream of experience an unremitting sense of practical purposiveness.

With almost remarkable ease, a present state of affairs taken for granted could be transformed into one of open problematic possibilities. Even small deviations from what she both expected and required to happen could occur to her as extraordinarily good or bad in their implications. She had achieved, at best, an unstable routinization of her daily rounds. One might expect that her concern for practical testing and the extensiveness of deliberateness, calculation, and the rest would be accompanied by the use of impersonal norms to assess her decisions of sensibility and fact, *i.e.*, that she knew what she was talking about, and that what she claimed to be so was indeed the case. Nothing of the sort was so. Agnes did not count her assessments of sensibility and fact right or wrong on the grounds of having followed impersonal, logico-empirical rules. Her rules of evidence were of much more tribal character. They could be summarized in a phrase: I am right or wrong on the grounds of who agrees with me. Particularly did she look to status superiors to test and maintain the difference between what in her situation she insisted were "true facts" and what she would count for "mere appearances." Being right or wrong was for Agnes a matter of being *in essence* correct or not. In matters relevant to her assessed chances of exercising her claimed rights to the status of the natural, normal female she did not take easily to the notion of being wrong in degree. For her the correctness of her assessments of events was a publicly verifiable one in the sense that other persons *typically like her* (*i.e.*, normal females) would experience what she had experienced in extremely close correspondence to the manner that she had experienced these events. She distrusted a characterization if its sense appeared to be peculiar or private to her and feared such an interpretation as unrealistic. Wanting to place the accent of actuality on events—fearing and suspecting supposition—she insisted that actual events were those which were verifiable by persons similarly situated. Similarly situated, to repeat, meant situated as a normal female. While she would allow that there were others in the world with problems like hers, neither with them nor with normal females was a community of understanding possible based upon their possible interchangeability of standpoints. "No one" Agnes insisted, "could possibly really understand what I have had to go through." In deciding the objectivity of her assessments of herself and of others Agnes counted, before anything, and sought to take for granted that she was normal and that she was like others.

### Agnes, the practical methodologist

Agnes' practices accord to the displays of normal sexuality in ordinary activities a "perspective by incongruity." They do so by making observable *that* and *how* normal sexuality is accomplished through witnessable displays of talk and conduct, as standing processes of practical recognition, which are done in singular and particular occasions as a matter of course, with the use by members of "seen but unnoticed" backgrounds of commonplace events, and such that the situated question, "What kind of phenomenon is normal sexuality?"—a member's question—accompanies that accomplishment as a reflexive feature of it, which reflexivity the member uses, depends upon, and glosses in order to assess and demonstrate the rational adequacy for all practical purposes of the indexical question and its indexical answers.

To speak seriously of Agnes as a practical methodologist is to treat in a matter of fact way her continuing studies of everyday activities as members' methods for producing correct decisions about normal sexuality in ordinary activities. Her studies armed her with knowledge of how the organized features of ordinary settings are used by members as procedures for making appearances-of-sexuality-as-usual decidable as a matter of course. The scrutiny that she paid to appearances; her concerns for adequate motivation, relevance, evidence, and demonstration; her sensitivity to devices of talk; her skill in detecting and managing "tests" were attained as part of her mastery of trivial but necessary social tasks, to secure ordinary rights to live. Agnes was self-consciously equipped to teach normals how normals make sexuality happen in commonplace settings as an obvious, familiar, recognizable, natural, and serious matter of fact. Her specialty consisted of treating the "natural facts of life" of socially recognized, socially managed sexuality as a managed production so as to be making these facts of life true, relevant, demonstrable, testable, countable, and available to inventory, cursory representation, anecdote, enumeration, or professional psychological assessment; in short, so as unavoidably in concert with others to be making these facts of life visible and reportable—accountable—for all practical purposes.

In association with members, Agnes somehow learned that and

how members furnish for each other evidences of their rights to live as *bona-fide* males and females. She learned from members how, in doing normal sexuality "without having to think about it," they were able to avoid displays that would furnish sanctionable grounds for doubt that a member was sexually what he appeared to be. Among the most critical of these displays were situated indexical particulars of talk. Agnes learned how to embed these particulars in vis-a-vis conversations so as to generate increasingly tellable, mutual biographies.

Agnes' methodological practices are our sources of authority for the finding, and recommended study policy, that normally sexed persons are cultural events in societies whose character as visible orders of practical activities consist of members' recognition and production practices. We learned from Agnes, who treated sexed persons as cultural events that members make happen, that members' practices alone produce the observable-tellable normal sexuality of persons, and do so only, entirely, exclusively in actual, singular, particular occasions through actual witnessed displays of common talk and conduct.

### Agnes, the doer of the accountable person

The inordinate stresses in Agnes' life were part and parcel of the concerted practices with normals, whereby the "normal, natural female" as a moral thing to be and a moral way to feel and act was made to be happening, in demonstrable evidence, for all practical purposes. Agnes' passing practices permit us to discuss two among many constituent phenomena that made up the normally sexed person as a contingent, practical accomplishment: (1) Agnes as a recognizable case of the real thing, and (2) Agnes the self-same person.

(1) *The case of the real thing.* In the ways Agnes counted herself a member to, and an object in, the environment of normally sexed persons, it included not only males with penises and females with vaginas but, because it included her as well, it included a female with a penis, and following the operation a female with a man-made vagina. For Agnes, and for the physicians who recommended the operation as the "humane" thing to do, the surgeons rectified nature's original mistake. Agnes' rueful admission, "Noth-

ing that man makes is as good as something that nature makes" expressed a member's realistic social truth about claims to normal sexuality. She, her family, and the physicians agreed that she had been granted a vagina as the organ which was rightfully hers, that she had resisted the anomaly as an accident of fate, and that because of a cruel trick she had been the victim of severe penalties of misunderstanding while she carried out the tasks of living as best she could as a misunderstood "case of the real thing." The operation furnished her and others evidences of the socially realistic character of her claims.

Agnes had witnessed in endless demonstrations by normals that and how normals believe that normal sexuality as a case of the real thing is an event in its own right and is assessable in its own terms, and that the accountability of normal sexuality could be made out from the study of how normally sexed members appear to common sense, lay or professional. Those were not her beliefs. Nor *could* she believe them. Instead, for Agnes in contrast to normals, the commonplace recognition of normal sexuality as a "case of the real thing" consisted of a serious, situated, and prevailing accomplishment that was produced in concert with others by activities whose prevailing and ordinary success itself subjected their product to Merleau-Ponty's "prejuge du monde." [8] Her anguish and triumphs resided in the observability, which was particular to her and uncommunicable, of the steps whereby the society hides from its members its activities of organization and thus leads them to see its features as determinate and independent objects. For Agnes the observably normally sexed person *consisted* of inexorable, organizationally located work that provided the way that such objects arise.[9]

(2) *The self-same person.* The ways in which the work and occasions of passing were obstinately unyielding to Agnes' attempts

[8] This and the observations in the remainder of this paragraph were obtained by revising the illuminating remarks by Hubert L. and Patricia Allen Dreyfus (in their translators' introduction to Maurice Merleau-Ponty, *Sense and Non-Sense* [Evanston, Ill.: Northwestern University Press, 1966], pp. x-xiii) so as to make their modified sense available to my interests.

[9] That knowledge loaned to her descriptions of this work an unavoidable "performative" character. This property of her descriptions of normal sexuality turned them into exhibitions which, as much as anything, distinguished for us her talk about normal sexuality from the talk about normal sexuality by normals.

to routinize her daily activities suggest how deeply embedded are appearances-of-normal-sexuality for members' recognition in commonplace scenes as unavoidable, unnoticed textures of relevances. Agnes' management devices can be described as measures whereby she attempted to exercise control over the changed content and the changed texture of relevances. Directed over their course to achieving the temporal identicality of herself as the natural, normal female, her management devices consisted of the work whereby the problem of object constancy was continually under solution. Her "devices" consisted of her work of making observable for all practical purposes the valuable sexed person who remains *visibly* the self-same through all variations of actual appearances.

Agnes frequently had to deal with this accountable constancy as a task and in a deliberate way. Her management work consisted of actions for controlling the changing textures of relevances. It was this texture that she and others consulted for evidences that she was the self-same person, originally, in the first place, and all along that she had been and would remain. Agnes was well aware of the devices that she used to make visible the constancy of the valuable, self-same natural, normal female. But her question, "Devices for what?" inseparably accompanied that awareness.

With that question Agnes mocked scientific discussions of sex roles that portray how members are engaged in making normal sexuality accountable. She found it flattering and innocent to consider a normal's activities and hers as those of role players or role makers who know, seek to establish, and enforce compliance to socially standardized expectancies of normal sexuality with their "functional consequences" that prior to encountering actual occasions in which they apply the normal can "talk about," given the various things he might be *doing* with something that's "said," and in the actual occasion use them to exercise choice among displays of appropriate talk and conduct. Equally flattering were the varieties of psychologically certified normally sexed persons whose possibilities, according to a favored version, are fixed early in life by the social structures of the childhood family as a complicated program of reinforcements; or the biological normal who is after all one sex or the other by the surplus that remains in the appropriate column when the signs are arithmetically evaluated; or the sociological normal for whom society is a table of organization so that sex "positions" and "statuses" and their possible departures are assigned and enforced as a condition for maintaining that table of organization and for other "good reasons."

Each furnishes a commonplace method for theorizing out of recognition a demonic problematic phenomenon: *the unrelieved management of herself as the identical, self-same, natural female, and as a case of the real and valuable person by active, sensible, judgmentally guided unavoidably visible displays in practical, common sense situations of choice.*

That this phenomenon was happening was Agnes' enduring concern. Her devices were continually directed to, indeed, they consisted of a Machiavellian management of practical circumstances. But to manage in Machiavellian fashion her scenes of activity she had to take their relevant features on trust and be assured that normal companions were doing so, too. She differed from the normals in whose company and with whose unacknowledged help she "managed" the production task of keeping this trust in good repair. Thereby we encounter her wit with, her sensitivity to, her discrimination in selecting, her preoccupation with and talk about, and her artful practices in furnishing, recognizing "good reasons" and in using them and making them true. To enumerate Agnes' management devices and to treat her "rationalizations" as though they were directed to the management of impressions and to let it go at that, which one does in using Goffman's clinical ideal, euphemizes the phenomenon that her case brings to attention. In the conduct of her everyday affairs she had to choose among alternative courses of action even though the goal that she was trying to achieve was most frequently not clear to her prior to her having to take the actions whereby some goal might in the end have been realized. Nor had she had any assurances of what the consequences of the choice might be prior to or apart from her having to deal with them. Nor were there clear rules that she could consult to decide the wisdom of the choice before the choice had to be exercised. For Agnes, stable routines of everyday life were "disengageable" attainments assured by unremitting, momentary, situated courses of improvisation. Throughout these was the inhabiting presence of talk, so that however the action turned out, poorly or well, she would have been required to "explain" herself, to have furnished "good reasons" for having acted as she did.

That persons "rationalize" their own and each other's past actions, present situations, and future prospects is well known. If I were speaking only of that, this report would consist of one more authoritative version of what everyone knows. Instead, I have used the case to indicate why it is that persons would require this of each other, and to find anew as a sociological phenomenon how "being able to give good reasons" is not only dependent upon but contributes to the maintenance of stable routines of everyday life as they are produced from "within" the situations as situations' features. Agnes' case instructs us on how intimately tied are "value stability," "object constancy," "impression management," "commitments to compliance with legitimate expectancies," "rationalization," to member's unavoidable work of coming to terms with practical circumstances. It is with respect to that phenomenon that in examining Agnes' passing I have been concerned with the question of how, over the temporal course of their actual engagements, and "knowing" the society only from within, members produce stable, accountable practical activities, *i.e.*, social structures of everyday activities.

# SIX

# "Good" organizational reasons
# for "bad" clinic records*

## The problem

Several years we examined selection activities of the Outpatient Psychiatric Clinic at the U.C.L.A. Medical Center, asking
"By what criteria were applicants selected for treatment?" Kramer's
method [1] for analyzing movements of hospital populations was
used to conceive the question in terms of the progressive attrition
of an initial demand cohort as it proceeded through the successive
steps of intake, psychiatric evaluation, and treatment. [2] Clinic records were our sources of information. The most important of these
were intake application forms and case folder contents. To supplement this information we designed a "Clinic Career Form"
which we inserted into case folders in order to obtain a continuing
record of transactions between patients and clinic personnel from
the time of the patient's initial appearance until he terminated con-

* In collaboration with Egon Bittner, The Langley Porter Neuropsychiatric
Institute.
[1] M. Kramer, H. Goldstein, R. H. Israel, and N. A. Johnson, "Application
of Life Table Methodology to the Study of Mental Hospital Populations,"
Psychiatric Research Reports, June, 1956, pp. 49-76.
[2] Chapter Seven reports this study in detail. Chapter One, pp. 18-24, reports
other aspects of this research.

tact with the clinic. Clinic folders contain records that are generated by the activities of clinic personnel, and so almost all folder contents, as sources of data for our study, were the results of self-reporting procedures.

In promised applicability and results, the cohort method was clear-cut and rich. There were no questions of access to the files. Hence, when we prepared the grant application we thought that closely supervised personnel could get the information from clinic folders that we needed. A pilot attempt to learn what information we could and could not get caused us to upgrade needed training and skill to the level of graduate assistants in sociology. We permitted coders to use inferences and encouraged diligent searching. Even so there were few items in our schedule for which we obtained answers. Some kinds of information that we had hoped to get from clinic files, that we got, with what estimated credibility is illustrated in Table 1. For example, patient's sex was obtained in practically all cases; patient's age in 91 per cent of cases; marital status and local residence in about 75 per cent; race, occupation, religion, and education in about a third of the cases; and occupational history, ethnic background, annual income, household living arrangements, and place of birth in less than a third. Of 47 items that dealt with the history of contacts between applicants and clinic personnel we had returns on 18 items for 90 per cent of our cases; for 20 other items we got information from between 30 per cent to none of the cases.

When, after the first year's experience, we reviewed our troubles in collecting information from the files, we came to think that these troubles were the result of our seeking information that we or anyone else, whether they were insiders or outsiders to the clinic, could probably not have, because any self-reporting system had to be reconciled with the routine ways in which the clinic operated. We came to tie the unavailable information to the theme of "good" organizational reasons for "bad" records. It is this theme to which our remarks are addressed.

### "Normal, natural troubles"

The troubles that an investigator can encounter in using clinic records can be roughly divided into two types. We may call the

TABLE 1

Availability of desired information and how it was obtained in the 661 cases

| Item of Information | Per cent of 661 cases for which | | | |
|---|---|---|---|---|
| | There was no information | Information was obtained by uncertain inference | Information was obtained by certain inference | Information was obtained by inspection |
| **(A) Patient's "Face Sheet" Characteristics** | | | | |
| Sex | 0.2 | - | 0.3 | 99.5 |
| Age | 5.5 | 2.9 | 0.4 | 91.2 |
| Marital status | .11.8 | 5.4 | 3.9 | 78.9 |
| Social area | 21.4 | 0.4 | 3.6 | 74.6 |
| Race | 59.5 | 0.2 | 0.6 | 39.7 |
| Occupation | 55.6 | 0.4 | 5.0 | 39.0 |
| Religion | 51.7 | 9.5 | 2.3 | 36.5 |
| Education | 60.7 | 1.4 | 2.6 | 35.3 |

Eliminated because of no information

Occupational history
Duration of marriage
Married first time or remarried
Ethnic background
Income
Household arrangements
Principal contributor to patient's support
Place of birth
Length of residence in California

| | | | | |
|---|---|---|---|---|
| **(B) First Contact** | | | | |
| How contact was made | 7.2 | 0.4 | 2.3 | 90.1 |
| If patient was accompanied, by whom | - | 2.0 | 2.0 | 96.0 |
| Type of referral | 3.5 | 0.4 | 7.8 | 88.3 |
| Outside persons involved in the referral | 2.5 | 0.2 | 3.0 | 94.3 |
| Clinic person involved in first contact | 3.6 | - | - | 96.4 |
| Number of clinic persons contacted | 4.8 | - | 2.0 | 93.2 |
| Disposition after first contact | 5.0 | 0.3 | 11.9 | 82.8 |
| **(C) Intake interview and psychological tests** | | | | |
| Patient's appearance at intake interview | 0.4 | 0.5 | 2.1 | 97.0 |
| Clinic person involved in intake interview | 0.3 | - | - | 99.7 |
| Outcome of psychological testing | 0.2 | 0.3 | 1.5 | 98.0 |
| If no psychological tests, reason | 16.3 | 2.5 | 17.5 | 63.7 |

TABLE 1 (cont.)

Availability of desired information and how it was obtained in the 661 cases

| Item of Information | Per cent of 661 cases for which | | | |
|---|---|---|---|---|
| | There was no information | Information was obtained by uncertain inference | Information was obtained by certain inference | Information was obtained by inspection |
| **(D)  Intake Conference and Treatment** | | | | |
| Scheduled or impro- vised intake conference | 44.6 | 10.9 | 34.9 | 9.6 |
| Staff member in charge of intake conference | 50.3 | - | - | 49.7 |
| Conference decision | 8.0 | 9.7 | 10.3 | 72.0 |
| If patient was assigned to therapist, name of therapist | 8.3 | - | - | 91.7 |
| Name of first therapist | 3.8 | - | - | 96.2 |
| If patient was on wait- ing list, outcome | - | 0.3 | 9.6 | 90.1 |
| If patient was not accepted, reason | 19.7 | 1.2 | 7.7 | 71.4 |
| If patient was not accepted, how notified | 31.5 | 2.7 | 6.8 | 59.0 |

Eliminated because of no information

Composition of intake conference
Number of prior admissions
Collateral cases
Scheduling of psychological testing
Scheduling of intake interviews
Number of appointments for intake interview
Notification of impending termination after intake interview
Psychological tests administered
Type of recommended treatment
Number of scheduled treatment sessions
Number of missed appointments
Number of interviews with spouses, parents, relatives, friends, etc.
Treatment supervisor
Planned visit regime
Actual frequency of visits
Reasons for termination after treatment

| | | | | |
|---|---|---|---|---|
| **(E)  Psychiatric Characteristics** | | | | |
| Nature of patient's complaints | 7.0 | 0.2 | 1.9 | 90.9 |
| Psychiatric diagnosis | 17.2 | - | - | 82.8 |
| Prior psychiatric experience | 19.0 | 1.7 | 46.5 | 32.8 |
| Motivation for therapy | 32.0 | 11.3 | 28.3 | 28.4 |
| "Psychological mindedness" | 40.2 | 14.0 | 23.9 | 21.9 |

TABLE 1 (cont.)

Availability of desired information and how it was obtained in the 661 cases

| | | Per cent of 661 cases for which | | |
|---|---|---|---|---|
| Item of Information | There was no information | Information was obtained by uncertain inference | Information was obtained by certain inference | Information was obtained by inspection |
| (F) Clinic Career | | | | |
| Point of termination | – | 0.9 | 6.2 | 92.9 |
| Circumstances of termination | 2.6 | 1.1 | 5.6 | 90.7 |
| Where was patient referred | 3.5 | 0.3 | 7.6 | 88.6 |
| Type of clinic career | 0.2 | 0.8 | 5.1 | 93.9 |
| Number of days in contact with clinic | 1.5 | 3.0 | 3.5 | 92.0 |
| Number of days outside of intreatment status | 2.0 | 3.8 | 3.9 | 90.3 |
| Number of days in treatment | 8.8 | 0.4 | 0.4 | 90.4 |

first type general methodological troubles, and the second "normal, natural troubles." We shall make very brief remarks about the first type; the burden of our interest is with the second.

*General methodological troubles* furnish the topic of most published discussions about the use of clinic records for research purposes. Interest in these troubles is directed by the task of offering the investigator practical advice on how to make a silk purse out of a sow's ear. Instead of "silk purse" we should say a container of sorts that might, with the investigator's sufferance, be permitted to hold a usable percentage of the sorry and tattered bits that are removed from the files and put into it. Such discussions attempt to furnish the investigator with rules to observe in bringing the contents of case folders to the status of warranted answers to his questions. What is generally involved here is the rephrasing of actual folder contents so as to produce something like an actuarial document that hopefully possesses the desired properties of completeness, clarity, credibility, and the like. The transformed content of the record lends itself more readily than the original to various kinds of social scientific analyses on the assumption, of course, that there exists a defensible correspondence between the transformed account and the way the information was meant in its original form.[3]

Any investigator who has attempted a study with the use of clinic records, almost wherever such records are found, has his litany of troubles to recite. Moreover, hospital and clinic administrators frequently are as knowledgeable and concerned about these "shortcomings" as are the investigators themselves. The sheer frequency of "bad records" and the uniform ways in which they are "bad" was enough in itself to pique our curiosity. So we were led to ask whether there were some things that could be said by way of describing the great uniformity of "bad records" as a sociological phenomenon in its own right.

We came to think of the troubles with records as "normal, natural" troubles. We do *not* mean this ironically. We are *not* saying, "What more can you expect?!" Rather, the term "normal, natural" is used in a conventional sociological sense to mean "in accord with prevailing rules of practice." "Normal, natural troubles" are troubles that occur because clinic persons, as self-reporters, actively seek to act in compliance with rules of the clinic's operating procedures that for them and from their point of view are more or less taken for granted as right ways of doing things. "Normal, natural" troubles are troubles that occur because clinic persons have established ways of reporting their activities; because clinic persons as self-reporters comply with these established ways; and because the reporting system and reporter's self-reporting activities are integral features of the clinic's usual ways of getting each day's work done—ways that for clinic persons are right ways.

The troubles we speak of are those that any investigator—outsider or insider—will encounter if he consults the files in order to answer questions that depart in theoretical or practical import from organizationally relevant purposes and routines under the auspices of which the contents of the files are routinely assembled in the first place. Let the investigator attempt a remedy for shortcomings and he will quickly encounter interesting properties of these troubles. They are persistent, they are reproduced from one clinic's files to the next, they are standard and occur with great

[3] For an account of social scientific uses of clinical records consult E. Kuno Beller, *Clinical Process* (New York: Free Press of Glencoe, Inc., 1962).

uniformity as one compares reporting systems of different clinics, they are obstinate in resisting change, and above all, they have the flavor of inevitability. This inevitability is revealed by the fact that a serious attempt on the part of the investigator to remedy the state of affairs, convincingly demonstrates how intricately and sensitively reporting procedures are tied to other routinized and valued practices of the clinic. Reporting procedures, their results, and the uses of these results are integral features of the same social orders they describe. Attempts to pluck even single strands can set the whole instrument resonating.

When clinic records are looked at in this way the least interesting thing one can say about them is that they are "carelessly" kept. The crux of the phenomenon lies elsewhere, namely in the ties between records and the social system that services and is serviced by these records. There is an organizational rationale to the investigator's difficulties. It is the purpose of this paper to formulate this rationale explicitly. Toward that end we shall discuss several organizational sources of the difficulties involved in effecting an improvement in clinic records.

### Some sources of "normal, natural troubles"

One part of the problem, a part to which most efforts of remedy have been directed, is contributed by the marginal utility of added information. The problem for an enterprise that must operate within a fixed budget involves the comparative costs of obtaining alternative information. Because there are comparative costs of different ways of keeping records, it is necessary to choose among alternative ways of allocating scarce resources of money, time, personnel, training, and skills in view of the value that might be attached to the ends that are served. The problem is in strictest terms an economic one. For example, information about age and sex can be had almost at the cost of glancing at the respondent; information about occupation puts a small tax on the time and skill of the interviewer; occupational history is a high-cost piece of information. The economic problem is summarized in the question that is almost invariably addressed to any recommended change of reporting procedure: "How much of the nurse's (or the resident's or the social worker's, etc.) time will it take?"

If the troubles in effecting an improvement amounted entirely to how much information the clinic could afford on a strict time-cost basis, the remedy would consist of obtaining enough money to hire and train a large staff of record keepers. But it is enough to imagine this remedy to see that there are other troubles in effecting "improvements" that are independent of the number of record keepers.

Consider a part of the trouble, for example, that is contributed by the marginal utility of information when the information is collected by clinic members according to the procedures of an archive—*i.e.*, where uniform information is collected for future but unknown purposes. An administrator may be entirely prepared to require of persons in his establishment that whatever is gathered be gathered consistently. But he must be prepared as well to maintain their motivation to collect the information in a regular fashion knowing that the personnel themselves also know that the information must be gathered for unknown purposes that only the future can reveal. Over the course of gathering the information such purposes may vary, in their appearances to personnel, from benign to irrelevant to ominous, and for reasons that have little to do with the archives.

Further, partisans in the clinic for one reporting program or another are inclined to argue the "core" character of the information they want gathered. Administrators and investigators alike know this "core" to be a troublesome myth. Consider, for example, that a sociologist might urge the regular collection of such minimum "face sheet" information as age, sex, race, marital status, family composition, education, usual occupation, and annual income. The question he must argue against competitors to archive rights is not "*Is* the information worth the cost?" but "*Will it have been* worth the cost?" One need not be a trained investigator to understand that by addressing almost any definitive question to the archives one can reveal the shortcomings of the collection enterprise. Whether or not it turns out that what has been gathered will not do after all, and will have to be gathered all over again, will depend upon what constraints the investigator is willing to accept that are imposed by the necessity of his having to frame questions for which the archives will permit answers. For such reasons, an administrator with an eye to the budgeted costs of his reporting procedures is apt to prefer to minimize the burden of present costs and to favor short-term peak load operations when the investigator has decided his needs in a formulated project.

There are the further difficulties of ensuring the motivation to collect "core" information that occur when "good reporting performance" is assessed according to research interest. Such standards frequently contradict the service interests of professional persons within the organization. Moreover, founded priorities of occupational responsibility may motivate vehement and realistic complaints as well as—and with greater likelihood—informal and hidden recording practices that permit the recorder to maintain the priority of his other occupational obligations while keeping the front office appropriately misinformed.

This point touches on a related source of troubles in effecting improvement, troubles having to do with ensuring compliance of self-reporting personnel to record keeping as a respectable thing for them to be doing from their point of view. The division of work that exists in every clinic does not consist only of differentiated technical skills. It consists as well of differential moral value attached to the possession and exercise of technical skills. To appreciate the variety and seriousness of troubles contributed by this organizational feature one need only consider the contrasting ways in which records are relevant to the satisfactory accomplishment of administrative responsibilities as compared with professional medical responsibilities and to the wary truce that exists among the several occupational camps as far as mutual demands for proper record-keeping are concerned.

Clinic personnel's feelings of greater or lesser dignity of paper work as compared with the exercise of other skills in their occupational life, are accompanied by their abiding concerns for the strategic consequences of avoiding specifics in the record, given the unpredictable character of the occasions under which the record may be used as part of the ongoing system of supervision and review. Records may be used in the service of interests that those higher up in the medical-administrative hierarchy are probably not able, but in any case are neither required nor inclined beforehand, to specify or give warning about. Inevitably, therefore, informal practices exist which are known about by everyone, that as a matter of course contradict officially depicted and openly acknowledged practices. Characteristically, the specifics of who, what, when, and where are well guarded team secrets of cliques and cabals in clinics, as they are in all bureaucratically organized settings. From the point of view of each occupational team, there are the specifics that facilitate the team's accomplishment of its occupational daily round which is none of the business of some other occupational team in the clinic. This is not news of course, except that any investigator has to confront it as a fact of his investigative life when, for example, in order to decide the import of what is in the record, he has to consult materials that are not in the record but are nevertheless known and count to someone.

Another source of troubles: clinic personnel know the realities of life in the clinic in their capacity as socially informed members, whose claims to "have the actual account of it" derive in good part from their involvements and positions in the social system, involvements and positions which carry, *as a matter of moral obligation*, the requirement that incumbents make good sense of their work circumstances. As a consequence of that moral obligation there is the long standing and familiar insistence on the part of self-reporters: "As long as you're going to bother us with your research why don't you get the story right?" This occurs particularly where standard reporting forms are used. If the researcher insists that the reporter furnish the information in the way the form provides, he runs the risk of imposing upon the actual events for study a structure that is derived from the features of the reporting rather than from the events themselves.

A closely related source of trouble stems from the fact that self-reporting forms—whatever they may consist of—provide not only categories with which clinic personnel describe clinic events, but simultaneously and inevitably, such forms constitute rules of reporting conduct. The self-reporting forms consist of rules that for personnel define correct self-reporting conduct as a work obligation. It is not startling that the investigator can obtain a description of clinic events precisely to the extent that the reporting form is enforced as a rule of reporting conduct upon reporting personnel. But then it should also come with no surprise that the information the investigator can have, as well as the information he cannot have, is subject to the same conditions that investigators are aware of in other areas of rule governed conduct: namely, that well known differences and well known sources of differences occur between rules and practices, differences that are notoriously recalcitrant to remedy.

Such differences are not understandable let alone remediable by attempting to allocate blame between reporters and investigators. Consider, for example, the case where a staff member may seek to report in compliance with what the investigator's forms provide, and, precisely because he attempts to take the reporting form seriously, finds it difficult to reconcile what he knows about what the form is asking with what the form provides as a rule for deciding the relevance of what he knows. For example, consider a question which provides the staff member with fixed alternative answers, *e.g.*, "Yes" or "No," yet from what he knows of the case he is convinced that a "Yes" or "No" answer will distort the question or defeat the inquirer's aim in asking it. Taking the study seriously the reporter might ask himself if a marginal note will do it? But then is he asking for trouble if he writes it? Perhaps he should wait until he encounters the investigator and then remind him of this case? But why only *this* case? He knows, along with other reporters like him, of many cases and of many places throughout the reporting form, so that his complaint is entirely a realistic one that were he to engage in marginal jottings, he might have innumerable remarks to make for many items in many cases.

The investigator, for his part, wants nothing more of the self-reporter than that he treat the reporting form as the occasion to report what the self-reporter knows *as he knows it.* Thus we find that the self-reporter may distort the reality of the case precisely because he wants to be helpful and thereby complies with the reporting form. He may know he is distorting and resent it or otherwise suffer it. One can easily imagine that his resentment and suffering are matched on the investigator's side.

Further, while the terminology in self-reporting forms is fixed, the actual events that these terms refer to, as well as the ways in which actual events may be brought under the jurisdiction of the form's terminology as descriptions, are highly variable. The relevance of the reporting form's terminology to the events it describes is subject to the stability of the on-going clinic operations and depends upon the self-reporter's grasp and use of the regular features of the clinic's operation as a scheme of linguistic interpretation. Upon any change of clinic policy, organization, personnel, or procedure the terms on the reporting forms may change in their meaning without a single mimeographed sentence being altered. It is disconcerting to find how even small procedural changes may make large sections of a reporting form hopelessly ambiguous.

Difficulties that are introduced either because the clinic members are reporting on their own activities or because the self-reporting activities are carried on with the use of prepared forms, may be extended and illuminated by considering that candor in reporting carries well known risks to careers and to the organization. Speaking euphemistically, between clinic persons and their clients, and between the clinic and its environing groups, the exchange of information is something less than a free market.

### A critical source of trouble:
### Actuarial versus contractual uses of folder contents

The foregoing troubles were introduced by recommending, as a context for their interpretation, that reporting procedures and results, as well as their uses by clinic persons, are integral features of the same orders of clinic activities they describe; that methods and results of clinic record-keeping consist of and are closely regulated by the same features they provide accounts of.

But though the above troubles *can* be interpreted with this context, nothing *about the troubles* requires it. The troubles we have discussed, one might argue, merely document some insufficiency in the rational control of clinic practices. We have enumerated, as troubles with reporting procedures, matters that strong management could undertake to remedy, and in this way the conditions that contribute to bad records could be eliminated, or their impact on record-keeping could be reduced.

But to think of such troubles as a managerial problem of bringing record-keeping performances under greater or more consistent control, overlooks a critical and perhaps unalterable feature of medical records as an element of institutionalized practices. We propose that the enumerated troubles—and obviously our enumeration is by no means complete—either explicate or themselves consist of properties of the case folder as a reconstructable record of transactions between patients and clinic personnel. This critical

feature of clinic records brings the enumerated troubles under
the jurisdiction of their status as "structurally normal troubles" by
relating reporting systems to the conditions of the clinic's viability
as a corporately organized service enterprise. We shall now en-
deavor to show that clinic records, such as they are, are not something clinic personnel get away with, but that instead, the records
*consist of procedures and consequences of clinical activities as a
medico-legal enterprise.*

In reviewing the contents of case folders it seemed to us that a
case folder could be read in one or the other of two contrasting
and irreconcilable ways. On the one hand it could be read as an
*actuarial* [4] *record.* On the other hand it could be read as the *record
of a therapeutic contract* between the clinic as a medico-legal
enterprise and the patient. Because our understanding of the
term "contract" departs somewhat from colloquial usage, but not
from the understanding which Durkheim taught, a brief explanation is in order.

Ordinarily "contract" refers to a document containing an explicit schedule of obligations, the binding character of which is
recognized by identifiable parties to the agreement. In contrast,
and because we are talking specifically about clinics, we use the
term "contract" to refer to the *definition* of normal transactions
between clientele and remedial agencies in terms of which agencies' services are franchised and available to clients. One of the
crucial features of remedial activities is that its recipients are
socially defined by themselves and the agencies as incompetent to
negotiate for themselves the terms of their treatment.

Thus it is the socially acknowledged normal course of affairs
that a patient "puts himself in the hands of a doctor" and is expected to suspend the usual competence of his own judgment about
his well being, what he needs, or what is best for him. The same
applies to the criminal, *mutatis mutandis*, who is the sole person

[4] David Harrah's model of an information-matching game is taken to define the meaning of "actuarial" procedure. See David Harrah, "A Logic of
Questions and Answers," *Philosophy of Science*, 28, No. 1 (January, 1961),
40-46. More extensive discussion that is compatible with Harrah's formulation is found in Paul E. Meehl, *Clinical Versus Statistical Prediction* (Minneapolis: University of Minnesota Press, 1954); and in Paul E. Meehl, "When
Shall We Use Our Heads Instead of the Formula?" *Minnesota Studies in the
Philosophy of Science*, Vol. 2 (Minneapolis: University of Minnesota Press,
1958).

barred from contributing his opinion to the formulation of a just sentence. Despite these limitations of competence, neither patients nor criminals lose their right to the "treatment they deserve." This is so because treatment consists of occasions for performances that in the eyes of participants accord with a larger scheme of obligations. The larger scheme of obligations relates the authorization in terms of which a remedial agency is deputized to act to the technical doctrines and practical professional ethics which govern the operations of the agency. By assuming jurisdiction in specific cases, medical and legal agencies commit themselves to honoring legitimate public claims for "good healing" and "good law." An indispensable though not exclusive method whereby clinics demonstrate that they have honored claims for adequate medical care consists of procedures for formulating relevant accounts of their transactions with patients.

Further remarks are needed about our use of the concept of contract. Even colloquial usage recognizes that what a contract specifies is not simply given in the document that attests to the contract's existence. Nor are terms, designations, and expressions contained in a document invoked in any "automatic" way to regulate the relationship. Instead, the ways they relate to performances are matters for competent readership to interpret. As is well known, culturally speaking, jurists are competent readers of most contracts; it is for *them* to say what the terms really mean. Indeed, the form in which legal contracts are put intends such readership.

Sociologically, however, legal contracts are only one variant of the class of contracts. The larger conception of contract, namely, its power to define normal relations, also requires that questions of competent readership be considered. Thus we were obliged to consider how the designations, terms, and expressions contained in the clinic folders were read to make them testify as answers to questions pertaining to medico-legal responsibility. In our view *the contents of clinic folders are assembled with regard for the possibility that the relationship may have to be portrayed as having been in accord with expectations of sanctionable performances by clinicians and patients.*

By calling a medical record a "contract" we are not claiming that the record contains only statements of what should have happened as opposed to what did happen. Nor are we proposing that a contractual reading of the medical record is even the most frequent reading, let alone the only reading that occurs. Clinic records are consulted upon many different occasions and for many different interests. But for all the different uses to which records may be put and for all the different uses that they serve, considerations of medico-legal responsibility exercise an overriding priority of relevance as prevailing structural [5] interests whenever procedures for the maintenance of records and their eligible contents must be decided.

Although folder materials may be put to many uses different from those that serve the interests of contract, *all* alternatives are subordinated to the contract use as a matter of enforced structural priority. Because of this priority, alternative uses are consistently producing erratic and unreliable results. But also because of this priority every last suggestion of information in a medical record can come under the scope of a contractual interpretation. Indeed, the contract use both addresses and establishes *whatsoever* the folder might contain as the elements of a "whole record" and does so in the manner that we shall now describe.

When any case folder was read as an actuarial record its contents fell so short of adequacy as to leave us puzzled as to why "poor records" as poor as these should nevertheless be so assiduously kept. On the other hand, when folder documents were regarded as unformulated terms of a potential therapeutic contract, *i.e.*, as documents assembled in the folder in open anticipation of some occasion when the terms of a therapeutic contract might have to be formulated from them, the assiduousness with which folders were kept, even though their contents were extremely uneven in quantity and quality, began to "make sense."

We start with the fact that when one examines any case folder for what it actually contains, a prominent and consistent feature is the occasional and elliptical character of its remarks and information. In their occasionality, folder documents are very much like utterances in a conversation with an unknown audience which, because it already knows what might be talked about, is capable

---

[5] By calling interests "structural" we wish to convey that the interest is not governed by personal considerations in advancing a cause but is related to demands of organized practice which the member treats as his real circumstances.

of reading hints. As expressions, the remarks that make up these documents have overwhelmingly the characteristic that their sense cannot be decided by a reader without his necessarily knowing or assuming something about a typical biography and typical purposes of the user of the expressions, about typical circumstances under which such remarks are written, about a typical previous course of transactions between the writers and the patient, or about a typical relationship of actual or potential interaction between *the writers and the reader.* Thus the *folder contents much less than revealing an order of interaction, presuppose an understanding of that order for a correct reading.* The understanding of that order is not one, however, that strives for theoretical clarity, but is one that is appropriate to a reader's pragmatic interest in the order.

Further, there exists an entitled use of records. The entitlement is accorded, without question, to the person who reads them from the perspective of active medico-legal involvement in the case at hand and shades off from there. The entitlement refers to the fact that the full relevance of his position and involvement comes into play in justifying the expectancy that he has proper business with these expressions, that he will understand them, and will put them to good use. The specific understanding and use will be occasional to the situation in which he finds himself. The entitled reader knows that just as his understanding and use is occasional to the situation in which he finds himself, so the expressions that he encounters are understood to have been occasional to the situations of their authors. The possibility of understanding is based on a shared, practical, and entitled understanding of common tasks between writer and reader.

Occasional expressions are to be contrasted with "objective" expressions, *i.e.,* expressions whose references are decided by consulting a set of coding rules that are assumed, by both user and reader, to hold irrespective of any characteristics of either one, other than their more or less similar grasp of these rules.

The documents in the case folder had the further feature that what they could be read to be *really* talking about did not remain and was not required to remain identical in meaning over the various occasions of their use. Both actually and by intent, their meanings are variable with respect to circumstances. To appreciate what the documents were talking about, specific reference to the circumstances of their use was required: emphatically *not* the circumstances that accompanied the original writing, *but the present circumstances of the reader* in deciding their appropriate *present* use. Obviously, the document readers to whom we refer are clinic persons.

A prototype of an actuarial record would be a record of installment payments. The record of installment payments describes the present state of the relationship and how it came about. A standardized terminology and a standardized set of grammatical rules govern not only possible contents, but govern as well the way a "record" of past transactions is to be assembled. Something like a standard reading is possible that enjoys considerable reliability among readers of the record. The interested reader does not have an edge over the merely instructed reader. That a reader is entitled to claim to have read the record correctly, *i.e.*, a reader's claim to competent readership, is decidable by him and others while disregarding particular characteristics of the reader, *his* transactions with the record, or *his* interests in reading it.

To recite investigators' troubles in the use of clinic folders is to remark on the fact that a negligible fraction of the contents of clinic folders can be read in an actuarial way without incongruity. An investigator who attempts to impose an actuarial reading upon folder contents will fill his notebook with recitation of "shortcomings" in the data, with complaints of "carelessness," and the like.

However, the folder's contents *can* be read, without incongruity, by a clinic member if, in the way that an historian or a lawyer might use the same documents, he develops a *documented representation* [6] of what the clinic-patient transactions consisted of as an orderly and understandable matter. The various items of the clinic folders are tokens—like pieces that will permit the assembly of an indefinitely large number of mosaics—gathered together not to describe a relationship between clinical personnel and the patient, but to permit a clinic member to formulate a relationship between patient and clinic as a normal course of clinic affairs when

---

[6] For further descriptions of documentary representation see Karl Mannheim, "On the Interpretation of 'Weltanschauung'," in *Essays on the Sociology of Knowledge*, ed. Paul Kecskemeti (New York: Oxford University Press, 1962); and Chapter Three in this volume.

and if the question of normalizing should arise as a matter of some clinic member's practical concern. In this sense, we say that a folder's contents serves the uses of contract rather than description, for a contract does not and is not used to describe a relationship. Rather it is used to normalize a relationship, by which is meant that the *quid pro quo* of exchanges is so ordered in an account of the relationship as to satisfy the terms of a prior and legitimate agreement, explicit or implicit.

Folder contents are assembled against the contingent need, by some clinic member, to construct a potential or a past course of transactions between the clinic and the patient as a "case," and thereby as an instance of a therapeutic contract, frequently in the interests of justifying an actual or potential course of actions between clinic persons and patients. Hence, whatever their diversity, a folder's contents can be read without incongruity by a clinic member if, in much the same way as a lawyer "makes the brief," the clinic member "makes a case" from the fragmented remains *in the course* of having to read into documents their relevance for each other as an account of legitimate clinic activity.

From this perspective a folder's contents consist of a single free field of elements with the use of which field the contractual aspect of the relationship may be formulated upon whatsoever occasion such a formulation is required. Which documents will be used, how they will be used, and what meanings their contents will assume, wait upon the particular occasions, purposes, interests, and questions that a particular member may use in addressing them.

In contrast to actuarial records, folder documents are very little constrained in their present meanings by the procedures whereby they come to be assembled in the folder. Indeed, document meanings are disengaged from the actual procedures whereby documents were assembled, and in this respect the ways and results of competent readership of folder documents contrast, once more, with the ways and results of competent actuarial readership. When and if a clinic member has "good reason" to consult folder contents, his purposes at the time define some set of the folder's contents as constituent elements of the formulated account. If, in the course of consulting the folder, his purposes should change, nothing is suffered since the constituent set of documents is not completed until the reader decides that he has enough. The grounds for stopping are not formulated beforehand as conditions that an answer to his questions has to satisfy. The possible use of folder documents might be said to follow the user's developing interests in using them; not the other way around. It is quite impossible for a user to say when he starts to work out a contract what documents he wants, let alone what ones he would insist on. His interests require a method of recording and retrieval that makes full provision for the developing character of his knowledge of the practical circumstances for the management of which the folder's contents must stand service. Above all, it is desired that folder contents be permitted to acquire whatsoever meaning readership can invest them with when various documents are "combinatorially" played against and in search of alternative interpretations in accordance with the reader's developing interests on the actual occasion of reading them. Thus the actual event, when it is encountered under the auspices of the possible use to be made of it, furnishes, on that occasion, the definition of the document's significance. Thereby, the list of folder documents is open ended and can be indefinitely long. Questions of overlap and duplication are irrelevant. Not only do they not arise but questions of overlap cannot be assessed until the user knows, with whatever clarity or vagueness, what he wants to be looking for and, perhaps, why. In any case questions of overlap and omission cannot be decided until he has actually examined whatever he actually encounters.

Further contrasting features of "duplication" and "omission" in the two reporting systems require comment. In an actuarial record, information may be repeated for the sake of expediency. But the statement of a present state of a bank account does not add any information to what can be readily gathered from the account's earlier state and the subsequent deposits and withdrawals. If the two do not match, this points irrefutably to some omission. The record is governed by a principle of relevance with the use of which the reader can assess its completeness and adequacy at a glance.

A clinical record does not have this character. A subsequent entry may be played off against a former one in such a way that what was known then, now changes complexion. The contents of a folder may jostle each other in bidding to play a part in a pending argument. It is an open question whether things said twice are repetitions, or whether the latter has the significance, say, of confirming the former. The same is true of omissions. Indeed, both come to view only in the context of some elected scheme of interpretation.

Most important, the competent reader is aware that it is not only that which the folder contains that stands in a relationship of mutually qualifying and determining reference, but parts that are not in it belong to this too. These ineffable parts come to view in the light of known episodes, but then, in turn, the known episodes themselves are also, reciprocally, interpreted in the light of what one must reasonably assume to have gone on while the case progressed without having been made a matter of record.

The scheme for interpreting folder documents may be drawn from anywhere at all. It may change with the reading of any particular item, change with the investigator's purposes in making a case of the documents he encounters, change "in light of circumstances," change as the exigencies require. What the relationship of any document's sense is to the "ordering schema" remains entirely a prerogative of the reader to find out, decide, or argue as he sees fit in each particular case, after the case, in light of his purposes, in light of his changing purposes, in light of what he begins to find, and so forth. The documents' meanings are altered as a function of trying to assemble them into the record of a case. Instead of laying out beforehand what a document might be all about, one waits to see what one encounters in the folders and from that, one "makes out," one literally finds, what the document was all about. Then, whether or not there is continuity, consistency, coherence between the sense of one document and another is for the reader to see. In no case are constraints placed upon the reader to justify beforehand or to say beforehand what in the folder counts for what, or what he is going to count or not count for what.[7]

---

[7] It is possible to deliberately design a system for reporting, search, and retrieval with such properties. For example, scholars may deliberately employ such a system precisely because their enterprise is such that they may not be willing to permit their knowledge of the situations that their reporting system is intended to permit an analysis of to be confined in its development by a method that places known limits to what is imaginable about the various readings and ideas they have encountered in their work. To their interests such an *ad hoc* system of classification and retrieval has the virtue of maximizing

In order to read the folder's contents without incongruity a clinic member must expect of himself, expect of other clinic members, and expect that as he expects of other clinic members they expect him to know and to use a knowledge (1) of particular persons to whom the record refers, (2) of persons who contributed to the record, (3) of the clinic's actual organization and operating procedures at the time the folder's documents are being consulted, (4) of a mutual history with other persons—patients and clinic members—and (5) of clinic procedures, including procedures for reading a record, as these procedures involved the patient and the clinic members. In the service of present interests he uses such knowledge to assemble from the folder's items a documented representation of the relationship.[8]

The clinic that we studied is associated with a university medical center. By reason of the clinic's commitment to research as a legitimate goal of the enterprise an actuarial record has high priority of value in the clinic's usual affairs. But the contract character of the contents of case folders has a competing priority of value which is associated with practical and prevailing necessities of maintaining viable relationships with the university, with other medical specialties, with the state government, with the courts,

---

opportunities for imaginative play. Not knowing as of any Here and Now what might develop later, yet wanting later developments to be used to reconstrue the past, an *ad hoc* strategy for collection and retrieval promises to permit the scholar to bring his corpus of documents to bear upon the management of exigencies that arise as a function of his actual engagement with a developing situation.

What the scholar might do on his own as an aid to thought is done by clinicians in each other's company, under the auspices of a corporately organized system of supervision and review, with their results offered not as possible interpretations but as accounts of what actually happened. Their uses of folders are entirely similar to the many methods of psychotherapy, just as both are legitimate ways of delivering clinical services. And, if one asks—be he insider or outsider—for the rational grounds of the procedure, in both cases too these grounds are furnished by the personnel's invocation of the clinic's ways as socially sanctioned medico-legal ways of doing psychiatric business.

[8] It is important to emphasize that we are not talking of "making some scientific best of whatever there is." Organizationally speaking, any collection of folder contents whatsoever can, will, even must be used to fashion a documented representation. Thus an effort to impose a formal rationale on the collection and composition of information has the character of a vacuous exercise because the expressions which the so ordered documents will contain will have to be "decoded" to discover their real meaning in the light of the interest and interpretation which prevails at the time of their use.

and with the various publics at large by making out its activities to be those of a legitimate psychiatric remedial agency in the first place.

Between the two commitments there is no question on the part of the many parties concerned, patients and researchers included, as to which of the two takes precedence. In all matters, starting with considerations of comparative economics and extending through the tasks of publicizing and justifying the enterprise, the conditions for maintaining contract folders must be satisfied. Other interests are necessarily lesser interests and must be accommodated to these.

To all of this it is possible to answer that we are making too much of the entire matter; that after all the clinic's records are kept so as to serve the interests of medical and psychiatric services rather than to serve the interests of research. We would answer with full agreement. This is what we have been saying though we have been saying it with the intent of tying the state of the records to the organizational significance of the priority that medical and psychiatric services enjoy over research concerns. Where research activities occur in psychiatric clinics one will invariably find special mechanisms whereby its research activities are structurally separated from and subordinated to the activities whereby the character and the viability of the clinic as a service enterprise are guaranteed. This is not to suggest that research is not pursued seriously and resolutely by clinicians.

SEVEN

# Methodological adequacy in the quantitative study of selection criteria and selection activities in psychiatric outpatient clinics *

Quantitative studies that describe how persons are selected for treatment in psychiatric outpatient clinics agree that the chances that an applicant will receive clinic treatment depend upon many factors besides the fact that he may be in need of it. Schaffer and Myers [1] compared applicants with those admitted to treatment at the Grace New Haven Hospital Psychiatric Outpatient Clinic and decided that the socio-economic status of the applicant was a relevant selection criterion. Hollingshead and Redlich [2] compared the class composition of patients affiliated with various treatment agencies and attributed to the processes of selection the over-representation in treatment at psychiatric clinics of middle class patients and the under-representation of lower class patients. Rosenthal and Frank [3] compared a population of all patients who contacted the Henry Phipps Psychiatric Clinic for the

* With the assistance of Egon Bittner, The Langley Porter Neuropsychiatric Institute.

[1] Leslie Schaffer and Jerome K. Myers, "Psychotherapy and Social Stratification: an Empirical Study of Practices in a Psychiatric Outpatient Clinic," Psychiatry, 17, 83-93.

[2] August B. Hollingshead and Frederick C. Redlich, Social Class and Mental Illness (New York: John Wiley & Sons, Inc., 1958).

[3] David Rosenthal and Jerome D. Frank, "The Fate of Psychiatric Clinic Outpatients Assigned to Psychotherapy," The Journal of Nervous and Mental Diseases, 127 (October, 1958), 330-343.

first time with those referred to treatment. They found that age, race, education, annual income, sources of referral, diagnosis, and motivation discriminated the two populations. Storrow and Brill [4] compared a population of all patients who made an inquiry in person at the U.C.L.A. Psychiatric Outpatient Clinic with the surviving population that appeared for at least one treatment interview. Psychoneuroses, shorter duration of illness, mild impairment in "occupational adjustments," the patient's desire for treatment, benefits wanted by the patient, secondary gain, economic status, religion, sex, age, the interviewer's reaction, the therapist's assessment of treatability, and the patient's evasiveness discriminated the two populations. They report an extensive list of "variables" which either did not discriminate or barely discriminated the two populations. Weiss and Schaie [5] compared a population of all patients who were discharged after completing either evaluation or treatment at the Malcolm Bliss Psychiatric Clinic with all who failed to return for scheduled further evaluation or treatment. They report that sex, marital status, source of referral, and diagnosis discriminated the two populations. No differences between the two were found for age, religion, place of birth, parents' place of birth, occupation, history of previous admission to a psychiatric hospital, status of first professional interviewer, duration of therapy, number of interviews, or number of changes of therapists. Katz and Solomon [6] compared three populations of all patients who were offered treatment after an intake interview at the psychiatric clinic of the Yale University School of Medicine and failed to return after the initial visit, after more than one but less than five visits, and after five or more visits. They reported that age, marital status, education, previous psychotherapy, source of referral, attitude of therapist toward the patient, and patients' interests in and ex-

[4] Hugh A. Storrow and Norman Q. Brill, "A Study of Psychotherapeutic Outcome: Some Characteristics of Successfully and Unsuccessfully Treated Patients." Paper presented at the meetings of the California Medical Association, San Francisco, February, 1959.

[5] James M. A. Weiss and K. Warner Schaie, "Factors in Patients' Failure to Return to Clinic," *Diseases of the Nervous System,* 19 (October, 1958), 429-430.

[6] Jay Katz and Rebecca A. Solomon, "The Patient and His Experience in an Outpatient Clinic," *A.M.A. Archives of Neurology and Psychiatry,* 80 (July, 1958), 86-92.

pectancies for treatment discriminated the different lengths of contact with the clinic.

A comparison of previous studies [7] discloses a number of categorical ideas that are presupposed in the descriptions of the selection process as an empirical phenomenon. These ideas are constitutive of the selection problem itself. Because of their constitutive character, reference to each of them is necessary for the adequate formulation of the selection problem. To simplify their exposition we shall call these constituent ideas the "parameters" [8] of the selection problem. We shall refer to these ideas by the terms "sequence," "selection operations," "an initial demand population," "the composition of a later population," and "a theory relating selection work and clinic load."

Not only did the studies handle these parameters differently, but each study failed to handle at least one. The result is that despite the care with which the studies were done, it is not possible to decide what is actually known thus far about selection criteria. Nor is it possible for the researcher to decide, from the published results, that patients were being selected on the re-

[7] Twenty-three previous studies are listed and analyzed in Table 1. Only quantitative studies which were primarily addressed to the topic of selection are included in this list. The list is not exhaustive.

[8] We use the term "parameter" because of the focus it permits on the essential point that a number of ideas define the conditions of complete description. For example, within the rules of physical theory, the concept of "sound-in-general" is defined by its constituent ideas of amplitude, frequency, and duration. Each parameter must be specified if an instance of the general case is to be clearly grasped. Thus to speak of a sound with a given amplitude and duration but with no frequency would be formal nonsense. However, one could refer to a sound whose amplitude and duration was known and which had *a* frequency though this frequency was unknown. All three parameters would be necessarily intended in speaking of "a sound" even though reference was explicitly made to only one or another. While one could address the amplitude alone as the object of interest, the clear grasp of this single parameter would presuppose a reference to the other parameters, and for the case of complete description, all three would need to be explicitly specified. We propose that just as amplitude, frequency, and duration are the parameters of the general concept of sound within the rules of physical inquiry, and serve the function for the researcher of defining adequate description of an instance of a sound, the ideas of "sequence," "selection operations," "an initial demand population," "the composition of a later population" and "a theory relating selection work and clinic load" are the parameters of "selection problem" within the program of sociological inquiry and serve to define for the researcher an actual instance of a selection problem and thereby the conditions of adequate description.

ported grounds, except by long chains of plausible inference which require the researcher to *presuppose a knowledge of the very social structures that are presumably being described in the first instance.*

What are these parameters? How are they necessarily presupposed? How did the studies handle them?

1. *"Sequence."* The first essential idea that informs the studies of patient selection is that the patient groups whose characteristics are compared populate two or more consecutive steps in a selection process. Each study conceives a set of populations as a succession, with each population related to a former one as a population selected from it.

This parameter is necessarily involved in the reported studies because each study not only intends the attributes it examines as possible discriminators of the compared patient populations, but in each study one of the compared populations is explicitly related to the other as the outcome of some set of selection activities.[9]

2. *"Selection operations."* The constituent idea of selection operations appears when a later population in a succession is viewed with respect to the processes whereby it is assembled. This parameter consists of *some* set of successive operations that are performed upon an initial population. The later population is by definition a product of some operations performed upon the former population by means of which the former population is transformed. Even if the operation that transforms the initial population into its successor remains unspecified, the recognition that it is a necessary term of the problem makes it at least possible to state what necessarily remains for further investigation.[10] Weiss and Schaie [11] are

[9] With the exception of the study by Weiss and Schaie these populations and the selection activities are related in a time sequence that is identical with the concrete sequences of actual clinic treatment. The Weiss and Schaie study compared populations of persons who completed scheduled services with those who did not complete scheduled services so that the idea of successive populations is retained in their comparisons though without reference to concrete sequences of actual clinic procedure.

[10] Of course selection criteria may be evaluated without respect for temporal sequences of selection operations, but this leaves the researcher without much to say about whether or how the discriminating criteria are relevant to the work whereby later populations are produced. See for example Rubenstein and Lorr, 1956. For example, if a later population was not discriminable in its age distribution from an earlier one, then just this lack of discriminability and no more would be as far as the researcher could go if he intended to talk literally about his findings. It is because researchers mean to ask whether a

talking to this point when, in concluding their paper, they write,

> It is our impression that those differences noted to be statistically significant in relationship to failure to return are of some importance in predicting rates of failure. . . . This type of cross sectional study, however, does not yield any insight into the dynamics of "breaking therapy. . . ."

Most of the other studies take due notice of "selection operations" in a mixture of conjecture and clinical interpretations.

3. *"An Initial Demand Population."* The parameter of an "initial population" is required by virtue of the fact that any program of sequential selection necessarily requires a reference to an initially given population. Given such a reference, one may ask what kind of an initial population is most appropriate to the study of clinic-selection activities and criteria.

It is not possible to restrict the conception of the initial population so that it consists of *a* population with attributes like age, sex, and the like whose status as selection criteria one seeks to evaluate. Regardless of what attributes are assigned to the initial population, a reference to their *legitimate* character is necessarily implied. This may be seen in the fact that the clinic continually receives claims upon its services of which no official notice is taken: for example, persons who call to ask if they may be given hypnosis or lysergic acid to see what it is like. The legitimate character of these attributes derives from the fact that any initial population must be characterized by the nature of the claims they have upon clinic services. The work of selection is in every case, therefore, at least tacitly conceived to occur through activities that are governed by medico-legal considerations. From the standpoint not only of clinic personnel, but in reciprocal fashion from the standpoint of patients, criteria must be capable of justification with respect to the medico-legal mandates within which the clinic operates. From the point of view of patients and clinic personnel, populations are not merely accepted or turned away—*i.e.,* "selected"—on grounds of "sex" or "age" or "socio-economic status" or "motivation" or "diagnosis."

---

lack of discriminability means that the selection transactions operated independently of age that the parameter of sequence must be settled on different terms. This problem is discussed later in the paper in connection with "out-out" comparisons.

[11] Weiss and Schaie, *op. cit.,* p. 430.

They are accepted or turned away on these grounds as "good reasons."

Because it is not sufficient from the person's point of view to say that an initial population is "distributed on some attribute," it is not sufficient from the researcher's point of view. Instead, the initial population is one that is distributed on some attribute with respect to which the outcome of selection is justifiable by the clinic if it is to ensure approval of its operations. The "initial population" that is appropriate to the problem of selection within the clinic conceived as an operation that is governed by a medico-legal order is therefore and necessarily a *legitimate initial population*.

But this does not rest the problem of deciding the appropriate initial population. A choice remains between whether the initial population is more appropriately considered an eligible or a demand population.

According to the doctrine of medico-legal responsibility, all members of the society constitute a potentially eligible population. Epidemiological studies are typically concerned with the task of defining eligible populations. An eligible population, however, cannot be the initial population that is appropriate to the study of clinic processes of patient selection. This can be seen in the fact that persons who are both eligible and in need of treatment must somehow manage to come to the attention of the psychiatric services. The theorist must provide for this if he is to avoid the assumption that populations in need and populations who appear for treatment are identical. The well known researches of Clausen and Yarrow and others [12] have demonstrated the "paths" to treatment. Such "paths" consist of a set of operations whereby a demand population is produced from a population of eligibles. Hence, if we compare a community population with a clinic population, as Hollingshead and Redlich [13] do, we learn only how the persons that the clinic accepted differ from those who can potentially exercise the right to treatment.

We are left with the conclusion that one wants to compare a population that is produced from the clinic's operations with

[12] J. A. Clausen and M. R. Yarrow, eds., "The Impact of Mental Illness on the Family," *The Journal of Social Issues,* 11 (1955), 3-64.

[13] See also the studies of Futterman *et al.*, 1947, Schaffer and Myers, 1954, Brill and Storrow, 1959 unpublished; analyzed in Table 1.

another population that is earlier in contact with the clinic. This earlier population would consist of an eligible population which has been changed by virtue of already having gone into the market for clinic services. More simply, it is a demand population.

Any population that is in contact with the clinic anywhere in the selection process is such a population. But if one wants to study the effect of clinic operations upon this demand population, then one wants an early demand population since the later in the sequence of clinic operations the demand population is first picked up, the more will the clinic operations confound the results of selection upon the demand population. Thus, for example, in the experience of the U.C.L.A. Outpatient Psychiatric Clinic, 67 per cent of all inquiries were made by phone. Approximately three quarters of these phone inquiries never followed up this contact. To count the demand population without taking these into account counts a population that has already been reduced by almost half (48 per cent).

To omit from a selection study as Schaffer and Myers [14] omitted from their study (a) patients who were referred for consultation only, (b) patients considered to have nonpsychiatric syndromes, (c) patients considered to need hospitalization, (d) patients whose referral was never followed by their appearance at the clinic, and (e) patients who, "following inadequate screening," were discovered to be able to afford private care, furnishes a demand population that the selection procedures have already worked over. The difficulties in assessing Schaffer and Myers results are seen if one asks how this portion of the demand population—which we think must have been sizable—compared in sex, age, class, etc. composition with the one that they used as the initial population. Only if the two populations were identical could we attribute the selection to the criteria that Schaffer and Myers cite. If the two populations differed, we would have to conclude that age, or sex, or class, or whatever had something to do with the story. In all but one of the previous studies [15] the initial populations that were used are subject to similar reservations.

[14] Schaffer and Myers, *op. cit.*, p. 86.

[15] A previous study excepted from this criticism is that by Auld and Eron, 1953, in which the problem of the study specifically required an initial population of persons who had received the Rorschach test.

We conclude that if the problem of selection is to be adequately framed, the legitimate demand population should consist of the demand as soon as it is first encountered. *Otherwise, the clinic's own selection operations confound the task of describing these selection procedures by using as a comparison population one that has already been selected in unknown ways.*[16]

[16] Comment is required to justify our insistence that the initial demand population is correctly defined at the point where it is first encountered. The point can be made by comparison with the criminologist's task.

Dr. Richard J. Hill asked if there was not a similarity in the situation of the criminologist who must decide where he will count in order to estimate the amount of real crime (or the number of real criminals), and our attempt to define the appropriate place to count in order to estimate the size of the initial demand population. The criminologist's problem would appear to be this: how to estimate the amount of real crime, given that the defining, detecting, reporting, and repressing activities may confound the movements of the phenomena being counted? (For example, an increase in police personnel or a change in legislation may alter a crime rate.) The criminologist settles for Thorsten Sellin's rule that the further along in the process of detection, arrest, and trial that the criminologist obtains his counts, the less credence is to be placed in the obtained count as a basis for estimating the parameters of real crime; hence the practical solution of using "crimes known to the police." Where the parameters of the initial demand population must be estimated, would not some such rule also obtain and for similar methodological reasons? *e.g.*, "all inquiries received by those clinic persons who are entitled to decide the occurrence of an inquiry about treatment."

It is our view that indeed there is a profound correspondence in the two cases, but that the correspondence rests on different grounds than the previous argument provides. The crux of the difference rests on the meaning of "real amount of crime" and "real demand." Our argument is as follows:

*Within the perspective of police activities* there exists a culturally defined "real amount of crime" committed by a culturally defined crime-producing population. Police use "crimes known to the police" to stand for or represent its features, like amount, trend, contributors, etc. Correspondingly, *from the point of view of clinic personnel* there exists a culturally defined "real demand for the clinic's services." Clinic personnel use actual inquiries to stand for or represent *its* features. Both situations—culturally defined real amount of crime for police, and culturally defined real demand for clinic services for clinic personnel—"exist" but only in the peculiar sense in which cultural objects, sociologically speaking, are said to "exist": *their existence consists only and entirely of the likelihood that socially organized measures for the detection and control of deviance can be enforced.*

Within the models and methods that the police use, real crime has the meaning that it occurs independently of the measures of crime repression. If the criminologist uses a similar model, his task of describing real crime is fraught with methodological difficulties for which Sellin's rule is an intended remedy. When, however, real crimes are defined in terms of the activities of repression, a procedure that Florian Znaniecki proposed in *Social Actions*, methodological difficulties are seen to *consist* of the very features of the socially

4. *"Composition of a later population."* This parameter stipulates that each resulting population is composed of two subpopulations: (a) the set of persons who are "in," with respect to which there exists (b) a complementary population of "outs." The sum of the two reproduces the preceding population. This parameter dictates the choice of populations that must be compared if the researcher is to decide the criteria that were used in selection. For the selection problem, the necessarily appropriate populations are the "ins" and "outs" at each step of the process.

---

organized activities whereby the existence of culturally defined real crimes is detected, described, and reported. As data in their own right, these "difficulties" consist of the very measures whereby real crimes are treated by police (and their clients) as objects in a culturally defined environment.

An exact parallel holds for the tasks of describing the initial demand population of the clinic. Methodological difficulties are encountered if the investigator tries to estimate the real initial demand population by using the clinic person's model of a demanding population. Like real crime, real demand is defined by the clinicians as existing independently of the measures whereby the real occurrence of psychiatric illness is socially and professionally defined and remedied. The medical "organism," for example, does heroic service in this practical respect.

The correspondence extends even further. Police and clinic personnel both claim, both are given, and both, in the particular ways of their respective professions, enforce a monopoly on the rights to define the real occurrence of these events and to advocate legitimate controls for them.

Thus, when real demand is defined in terms of the socially organized and socially controlled measures for its detection and treatment, the demand for clinic services has as its otherwise suppressed feature, that it consists of clinic persons' claims that their services are being demanded. Thereby the methodological difficulties in estimating the initial demand population are seen to consist of the very features whereby the existence of a culturally defined real demand is known and is treated as an object in the culturally defined environments of clinic persons and clients.

In cases of describing real crime and initial demand, the investigator's solution consists of the literal description of how the occurrence of an instance of a "criminal" or a "patient" is socially recognized, *i.e.*, procedurally speaking, how it occurs that those who are empowered by the society to detect its presence via their social judgments detect it. Hence the insistence in this paper that the investigator who addresses the selection problem is required to use an initial demand population that is necessarily found at the first opportunities that clinic persons have to recognize the existence of a claim upon their services as socially empowered remedial agents and employees of the clinic. It happens that a large percentage of the occasions on which the "demand is represented" at the U.C.L.A. clinic occurs through phone calls, letters, and walk-ins directed to persons "out front." The same must be true at other clinics as well. This is not to say, of course, that there are not other channels through which the demand may be "communicated." An adequate description would be required to take them into account as well.

With the exception of studies by Weiss and Schaie, and Kadushin, and disregarding eligible/in comparisons,[17] previous studies either compared an "in" population with a later "in" population, or an "out" population with a later "out" population. The reasoning would appear to be that if a later surviving population showed different characteristics from an earlier one, then the selection is to be assigned to the characteristics that discriminate the two.

Given the constituent idea of selection from successive populations, both "in-in" and "out-out" comparisons are procedurally incorrect. How is this so?

### "In-in" comparisons

For the studies that used an "in-in" procedure, a moment's reflection will show (a) that while an in-in comparison was used, the intent of the comparison was "in-out," with the result that actual and intended comparisons do not coincide. Further, (b) if the usual associational statistics, for example, chi-square,[18] are used to evaluate the presence of an association between criteria and survival, then only the intended comparison is the correct one.

Consider point (a). The very reasoning and method used in the in-in procedure involves the comparison of a surviving population with one that did not survive. The proof of this assertion consists in the fact that the earlier population consists of two groups: those who are "in" at the initial step and who will be "in" later, and those who are "in" at the initial step, but who will be "out" later when the characteristics of the "ins" are consulted. A comparison directed to successive "in" populations confounds the intent of the comparison which is directed to the criteria whereby the attrition of an original population was produced. Because we are necessarily dealing with the progressive attrition of an initial population, the criteria of selection must operate at any given "point" to discriminate those that remain from those who drop out at that point. Hence, even if the steps are undifferentiated, at least one step is necessarily meant by the terms of the problem itself, and for this one step the comparison is necessarily one of an "in" with an "out" population.

[17] These were considered and criticized above.
[18] We are indebted to Dr. Richard J. Hill for pointing out that our argument held for the usual associational statistics.

Consider point (b). Because both "in" and "out" populations of some later step are constituents of the population at the preceding step, the "ins" and "outs" at any step are complementary in their composition. If the researcher uses chi-square to decide selection criteria, care is required in comparing an "in" population with a later "in" population to avoid comparing a large part of the earlier population with itself. Further, in order to treat the earlier and later populations as independent distributions, a condition that must be satisfied for the correct use of chi-square, the initial population in a one-step operation would have to constitute the marginals. The survivors would then be compared with its complement who are "outs" at a later step. Statisticians [19] that we consulted were agreed that the use of chi-square to compare successive "in" populations is incorrect, but opinion was divided as to whether this procedure is incorrect because the correlation would depress the result, or because a chi-square comparison of successive in-populations in a case involving conditional frequencies has no clear meaning. In either case, the consequence is that the comparison of successive "ins" would obscure a judgment about the presence of discriminating attributes. All of the previous studies that used in-in comparisons used chi-square to compare the two populations, but none mentioned this problem.

### "Out-out" comparisons

Given that the task of deciding the presence of selection criteria is solved by employing a scheme of inference that must provide for the attrition of an initial population, an out-out comparison is incorrect because it employs an inappropriate scheme of inference. The difference between the scheme of inference that an out-out comparison uses, and the scheme that is appropriate to the selection problem can be demonstrated in the study by Katz and Solomon [20] which used out-out comparisons.

Katz and Solomon used an original cohort of 353 patients. Three possible things could happen to this original cohort: some part of

[19] Drs. Wilfred J. Dixon, Richard J. Hill, Charles F. Mosteller, William S. Robinson.
[20] Katz and Solomon, *op. cit.*, pp. 86-92.

it could be out after one visit ($O_1$); another part of it could be out after two to four visits ($O_{2\text{-}4}$); a third part could be out after five or more visits ($O_5$). More formally, we can say that the original cohort (OC) was partitioned by three possible occurrences $O_1$, $O_{2\text{-}4}$, and $O_5$. Any "cross-break," like the attribute, "patient's interest in clinic treatment," represents a partitioning rule. For example, one partitioning rule that Katz and Solomon tested was: send low interest patients out early; send high interest patients out late. An alternative partitioning rule was: send patients out early or late irrespective of their interest in treatment. Expected $O_1$, $O_{2\text{-}4}$, $O_5$ populations were compared with observed populations in order to establish the extent of departure of observed from expected populations. It was decided that selection criteria had operated when observed distributions departed significantly from distributions that were expected according to the partitioning rule of no association.

To demonstrate the inappropriateness of this procedure for the selection problem, it is necessary to show that it does not permit inferences about selection criteria without gratuitous reference to the terms of the selection problem.[21]

The procedure that Katz and Solomon used to partition the original cohort can be represented by the following lattice. It describes the relationship between the original cohort and the successive populations that a partitioning rule produces:

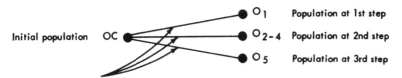

Initial population OC    $O_1$ Population at 1st step    $O_{2\text{-}4}$ Population at 2nd step    $O_5$ Population at 3rd step

Partitioning rule, e.g.,
patients' interest in treatment

An inspection of this lattice reveals (a) that the domain of possible occurrences consists of $O_1$, $O_{2\text{-}4}$, $O_5$; (b) that the original

[21] We are using the term "selection problem" to refer to the tasks of conceiving the sequence of populations where their successive attrition from an initial population is the event of interest. Obviously the term "selection problem" could be used to refer to a sequence of populations where successive attrition was not of interest.

cohort is reproduced as the sum $O_1 + O_{2-4} + O_5$; and (c) that the meaning of succession is gratuitous since, with respect to the original cohort as the "beginning," the branches can be rotated and the populations can be substituted for each other without altering the meaning of the lattice. Hence, although $O_1$, $O_{2-4}$, and $O_5$ each means a different duration of treatment, reference to their succession is no part of their necessary meaning. One might arrange them in the "natural order" of increasing magnitude of duration, but there is no more necessity to this arrangement than there is to any arrangement that accords with the meaning that duration of treatment has within this lattice, i.e., that each of the three durations is a different duration. If the researcher nevertheless refers to succession, he can do so only by lending the structure a gratuitous property.

There corresponds to each lattice a scheme of inference [22] which is constructed by ordering the domain of possible events according to the rule of inclusion. The set of necessary inferences consists of those which exhaust the domain of possible events. These inferences are obtained by comparing all the subdomains that exhaust the superordinate domain which the subdomains partition.

The scheme of inference that corresponds to the lattice used by Katz and Solomon is as follows:

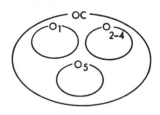

In this scheme the subdomains are $O_1$, $O_{2-4}$, and $O_5$. Again it will be seen that these possibilities may be ordered according to duration of contact but the meaning of successive populations is neither an integral feature of the domain of possible occurrences nor is

[22] We use the term "scheme of inference" to mean a grammar or set of rules that will reproduce the set of possible occurrences from a set of elementary units in terms of observed occurrences. The scheme of inference is therefore identical in meaning with an explicit theory of these observed occurrences.

there any comparison within this scheme whereby the meaning of successive populations is necessarily entailed. Instead, all inferences from this scheme are controlled by the necessity that they be compatible with the assumption that none of these three outcomes include the others in their meanings. Whatever the researcher says about these three populations must be compatible with the assumption that there is no necessary relationship of sense between how long a population has survived and how long it will have survived.

An original cohort that was partitioned while providing for the meaning of successive populations as an integral feature of the domain of possible occurrences would appear in the following lattice:

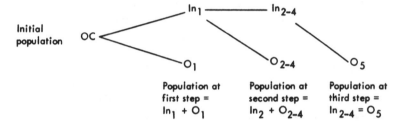

Initial
population     OC

$In_1$ ——————— $In_{2-4}$

$O_1$          $O_{2-4}$          $O_5$

Population at          Population at          Population at
first step =           second step =          third step =
$In_1 + O_1$          $In_2 + O_{2-4}$        $In_{2-4} = O_5$

It will be seen that the set of possible outcomes now consists of $In_1$; $O_2$; $In_1$-followed-by-$In_{2-4}$; $In_1$-followed-by-$O_{2-4}$; $In_1$-followed-by-$In_{2-4}$-followed-by-$O_5$. When this lattice of possible outcomes is ordered according to the rule of inclusion, the following scheme of inference results:

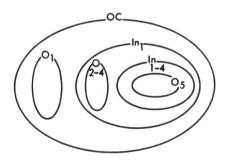

It will be seen that any rearrangement of populations in the lattice changes their meaning. Duration and succession are necessarily related.

Whereas the original cohort of Katz and Solomon is described as OC (100%) = $O_1$ + $O_{2-4}$ + $O_5$ the original cohort demanded by the parameter of sequence is described as OC (100%) [23] = $O_1$ + (In$_1$-followed-by-$O_{2-4}$) + (In$_1$-followed-by-In$_{2-4}$-followed-by-$O_5$).

The scheme of inference in the Katz and Solomon study involves a comparison of the subdomains of $O_1$, $O_{2-4}$, and $O_5$ for OC. By following Katz and Solomon's interpretation of the selection problem, survival chances are described by comparing the outs at each step as a fraction of the *original cohort*.

The scheme of inference that results from building the parameter of sequence into the conception of the selection problem involves a comparison of the subdomains of In$_1$ and $O_1$ for OC: In$_{2-4}$ and $O_{2-4}$ for In$_1$; and $O_5$ for In$_{2-4}$. Following this procedure, survival chances are described by comparing ins and outs at each step as fractions of those that survived the *preceding step*.

That these differences make a difference for Katz and Solomon's findings is illustrated in the following tables that were recalculated from Table 7 [24] in Katz and Solomon's article. Their table purported to describe the relationship between source of referral, duration of treatment, and patients' interests in treatment.

According to Katz and Solomon's procedure we find the following:

[23] Although this sum is identical with the sum in Katz and Solomon's procedure, the events summed are different. Katz and Solomon added terminations. Here we are summing careers that originate with an initial contact and have termination as their final occurrence.

[24] Katz and Solomon, *op. cit.*, p. 89. Katz and Solomon's published table reported different grades of interest in treatment as percentages of different durations of treatment. We have re-arranged their table to express the durations of treatment as percentages of different grades of interest, following the convention of calculating percentages in the direction of the "causal sequence." This re-arrangement does not affect our characterization of Katz and Solomon's procedure or our arguments about it.

| | Patients referred to "open clinic" from hospital wards, clinics, and emergency room who terminated treatment after | | | | Patient referred to "regular clinic" by self-referral or by physicians who terminated treatment after | | | |
|---|---|---|---|---|---|---|---|---|
| Patients' interest in treatment | Original cohort (N) | 1 visit % | 2 to 4 visits % | 5 or more visits % | Original cohort (N) | 1 visit % | 2 to 4 visits % | 5 or more visits % |
| Clearly expressed | (22) | 31.8 | 45.4 | 22.8 | (132) | 8.3 | 4.5 | 87.2 |
| Had to be encouraged | (28) | 35.8 | 42.9 | 21.3 | (43) | 20.9 | 20.9 | 58.2 |
| Little or no interest | (64) | 67.2 | 23.5 | 9.3 | (28) | 42.8 | 39.3 | 17.9 |
| Total | (114) | | | | (203) | | | |

When Katz and Solomon's data were recalculated to provide for the necessary meaning of succession, their findings took a different turn:

| | | | | | | | | |
|---|---|---|---|---|---|---|---|---|
| Clearly expressed | (22) | 31.8 | 66.7 | * | (132) | 8.3 | 4.9 | * |
| Had to be encouraged | (28) | 35.8 | 66.7 | * | (43) | 20.9 | 26.5 | * |
| Little or no interest | (64) | 67.2 | 71.5 | * | (28) | 42.8 | 68.8 | * |

* All percentages in this column are 100 per cent, since all persons out after five or more visits are those who survived two or more visits.

Katz and Solomon's original table states the following: When it was assumed that how long a person has been in contact with the "open clinic" and how long he would remain can occur independently of each other, the finding was that after one visit persons with little or no interest in psychiatric treatment dropped out at a proportionately higher rate than those with greater interests in treatment. Thereafter, persons with little or no interest dropped out at a proportionately lower rate than those with stronger interests. Persons with little or no interests dropped out after the first visit; persons with stronger interests dropped out later.

The recalculated table is based on the assumption that how long a person, referred to open clinic, would have remained includes as a dependent condition how long he has been in contact. The finding is that persons with little or no interest in treatment dropped out after one visit to a disproportionately high degree, whereas interest in treatment did not discriminate drop outs after two to four visits.

For persons who were referred to "regular clinic" Katz and Solomon found that the rates at which differentially interested persons dropped out did not change between the first visit and the second to fourth visits. The recalculated data states that these rates did change: the rate of drop outs rose sharply after two or more visits for persons who had little or no interest in treatment.[25]

In all cases where there is a necessary relationship between how long a person has been in and how long he will stay, in which the researcher treats these possibilities as if they occur independently of each other—which he does by using out-out comparisons—if the researcher describes his findings literally, he will have reported them incorrectly. Should the researcher, nevertheless, treat his findings obtained by out-out comparisons as if they involved a set of successively selected populations, his findings cannot be demonstrated from the data itself but will require instead that he go outside of his study in order to assign to his data their status as findings of the study.

The foregoing criticisms of studies that used in-in and out-out comparisons do not apply to the Weiss and Schaie study, since in their study the set of persons who failed to meet scheduled services is by definition an "out" population; persons who completed sched-

---

[25] Because of the wide interest in the Yale groups's work on social class as a selection factor, Table 3 in the report of Myers and Schaffer, 1954, was recalculated using an in/out procedure. The original table is as follows:

|  | SOCIAL CLASS | | | |
|---|---|---|---|---|
| Total times seen in clinic | II | III | IV | V |
| One | 17.6 | 23.1 | 38.9 | 45.2 |
| 2-9 | 29.4 | 28.8 | 40.3 | 42.9 |
| 10 or more | 52.9 | 48.1 | 20.9 | 11.9 |
|  | 99.9 | 100.0 | 100.1 | 100.0 |

*The recalculated table is:*

|  | II | III | IV | V |
|---|---|---|---|---|
| One | 17.6 | 23.1 | 38.9 | 45.2 |
| 2-9 | 35.7 | 38.5 | 66.0 | 78.3 |
| 10 or more | – | – | – | – |

Obviously, Myers and Schaffer could have insisted more strongly than they did, not only on the presence but the regularity of the gradient.

uled services constitute the "in" population. Neither do these criticisms apply where only two out populations were compared. In this case in-out and out-out comparisons yield identical results.[26]

5. Discussion will be deferred of the fifth "parameter." It concerns the necessity of a choice that the researcher must make in deciding how he will conceive the relationship between the work [27] that produces an "in" and an "out" population and the clinic load at that, or past, or future steps. Quotation marks are used in referring to this consideration as a parameter of an adequately defined selection problem since, correctly speaking, it consists of a statement of the related character of the previous four parameters of "sequence," "selection operations," "initial demand population," and "composition of compared populations." Their related character is furnished by the researcher's selection of some theory which conceives the relationship between the work that produces an "in" and "out" population and the clinic load. This theoretical election will necessarily determine the sense of the findings that he assigns to the results of his statistical methods. The critical character of

[26] This may be demonstrated by considering that where two groups are compared the lattice for an in/out comparison is

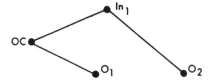

The corresponding scheme of inference is

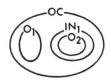

Thus $OC = (In_1 \rightarrow O_2) + O_1$. It will be seen that $In_1 = O_2$. Therefore the comparison $In_1/O_1 = O_2/O_1$. Studies to which this reasoning applies are Katkov and Meadow, 1953; Imber, Nash, and Stone, 1955; Frank, Gliedman, Imber, Nash, and Stone, 1957.

[27] The clinic load may be conceived as an assembly that is assembled by the activities of patients and staff. The term "work" is used to call attention to the point that the clinic load and whatever activities produce it are related to each other in the fashion of program and product.

**TABLE 1**  Comparison of methodological decisions on parameters of the selection problem in previous studies

| Study | Selection criteria considered | Sequence | Selection operations |
|---|---|---|---|
| Futterman, Kirkner, and Meyer (1947) | 18 attributes from VA claims folder | Army NP discharges→ In-treatment at VAMH clinic | Ad hoc comments |
| Ginsburg and Arrington (1948) | Attributes from case records. Unspecified except for those that were cited as "findings" | All patients for whom a record existed in 4 clinics→ Various numbers of visits up to five-or-more. Specific steps unspecified. | Ad hoc comments |
| Tissenbaum and Harter (1950) | Diagnosis, consultations, improvement and medical disposition. No "face sheet" attributes considered. | All admissions to treatment→out after 1 month or less→1-3 months→3-6 months 6-12 months→1-2 years→after 2 years or more | Ad hoc comments |
| Mensh and Golden (1951) | 23 attributes from cage records | Accepted for therapy→out after 1-4 5-9→10-19→20 or more therapeutic sessions | Ad hoc comments |
| Garfield and Kurz (1952) | Length of treatment, source of referral, types of cases, responsibility for termination, clinician's assessments of improvement. Information from case records | Offered treatment→out after less than 5 →5-9→10-14→15-19→20-24→25 or more interviews | Ad hoc comments |
| Katkov and Meadow (1953) | Rorschach signs | All patients with Rorschach records in test files→ceased keeping appointments without therapist's consent before 9th therapeutic session→attended first 9 therapeutic sessions | No mention |
| Auld and Eron (1953) | Rorschach signs | All patients with records in test files→out after less than 9 interviews→out after more than 9 interviews or terminated before 9 interviews with therapist's consent | No mention |
| Myers and Schaffer (1954) | Social class (Hollingshead) | (I) Accepted by intake interviewer for presentation at intake conference→out after less than one week→out after 1-9→out after 10 or more weeks. (II) Accepted→out after being seen one →2-9→10 or more times | Ad hoc comments |
| Schaffer and Myers (1954) | Social class (Hollingshead) | (I) Accepted by intake interviewer for presentation at intake conference→out after one week or less→out after 2-4→5-9→10-24 →25 weeks and over (II) Same first step as (I) →accepted for treatment →referred to other agencies →rejection (III) Eligible→ In | Ad hoc comments; Partial description; Partial description |
| Auld and Myers (1954) | Social class (Hollingshead) | Accepted by intake interviewer for presentation at intake conference→out after 7 or less→8-19→20 or more interviews | Used this data as test of the hypothesis that "in the interaction process... there are more rewards for both patient and therapist when the patient belongs to the middle class." |

| Initial demand population consisted of | Composition of compared populations | Theory relating selection activities and clinic load | | | Remarks |
| | | Populations related for purposes of inference as | Statistic | Theory that justifies choice of statistic | |
| --- | --- | --- | --- | --- | --- |
| Intakes who closed after treatment. N = 483 | Eligible/in | Independent sets | Inspection of percentages | No mention | Los Angeles VAMH clinic. Differences in populations were cited whenever the two populations were compared, i.e., 13 in 18 attributes |
| Records of "all patients seen during a 2 month period" for 3 clinics and for a 12 month period in a 4th clinic "in order to obtain a comparable sample." N = 288 | In/out | Successive populations are referred to but are not specified numerically | Inspection of percentages | "Tested" possibilities of sequential effects | Populations not numerically specified. Procedure for deciding the presence of sequential effects is too vaguely described to be replicated. Clinics in NYC but not identified |
| All veterans "the clinic had contact with for treatment purposes." Called "admissions." N = 5655 | Out/out | Independent sets | Inspection of graphs of actual counts | No mention | Study done in "a large VAMH clinic," Brooklyn, NYC. In/out procedure yields different findings |
| Total sample of male veterans seen therapeutically over 2 year period "in a VAMH Contract Clinic." Omits all prior steps of clinic contact. N = 575 | Out/out | Independent sets | $x^2$ | No mention | In/out procedure yields different findings. |
| All case records for closed cases of veterans who appeared and were interviewed by psychiatrists. N = 1216 | Out/out | Independent sets | Inspection of percentages | No mention | VAMH Clinic, Milwaukee, Wis. In/out procedure yields different findings |
| All patients with Rorschach records in test files. N = 52 | Out/out | Independent sets | Discriminant function to predict continuation | No mention | VAMH Clinic, Boston, Mass. Same as in/out because only two groups were compared. |
| All patients with Rorschach records in test files who were treated by regular staff. N = 33 | Out/out | Independent sets | $x^2$; biserial r, Festinger d, tetrachloric r | No mention | Psychiatric Outpatient Clinic, New Haven Hospital. Criticism of Katkov and Meadow prediction formula. See also Gibby, Stotsky, Hiler and Miller, Journal of Consulting Psychology, 18: 185-191, 1954. |
| Case records of all persons who appeared and were accepted by an intake interviewer for presentation at intake conference. N = 195 | Out/out | Independent sets | $x^2$ | No mention | Psychiatric Outpatient Clinic, New Haven, Conn. In/out analysis yields different findings. See footnote 25. |
| Case records of all persons who appeared for and were accepted by an intake interviewer for presentation at intake conference. N = 195 | Out/out | Independent sets | $x^2$ | No mention | Psychiatric Outpatient Clinic, New Haven, Conn. |
| | In/in | Independent sets | $x^2$ | No mention | |
| | Eligible/in | Independent sets | $x^2$ | No mention | |
| Same as Myers and Schaffer (1954) N = 65 | Out/out | Independent sets | Biserial r | No mention | Psychiatric Outpatient Clinic, New Haven, Conn. |

| Study | Selection criteria considered | Sequence | Selection operations |
|---|---|---|---|
| Winder and Hersko (1955) | Social class (Hollingshead 2 factor index) age, and sex | Received or were receiving treatment→ out after 1-9→10-19→20 or more treatment sessions | No mention |
| Myers and Auld (1955) | Manner in which treatment is terminated | In-treatment with senior staff and residents→ out after 1-9→10-19→20 or more interviews | Ad hoc comments |
| Imber, Nash and Stone (1955) | Social class | "All patients'→out after 0-4→after 5 or more interviews | No mention |
| Kurland (1956) | Team responsibility, and re-admissions | Applicants—out after work up only→ out after 1-2 $R_x$→3-5 $R_x$—up to 3 months→3-6 months→6-12 months→ 1-3 years→more than 3 years | Ad hoc comments |
| Rubenstein and Lorr (1956) | Personality inventory, modified F Scale, self-ratings, vocabulary test, "face sheet" items | Accepted for intensive treatment→5 or fewer visits→26 or more visits | Ad hoc comments |
| Frank, Gliedman, Imber, Nash, and Stone (1957) | Patient's "face sheet" and psychological features; treatment situation; relation of treatment situation to patient's life situation; treatment itself; therapist attributes | Actual appearance at clinic→out after 3 or fewer→out after 4 or more treatment sessions | Ad hoc comments |
| Kaduskin (1958) | Types of patients decisions re: origin of his problem; diagnosis, income, occupation | Appearance at clinic→not retained→ retained and dropped out→retained and remained | Manner in which problem was felt by client to originate was compared with other situational factors as prognosticators of careers. Emphasis is on relevance of these to patient as factors in his situation. |
| Katz and Solomon (1958) | Face sheet items, source of referral, diagnosis complaints, therapist's attitude toward patient, patient's interest in treatment, therapist's characteristics, use of drugs | Persons offered treatment→out after only 1→out after 2-4—out after 5 or more visits | Ad hoc comments |
| Weiss and Schaie (1958) | Face sheet items, source of referral, diagnosis, previous hospitalization, clinic personnel, duration of therapy and number of interviews | Functional sequence of completion or not of clinic services | Raised as critical question |
| Rosenthal and Frank (1958) | Face sheet items, source of referral, diagnosis, patient motivation, discharge status, length of therapy | (I) Initial visit→in treatment <br><br>(II) Offered treatment→out after 5 or fewer hours→out after 6 or more hours | Ad hoc comments |

|  |  | Theory relating selection activities and clinic load | | | |
| Initial demand population consisted of | Composition of compared populations | Populations related for purposes of inference as | Statistic | Theory that justifies choice of statistic | Remarks |
| --- | --- | --- | --- | --- | --- |
| Case records of random selection from total population of patients who had received or were receiving psychotherapy. N = 100. Population = 1250 | Out/out | Independent sets | $x^2$ | No mention | VA Mental Hygiene Outpatient clinic. In/out procedure strengthens reported findings |
| Same cases as those studied by Schaffer and Myers (1954) but with cases assigned to medical students omitted. N = 126 | Out/out | Independent sets | $x^2$ | No mention | Psychiatric Outpatient Clinic, New Haven, Conn. Used $x^2$ after combining cells to remedy small frequencies, although this altered the original purpose of the comparison |
| "All patients" between 18-55 "were included except those with organic disease, antisocial character disorder, alcoholism, overt psychosis and mental deficiency." N = 60 | Out/out | Independent sets | $x^2$ | No mention | Outpatient department, Henry Phipps Psychiatric Clinic, Johns Hopkins University Hospital. Same as in/out because only two groups were compared. |
| All patients for 9 years for whom a record was available N = 2478 | Out/out | Independent sets | $x^2$ | No mention | VA Mental Hygiene Clinic, Baltimore, Md. In/out procedure yields different findings. |
| Sample from all patients in 9 VA Mental Hygiene Clinics accepted for treatment who had either 5 or fewer visits or 26 or more. N = 128 | Out/out | Independent sets | $x^2$ | No mention | Clinics "throughout the country." Design specifically intended to handle duration without succession. |
| All white patients who appeared at clinic, and excepting those who met clinic's criteria for referral elsewhere. N = 91 | Out/out | Independent sets | $x^2$ | No mention | Outpatient dept., Henry Phipps Psychiatric Clinic, Johns Hopkins Hospital. Same as in/out because only 2 groups were compared. Attempted control for therapists; and therapists and patients "urged to remain in contact for at least 6 mos." |
| Sample of "larger population of clinic" consisting of persons awaiting intake interview, of which 1/3 were interviewed after waiting for and having intake interview. N = 110 | Three types of careers (1) Appearance — out (2) Appearance — retained — out (3) Appearance — retained — remained In/out | Idea of succession retained in comparison | Inspection of percentage | No mention | Religio-Psychiatric Clinic of American Foundation of Religion and Psychiatry, New York City |
| Charts of all patients seen in the clinic excluding those referred to other agencies after intake interview. N = 353 | Out/out | Independent sets | "Significant differences" cited but with no mention of the statistic | No mention | Outpatient Psychiatric Clinic, Yale University School of Medicine. In/out procedure yields different findings |
| Consecutive closed case files of persons scheduled for a program of clinic services. N = 603 | In/out | Independent sets | $x^2$ | No mention | Malcolm Bliss Psychiatric Clinic, St. Louis, Mo. |
| I Reporting form designed for the study and filled out by clinic persons to record assessment and treatment steps and services. N = 3413 | In/in | Independent sets | $x^2$ | No mention | Henry Phipps Psychiatric Clinic, Johns Hopkins University, School of Medicine. |
| II Reporting forms for patients offered treatment N = 384 | Out/out | Independent sets |  | No mention |  |

TABLE 1 (cont.) Comparison of methodological decisions on parameters
of the selection problem in previous studies

| Study | Selection criteria considered | Sequence | Selection operations |
|---|---|---|---|
| Hollingshead and Redlich (1959) | Social class (Hollingshead) | Eligible New Haven population→in treatment | Partial description |
| Rogers (1960) | Only drop out rates considered | Referrals→(number of interviews at time of termination handled as a continuous series from 1 to 144) | Formulated several questions |
| Storrow and Brill (unpublished 1959) | 44 items from reporting forms designed as "statistical" records administered at initial interview | First actual appearance→in treatment | Ad hoc comments |
| Brill and Storrow (unpublished 1959) | Age, sex, religion, marital status, education, area of birth, income, social class (Hollingshead) | General population of Los Angeles County →"Seeking treatment" | Ad hoc comments |

the choice is particular to studies of social selection. The necessity of this election will be discussed later in the paper when its character can be more easily demonstrated.

Table 1 summarizes the methodological decisions that previous studies made with respect to the parameters of an adequately defined problem of selection procedures.

We shall now show that a study of selection criteria that meets all the conditions of this review produces different results from those of previous studies, while raising further issues with respect to methodological adequacy.

### The data

A study was done at the Outpatient Psychiatric Clinic of the School of Medicine at the University of California, Los Angeles, using whatever data was available from the files for patients who had contacted and terminated contact with the clinic from July 1, 1955, when the clinic began its operation, until December 31, 1957. A count was made of all cases by counting all file folders, phone memoranda, and letters of inquiry. There were 3,305 cases.[28] These

[28] The 3305 cases is to be counted a "best" rather than a complete enumeration. There were 9 additional cases for which there was so little information that it was impossible to code them beyond the item that they had contacted the clinic. There was another set of cases about which there was knowledge among clinic persons that they existed but for which no record could be found. We estimated that there were 40 such cases.

| Initial demand population consisted of | Composition of compared populations | Populations related for purposes of inference as | Statistic | Theory that justifies choice of statistic | Remarks |
|---|---|---|---|---|---|
| Eligible population from U.S. Census of New Haven. In-treatment population from census of persons in treatment conducted by the investigators. N = 155. | Eligible/in | Independent sets | $x^2$ | No mention | Persons from New Haven area in treatment in "Public Clinics" in New Haven, Conn. and environing states |
| Author combined all referrals from reports provided by 5 state departments of mental health and one VA clinic. N = 904 patients from 53 separate clinics. | Out/out | Independent sets | Inspection of percentages | No mention | State Departments of Mental Health: California 1957; Iowa 1954; Kansas 1956; Texas 1956; Wisconsin 1956; VA Denver 1957 |
| All in-person applicants for whom standard reporting form for persons 18 years old and older was completed N = 433 | In/in | Independent sets | $x^2$ | No mention | Psychiatric in-patient and out-patient units, U.C.L.A. Medical Center |
| Consecutive in-person applicants from whom standard reporting form for persons 18 years old or older was completed. N = 620 | Eligible/in | Independent sets | $x^2$ | No mention | Psychiatric out-patient clinic, U.C.L.A. Medical Center |

were treated as the initial demand population. Every fifth record was selected which yielded a sample of 661 cases. The contents of these records were coded [29] with respect to the items listed in Table 4. For the information that he was able to obtain, the coder recorded whether he had obtained the information by inspection of the records, by certain inference, or by uncertain inference. The results are presented in Tables 2 to 4. All cases were used on which there was information on a given item regardless of the degree of confidence in the information that the coder had indicated. Within this condition the materials reported in this paper are based on the best [30] information that was available. Whether the cases of no information on the particular items that are reported would have given different results is difficult to say. In order to make the best of a bad situation, item distributions for which there were any cases of no information were compared with the sex composition of that item since we lacked information on sex in only one case. Unfortunately, we had our most complete information only on sex. In 21 comparisons all chi-squares were

[29] The coding was done by a project assistant, an advanced candidate for the Ph.D. degree in Sociology at U.C.L.A.

[30] By "best" information we refer to those items on patient attributes with less than 25 per cent no information, and accomplished steps in the clinic career.

TABLE 2

Frequency of no-information in each item

| | All cases | Cases with information | Cases with no information | |
|---|---|---|---|---|
| | | | Number | Per cent |
| Terminating point | 661 | 661 | 0 | 0.0 |
| Sex | 661 | 660 | 1 | 0.2 |
| Source of referral | 661 | 639 | 22 | 3.3 |
| Age | 661 | 624 | 37 | 5.6 |
| Male age groups | 284 | 272 | 12 | 4.2 |
| Female age groups | 376 | 352 | 24 | 6.4 |
| How first contact was made | 661 | 613 | 48 | 7.3 |
| Marital status | 661 | 583 | 78 | 11.8 |
| Prior psychiatric experience | 661 | 535 | 126 | 19.1 |
| Social rank of residential census tract | 661 | 519 | 142 | 21.5 |

TABLE 3

Frequency of no-information after various terminating points

| | All useable cases | After first contact | | After intake interview | | After intake conference | | After treatment | |
|---|---|---|---|---|---|---|---|---|---|
| | | Out | In | Out | In | Out | In | Out | In |
| All cases | 661 | 419 | 242 | 54 | 188 | 92 | 96 | 16 | 80 |
| Sex: | | | | | | | | | |
| Male | 284 | 187 | 97 | 19 | 78 | 33 | 45 | 4 | 41 |
| Female | 376 | 231 | 145 | 35 | 110 | 59 | 51 | 12 | 39 |
| Total | 660 | 418 | 242 | 54 | 188 | 92 | 96 | 16 | 80 |
| Source of referral | 639 | 408* | 231* | 50* | 181* | 89* | 92* | 16 | 76* |
| Male age group | 272 | 176* | 96 | 19 | 77 | 32 | 45 | 4 | 41 |
| Age | 624 | 383* | 241 | 54 | 187 | 91 | 96 | 16 | 80 |
| Female age group | 352 | 207* | 145 | 35 | 110 | 59 | 51 | 12 | 39 |
| How first contact was made | 613 | 402* | 211* | 46* | 165* | 83* | 82* | 16 | 66* |
| Marital status | 583 | 343* | 240* | 53 | 187 | 91 | 96 | 16 | 80 |
| Prior psychiatric experience | 535 | 304* | 231* | 52* | 179* | 86 | 93* | 16 | 77* |
| Social rank of residential census tract | 519 | 289* | 230* | 51* | 179* | 85 | 94* | 15 | 79 |

* marks instances where 2 or more cases lacked information.

nonsignificant.[31] Therefore we shall proceed as if cases with or without information on a given attribute were not discriminable and that the survival experience of cases with information on an attribute describes the experiences for the entire cohort.

## The conception

During some interval of time some number of persons, through phone calls, letters, and personal appearance make themselves known to the clinic personnel as potential "patients." Call any set of these persons with a common characteristic like age, sex, and the like, a cohort. The members of each cohort proceed through a number of successive steps, all of which begin, by definition, with a first contact. At each successive step they are of interest to themselves and to various clinic personnel in different ways. Personnel at the U.C.L.A. clinic referred to these successive types of interest in potential patients as "first contact," "intake interview," "psychological tests," "intake conference," "waiting list," "in-treatment," and "terminated." For the purposes of this paper we shall consider only "first contact," "intake interview," "intake conference," "in-treatment," and "termination." After some period of time all the members of a cohort have terminated. These steps can be represented with the following diagram:

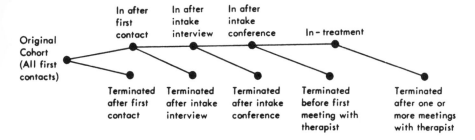

**FIGURE 1.**

[31] Two in 21 comparisons did not reach the .10 level of significance; the other 19 failed to reach the .25 level. Most of the cases of no information occurred for patients that had no further contact with the clinic after an initial inquiry.

TABLE 4

Availability of information and how it was obtained in the 661 cases

| Item of Information | There was no information | Per cent of 661 cases for which | | |
|---|---|---|---|---|
| | | Information was obtained by uncertain inference | Information was obtained by certain inference | Information was obtained by inspection |
| (A) Patient's "Face Sheet" Characteristics | | | | |
| Sex | 0.2 | - | 0.3 | 99.5 |
| Age | 5.5 | 2.9 | 0.4 | 91.2 |
| Marital status | 11.8 | 5.4 | 3.9 | 78.9 |
| Social area | 21.4 | 0.4 | 3.6 | 74.6 |
| Race | 59.5 | 0.2 | .6 | 39.7 |
| Occupation | 55.6 | 0.4 | 5.0 | 39.0 |
| Religion | 51.7 | 9.5 | 2.3 | 36.5 |
| Education | 60.7 | 1.4 | 2.6 | 35.3 |

Eliminated because of no information

Occupational history
Duration of marriage
Married first time or remarried
Ethnic background
Income
Household arrangments
Principal contributor to patient's support
Place of birth
Length of residence in California

| Item of Information | There was no information | Information was obtained by uncertain inference | Information was obtained by certain inference | Information was obtained by inspection |
|---|---|---|---|---|
| (B) First Contact | | | | |
| How contact was made | 7.2 | 0.4 | 2.3 | 90.1 |
| If patient was accompanied, by whom | - | 2.0 | 2.0 | 96.0 |
| Type of referral | 3.5 | 0.4 | 7.8 | 88.3 |
| Outside persons involved in the referral | 2.5 | 0.2 | 3.0 | 94.3 |
| Clinic person involved in first contact | 3.6 | - | - | 96.4 |
| Number of clinic persons contacted | 4.8 | - | 2.0 | 93.2 |
| Disposition after first contact | 5.0 | 0.3 | 11.9 | 82.8 |
| (C) Intake interview and psychological tests | | | | |
| Patient's appearance at intake interview | 0.4 | 0.5 | 2.1 | 97.0 |
| Clinic person involved in intake interview | 0.3 | - | - | 99.7 |
| Outcome of psychological testing | 0.2 | 0.3 | 1.5 | 98.0 |
| If no psychological tests, reason | 16.3 | 2.5 | 17.5 | 63.7 |
| (D) Intake Conference and Treatment | | | | |
| Scheduled or improvised intake conference | 44.6 | 10.9 | 34.9 | 9.6 |
| Staff member in charge of intake conference | 50.3 | - | - | 49.7 |

TABLE 4 (cont.)

Availability of information and how it was obtained in the 661 cases

| Item of Information | There was no information | Information was obtained by uncertain inference | Information was obtained by certain inference | Information was obtained by inspection |
|---|---|---|---|---|
| | | Per cent of 661 cases for which | | |
| Conference decision | 8.0 | 9.7 | 10.3 | 72.0 |
| If patient was assigned to therapist, name of therapist | 8.3 | - | - | 91.7 |
| Name of first therapist | 3.8 | - | - | 96.2 |
| If patient was on waiting list, outcome | - | .3 | 9.6 | 90.1 |
| If patient was not accepted, reason | 19.7 | 1.2 | 7.7 | 71.4 |
| If patient was not accepted, how notified | 31.5 | 2.7 | 6.8 | 59.0 |

Eliminated because of no information

Composition of intake conference
Number of prior admissions
Collateral cases
Scheduling of psychological testing
Scheduling of intake interviews
Number of appointments for intake interview
Notification of impending termination after intake interview
Psychological tests administered
Type of recommended treatment
Number of scheduled treatment sessions
Number of missed appointments
Number of interviews with spouses, parents, relatives, friends, etc.
Treatment supervisor
Planned visit regime
Actual frequency of visits
Reasons for termination after treatment

(E) Psychiatric Characteristics

| | | | | |
|---|---|---|---|---|
| Nature of patient's complaints | 7.0 | 0.2 | 1.9 | 90.9 |
| Psychiatric diagnosis | 17.2 | - | - | 82.8 |
| Prior psychiatric experience | 19.0 | 1.7 | 46.5 | 32.8 |
| Motivation for therapy | 32.0 | 11.3 | 28.3 | 28.4 |
| "Psychological mindedness" | 40.2 | 14.0 | 23.9 | 21.9 |

(F) Clinic Career

| | | | | |
|---|---|---|---|---|
| Point of termination | - | 0.9 | 6.2 | 92.9 |
| Circumstances of termination | 2.6 | 1.1 | 5.6 | 90.7 |
| Where was patient referred | 3.5 | 0.3 | 7.6 | 88.6 |
| Type of clinic career | 0.2 | 0.8 | 5.1 | 93.9 |
| Number of days in contact with clinic | 1.5 | 3.0 | 3.5 | 92.0 |
| Number of days outside of in-treatment status | 2.0 | 3.8 | 3.9 | 90.3 |
| Number of days in treatment | 8.8 | 0.4 | 0.4 | 90.4 |

Call each point a "status." Call any two joined points a "step." Call any set of two or more joined points that begin with first contact and end with termination a patient's "career." Call the connecting lines "activities of selection." Call the set of connected points a "tree."

The point of first contact is fixed by definition. After that any conceivable joining of the remaining points is possible. Figure 1 is one instance of a tree. It represents the successive selection activities, their related statuses, and the possible careers described in the U.C.L.A. Outpatient Psychiatric Clinic's Manual of Clinic Procedure. It may properly be regarded as the clinic's officially understood selection procedure. The tree that cohorts describe by their actual movements would be expected to differ from the official portrait of "proper selection procedures." For example, although the official portrait depicts the steps as the strict sequence, First-Contact-to-Intake Interview-to-Intake Conference-to-In-treatment, with termination possible after each step, the actual cohort of 661 cases described different paths. Seventy of the 661 cases followed paths in which steps were either omitted or transposed. Because all 70 cases occurred after the first contact, and because 419 of the 661 cases terminated after the first contact, the 70 "anomalous" careers represent 29 per cent of all those who could have shown departures from the careers prescribed by the Manual of Procedures. Fifty-one of the 70 anomalous careers either omitted psychological tests or reversed the sequence, Psychologicals-to-Intake Conference. By collapsing the steps of Psychologicals and Intake Conference, it was possible to treat most of the cases as if the actual careers followed a strict sequence. The distortion introduced by this method is represented by 27 per cent of the anomalous careers; 3 per cent of all cases.

For the purposes of this paper, the tree delineates the essential features of clinic-patient transactions conceived as a sequence of population transforming operations.[32] The tree represents the successive activities of selection which produce two populations from the population of persons that are in contact with the clinic at a

[32] We use the formal and empty notion of "operations" so as to avoid taking a position too early on the nature of these selection procedures, while permitting rigor in conception and definite description.

prior point: an "in" and an "out" population at the succeeding step. The tree thus permits four sets of comparisons of persons still in contact and persons terminated after each successive place at which selection activities occurred. These four successive comparison points are listed in Table 5 which also describes the successive "in" and "out" experiences of the original cohort of 661 persons.

TABLE 5

Attrition of the original cohort at successive steps in the tree

| Steps in the tree | Number In | Number Out | Cumulative per cent of original cohort In | Cumulative per cent of original cohort Out | Per cent of survivors of nth step who were "in" and "out" at the n + 1st step In | Per cent of survivors of nth step who were "in" and "out" at the n + 1st step Out |
|---|---|---|---|---|---|---|
| Original cohort | 661 | | 100.0 | | 100% | |
| After first contact | 242 | 419 | 36.6 | 63.4 | 36.6 | 63.4 |
| After intake interview | 188 | 54 | 28.4 | 71.6 | 77.7 | 22.3 |
| After intake conference | 96 | 92 | 14.5 | 85.5 | 51.1 | 48.9 |
| For the first meeting with the therapist | 80 | 16 | 12.1 | 87.9 | 83.3 | 16.7 |

Note: Arrows indicate the percentage distribution between "in" and "out" at the succeeding step of all survivors of the preceding step.

Did the age, sex, marital status, etc., cohorts differ with respect to their chances of surviving the $n^{th}$ step? The notion of the clinic as a population transforming operation will be used as a method for conceiving this question and its appropriate answers, particularly as both bear on the problem of selection criteria.

The method is this. Conceive the transactions between patients and clinic personnel, depicted in some tree, as a population transforming operation. An initial cohort, which is a demand population, is distributed between some set of categories, e.g., between male and female, among age groups, among marital statuses and the like. Call any such distribution, wherever it occurs in the tree, a population. An operation is performed upon the initial cohort which sends some fraction of it to the succeeding step and terminates the remaining fraction. Thus, the activities of the tree alter the properties of size and composition of the successive "in" populations. At the $n^{th}$ step there is an in-population and an out-population. Patient–clinic transactions after each $n^{th}$ step are unknown operators which produce from the preceding in-population a succeeding division of "ins" and "outs" at the $n$-plus-one$^{th}$ step. The process continues until all members of the initial cohort have been terminated. This process consists essentially of the progressive attrition of an initial demand population.

According to this conception, the question, "Did the age, sex, marital status, etc., cohorts differ with respect to their chances of surviving the $n^{th}$ step?" is identical with the question, "Were the successive in and out populations of each step discriminable on the particular attribute?" Whether this question, however, *which other studies as well as the present one answers,* is identical with the question, "Which criteria were used to select persons for treatment?" remains to be seen later.

An operation may be described according to either one or the other of the following rules, but not both:

*Rule 1:* Reduce the survivors of the $n^{th}$ step by some fraction while holding the ratios of persons on the characteristic invariant to the size reduction. Send on one part to the $n$-plus-one$^{th}$ step and terminate the remainder.

*Rule 2:* Reduce the survivors of the $n^{th}$ step while changing the ratios of persons on the characteristic. Send one part on to the $n$-plus-one$^{th}$ step and terminate the remainder.

If the observed successive "in" and "out" populations are *not* statistically discriminable from the expected successive populations generated by Rule 1, then we shall say that Rule 1 describes the observed "in" and "out" populations with respect to the processes for assembling them. If the observed "in" and "out" populations *are* statistically discriminable from the expected successive populations generated by Rule 1, then we shall say that Rule 2 describes the above "in" and "out" populations with respect to the processes for assembling them.

Thus, the question of whether age, sex, etc., cohorts had dif-

ferent experiences with respect to selection is answered by electing one or the other rule as the applicable one. Since there are
four [33] steps, there are four occasions on which a decision must
be made between one or the other rule as the applicable one.
Hence the four rules can be combined in various ways. Call any
possible combination of Rules 1 and 2 for the set of four successive
steps, a "selection program."

The method for deciding between the two rules at any step or
set of steps is furnished in Appendix I. Table 5 which describes the
chances of survival and termination [34] for the undifferentiated cohort at successive steps in the tree also specifies Rule 1 for producing
a set of careers in which persons are passed along the entire chain
of applicancy, candidacy, and treatment without respect for their
characteristics either at any particular step or over a succession
of them.

## Findings

*Selection Program 1:* Rule 1 describes the results of processing
the cohorts of (a) age, (b) sex, (c) social rank of census tract of

[33] Although four "out" and "in" populations are shown in Figure 1 and
Tables 5 and 6, the "out" and "in" populations after treatment were not used
in the analysis reported in this paper. Instead, all cases that were "in" after
Intake Conference were treated as all cases "out" after In-treatment. Thus
the fourth step was omitted, and the programs were concerned with three
steps. The fourth step in all programs consisted of the rule, "Terminate the
remainder." The fourth step was omitted in order to simplify the analysis.
There were comparatively few "outs" after being accepted for treatment but
before the first meeting with the therapist. Hence many cells had very small
or no entries. In order to use the computing procedure reported in Appendix I
for $X^2$ we would have had to combine cells at this step. But then to make
these findings comparable with the preceding steps would have required com-
bining them as well. Since we are not interested in this paper in the actual
chi-square values as much as in presenting a method of evaluation that is appropriate to the selection problem, a decision to combine the cells of the preceding steps so as to retain the conditions of chi-square while altering the
sense of the paper's task would have permitted the tail to wag the dog.

[34] We used observed frequencies as probabilities. We are concerned with
a study of the selection problem and are using materials from the U.C.L.A.
clinic to illustrate the argument as compared with being concerned with the
question of what the actual transition probabilities were for the U.C.L.A.
clinic. Therefore the question of whether the transition probabilities are other
than what we reported them to be is irrelevant.

residence,[35] (d) marital status, and (e) female age groups over the four steps. Populations in contact or terminated at each step were reproducible according to the following procedure: Terminate two thirds of the original applicants after the initial inquiry; terminate approximately one fifth of the survivors after the intake interview; terminate at the intake conference one-half of those that were considered; and terminate one sixth of those accepted for treatment before they appear for their first treatment with the therapist. At each reduction, disregard the fact that the persons were male or female; or are either children, adolescents, early, middle or late adults, or aged; or come from low, middle, or high socially ranked areas of the western sector of Los Angeles; or are less than sixteen and therefore ineligible for marriage, or are single, married, or separated, divorced, or widowed.

*Selection Program 2:* A second procedure is required to reproduce the "in" and "out" populations with respect to (a) the male age grades of the applicants, (b) how persons first contacted the clinic, and (c) how persons were referred to the clinic. The program for reproducing each of these groups states: selectively terminate each of these cohorts with respect to each of these three characteristics but do so only at the first contact. After the first contact, disregard these characteristics: pass or terminate the survivors in accordance with Rule 1.

The specific experience of these three cohorts was as follows:

(a) *Male age groups:* As an examination of Table 6 discloses, after first contact adolescent and late adult males were terminated in excess of expected numbers. Children and early and middle adults were terminated at about expected numbers. Aged males were terminated less frequently than expected. Three fifths of the chi-square for the entire table was contributed by these comparisons. The remaining differences were distributed throughout the process. Discriminations with respect to male age groups occurred

[35] Social rank of the patient's residential area was determined by his address. For this determination we used a table of social ranks of census areas prepared by the Laboratory in Urban Culture, Occidental College, Los Angeles, California, May, 1954, based on the 1950 census, and prepared according to the procedure described in Shevky, Eshref and Wendell Bell, *Social Area Analysis* (Stanford, Cal.: Stanford University Press, 1955) and Shevky, Eshref and Marilyn Williams, *The Social Areas of Los Angeles: Analysis and Typology* (Berkeley and Los Angeles: University of California Press, 1949).

at the first step and were concerned there with only 27 per cent of all the male age grades that contacted the clinic. Later discriminations, although they occurred, were of little predictive value either with respect to proportionate size or composition.

(b) *How first contact was made:* Selections with respect to the nature of the first contacts were heavily concentrated at first contact. Seventy per cent of persons who applied by letter or phone, or for whom someone else appeared on their behalf, terminated after the initial inquiry. Almost 98 per cent of the chi-square for the entire process was contributed by the difference between persons at this step. After this step the populations of survivors and terminators were indistinguishable.

(c) *Source of referral:* Persons who were either self-referred or were referred by lay-persons were not distinguishable in their drop out rate at first contact, and both of these groups dropped out in larger than expected numbers. In contrast, persons who were referred by professional medical or psychiatric sources dropped out much below expected numbers. This effect was overwhelmingly limited to the initial contact. Survivors of the initial contact proceeded through the remainder of their careers without the manner of referral showing up again. Most of the differences between these groups occurred at this step: 85 per cent of the table chi-square was contributed here.

*Selection Program 3:* A third program is required to reproduce the "in" and "out" populations that correspond to the type of prior experience with psychiatric remedies. Type of prior psychiatric experience was associated with survival chances at the initial contact and again at the intake conference. The survival chances at first contact of persons who had a history of contact with a public mental institution were poorer than expected. Survival chances were somewhat better than expected for those with prior experience with public psychiatric clinics. This pattern was repeated after the intake conference. Rule 1 reproduces the ins and outs at intake conference and in-treatment.

## The problem of selection

The three programs that were described answer the question: "Were the successive in and out populations discriminable on the particular attributes?" Is this question identical with the question that a study of patient selection actually seeks an answer to, namely: "What criteria were used to select persons for treatment?" Does the fact that the in and out populations for the age cohort are programmable according to Rule 1 mean that the work of selection by clinic personnel is described by Rule 1? Rule 1 states that the initial demand population after first contact be proportionately reduced in size by two thirds so as to reproduce the initial ratios of males and females. The rule is clearly an instruction to the programmer. Does Rule 1 describe the use of the age criterion in a way that permits us to say how the criterion is actually administered in the course of the selection activities?

An unequivocal answer to these questions is not possible until the researcher decides upon a theory to conceive the relationship between the work of selection and the clinic load. That some theory is necessarily elected recalls us to the fifth "parameter"[36] of an adequately defined problem of selection.

How we answer these questions depends upon how we elect to conceive the relationships between the work of selection and the clinic load. The choice of a theory is not only unavoidable but is critical to the task of deciding what will count as a finding. This election of theory furnishes the researcher the grounds for deciding what the results of his statistical evaluations are to stand for as findings. *Statistical tests that yield identical results*[37] *will yield incompatible findings in accordance with the use of different theoretical decisions that are made with respect to the relationship of selection work to clinic load.*

Ideally, one wants a method that corresponds in its logical structure to the intended features of the events under study. One wants to assume that the actual observations and the intended observations are identical in meaning. The results of applying the method

[36] The reader's attention is called to p. 210 where the reason for using "parameter" in quotation marks is discussed.

[37] We used the term "results" to refer to the set of *mathematical* events that are possible when the procedures of a statistical test, like chi-square, for example, are treated as grammatical rules for conceiving, comparing, producing, etc., events in the mathematical domain. We use the term "findings" to refer to the set of *sociological* events that are possible when, under the assumption that the sociological and mathematical domains correspond in their logical structure, sociological events are interpreted in terms of the rules of statistical inference.

of chi-square acquire the status of a finding only and exclusively in accordance with the rules that the researcher uses in defining the correspondence between the logical structure of the events of the test and the logical structure of the events that he purports to have under observation. This much is obvious and hardly requires pointing out. How is this rule relevant to the researcher's purposes of deciding how persons were selected?

That different findings would correspond to identical statistical results can be illustrated by considering some of the above results. Chi-square was nonsignificant for the successive in and out populations for the age cohort. This result could be treated as the finding that when persons were passed on to succeeding steps, the criterion of age was disregarded. On the other hand, the identical nonsignificant chi-square could be treated as a contrasting finding *i.e.*, that the clinic personnel made their selections with respect to the age distribution of the original cohort which served them as a norm governing their selections. The age distribution of the original cohort defined for them a desirable composition of the population that selectors by their decisions sought to produce at later steps. According to this conception of the relationship between the work of selection and the clinic load, a nonsignificant chi-square is a measure of the extent to which the selection activities of clinic personnel conformed to desired practices. Thus, using the identical chi-square result, nothing could be *less* relevant than the age of the applicant in the first case; nothing could be *more* relevant than the age of the applicant in the second.

Where a significant chi-square occurred—consider, for example, sources of referral—one finding is that discrimination operated at first contact; afterwards, source of referral was disregarded. An alternative finding would be that special consideration was given to professional referrals in accordance with the attempt of the clinic to encourage professional referrals and maintain its ties with professional agencies. This obligation is discharged after the first contact. From then on a just distribution provides that persons be accepted in proportion to the frequency with which they appear in following up their interests in clinic evaluation and therapy. In the latter case, source of referral would continue throughout the successive steps to be a relevant consideration governing selection work whereby successive in and out populations were generated, whereas in the first case source of referral was irrelevant after the first contact.

These examples should suffice for the point: the choice of conception is unavoidable if the researcher is to assign a sense to a statistical result, as a finding about the work of selection and the populations that it produces.

Not only is the choice of a conception unavoidable; the choice is a critical one as well because *an identical statistical result will correspond in every different theoretical case to a different specific finding.* This variation depends entirely upon the theory of the selection procedures themselves that the researcher elects to use. Indeed, without the researcher's choice of a theory, he can neither decide which test to employ nor can he decide the appropriate operations for conducting them. If tests are done nevertheless, the results will stand on behalf of the findings in the identical logical fashion that the fur of the bear stands for the bear, or stands for any other object that the researcher, by any slight exercise of clinical wit, is able to conceive or is able through plausible reasoning to justify. In a word then, identical statistical results will yield different findings about selection criteria.

Obviously, we are interested in deciding *findings* about selection criteria. If, in a comparative way, we review several choices that are available with respect to this "parameter," further considerations of adequacy can be demonstrated.

One choice is to conceive the relationship between selection work and clinic load as a linear causal sequence with successive populations conceived as a series of independent events. Call this a *chi-square model.* Another choice is to conceive the relationship as a linear causal sequence but to treat this sequence as a finite Markov process with fixed transition probabilities. Call this a *Markov model.* In both cases, the probable distribution of characteristics in a later population is governed only by (a) the characteristics of the population at the preceding step and (b) by an operation upon that population that sends one part of it "in" and sends the remainder "out" at the succeeding step. A third conception relates selection work and clinic load as a process whereby selectors' selections are governed in their occurrence by the desired or perhaps justifiable composition that the selection process is expected by selectors to produce at some later step. Call this theory a *"steering"* model.

A theorist who used a *chi-square model* in conjunction with the chi-square method to decide a finding would be committed to report the following findings under the occurrence of a nonsignificant chi-square with respect to the sex cohort. The nonsignificant chi-square describes the two populations as the outcome of the total set of selection decisions, each decision having occurred independently of the others, in which sex was an irrelevant consideration in the decision. The condition of independence furnishes the additional features that the selections were made by selectors who treated also as irrelevant the composition of the entire population, the occasion of the selection, and the anticipated disposition of those that would remain "in" at later steps.

If the theorist used a *Markov model* the nonsignificant chi-square describes a later two in and out populations as the outcome of the total set of selection decisions in which persons were sent in or out without respect to their sex. But there is added to the results that the selections were made by selectors who took the size and proportionate composition of the population at the immediate prior step into account, but only at the prior step, and who counted the occasion of the selection as relevant but only in its sense as the occasion that followed the preceding step. For the rest, they disregarded the anticipated final disposition but administered instead a fixed percentage rule for selecting ins and outs that was appropriate to the proportionate numbers that had to occur as ins and outs at the succeeding step.[38]

If the *"steering"* model is used, a nonsignificant chi-square describes the two populations as the outcomes of individual selection decisions, each having been made with respect to both available and accumulating products, with the accumulating product being governed by what the final outcome for that set would have become as well as by the terminal goal of the entire set of remaining steps, and with the aim in the course of selections being to produce a distribution of ins and outs *that corresponds to the rule*

---

[38] Our remarks have taken only a few properties of Markov chains into account. Obviously many more things could be said about deciders and decisions as additional features of the Markov model were reviewed.

*of irrelevance* as a sanctioned mode of selection behavior. A non-significant chi-square would mean that sex was definitely taken into account by the selectors and that sex was so taken into account by them as to produce a population that conformed with a justifiable size and sex composition of a later clinic load.

By no means are these the only available models. And of course no rule exists whereby the number of available choices might be limited. How is one to make a choice?

Because the choice will direct the sense to be made of the statistical result, and because one would want the method to correspond to actual selection activities, the obvious rule is to select a conception that most closely corresponds to the actual activities whereby persons are selected in the clinic. Problems of adequacy accompany this rule.

Were we to base our choice on this rule, there were features of selection activities at U.C.L.A. that might be cited as grounds for preferring the *steering model* to the other two. For one thing, clinic personnel had definite ideas about the properties that the clinic load should show. Their ideas were concerned with the load at each step beginning with the composition of the demand population, but these ideas were most definite with respect to the in-treatment load. Further, there was the phenomenon at the U.C.L.A. clinic of the nonexistent waiting list. Persons were asked to "wait." They were told that they had been accepted for treatment and would be contacted as soon as a place was available. The pool was established to meet anticipated but indefinite contingencies. Selections were made from the "pool" to repair "deficiencies" in the loads of the residents as the residents momentarily decided lacks and surpluses. Further rough assurance of the realistic character of the *"steering"* model is obtained from the fact that clinic personnel complained to the researchers that their work was not being accurately and *justly* represented when their selections were portrayed to them as being made without respect for the legitimate size and composition of the load that they were expected to produce.

Despite its plausibility, there are several obvious shortcomings of the *"steering"* model. First, many criteria were used in selections that U.C.L.A. clinic personnel were unaware of. For example, psychiatric residents insisted upon the relevance of technical psychiatric considerations in their selections of patients, and discounted the relevance of criteria that minimized the risks of a diminution or loss of professional reputation. For another example, clinic personnel generally stressed that time was wasted on psychopathic personalities because such persons are so resistant to treatment. But clinic personnel generally failed to mention the organizational importance of being able to count upon regularly scheduled treatment sessions; psychopaths are for them "pests" in the same way that any others are "pests" whose demands complicate and obstruct established and respected routines. If the *"steering" model* is to be used, methods would have to be developed to demonstrate the occurrence of events it provides for.

A second shortcoming of the *"steering" model* consists in the control that it implies that clinic personnel exert over the composition of successive populations. Neither the *chi-square model* nor the *Markov model* requires the researcher to answer this point, though it is a most difficult one to conceive for the purposes of rigorous empirical demonstration. It is easy enough to show for the U.C.L.A. clinic that if clinic personnel do control the composition of a later population, they do so at the point of first contact and again at the intake conference. But even at these steps there is no better than a marked association between the step in the process and the division of responsibility between patient and clinic for the decision to continue or terminate. Enough of the outcome is dependent upon the patient and unknown features of patient-clinic personnel interaction to change considerably the size and composition of later in and out populations. At the other steps the selection operators are complicated in the extreme. At best, then, the *"steering" model* is merely plausible, and would remain so as long as it is not factually known let alone conceptually clear as to how the criteria work into the transactions between patients and clinic personnel.

A discussion of the adequate framing of the selection problem would not be complete without addressing Weiss and Schaie's observation that the "cross sectional" method is sufficient for the "limited but important purposes of prediction." Weiss and Schaie speak for accepted opinion when they say that although the "cross sectional" method has nothing to say about "dynamics," it still retains predictive value. What Weiss and Schaie call predictive value is identical in sense with our statement that successive in and out populations are programmable. With full acknowledgement of the care and modesty with which their statement was formulated, we think it necessary, nevertheless, to consider some qualifications of this "predictive value."

(1) That survival chances can be programmed is not a virtue owned exclusively by the "cross sectional" method. The researcher's decision to restrict a study to "cross sectional" method does not achieve an advantage over studies that addressed the task of programming survival chances while explicitly providing for the five parameters. Indeed, we have seen that the virtue of "predictive" statements based upon a "cross sectional" method may be swamped by the indeterminacy of results.

(2) A program for the U.C.L.A. clinic may happen not to describe populations at other clinics. If we restrict ourselves to the Weiss-Schaie advice, we would be unable to decide even from the reported differences whether or not different selection criteria were being used in the different clinics.

(3) A program such as that described in Tables 5, 6 and 7 holds as long as the criteria for referring persons in and out of the clinic process are not altered by such factors as administrative rulings, size and composition of clinic personnel, the clinic's relationships with outside groups—in a word, the features of patient-clinic transactions as a socially organized system of activities.

(4) But even this formulation assumes that predictive criteria are identical with selection criteria. This identity, however, is in no sense a necessary one. To use the identity nevertheless, may preclude the research that is required to clarify the relationship between the two. Consider, for example, that a predictive criterion may always be partitioned among the selection decisions of selectors. The identical predictive criterion can be assembled by many different sets of decisions, the grounds of which showed a variability that the unified character of the predictive criterion masked. The remedy is not as Weiss and Schaie suggest that attention be addressed to predicting the outcome for individual cases. Instead, the remedy is to show the correspondence between the criteria operating in individual decisions and the predictive criteria by depicting the predictive criteria as an assembly of the decisions made in individual cases. This criticism is identical with the

**TABLE 6**

Attrition of original cohort at successive steps in the tree by selected cohort attributes

| Attributes | Original cohort 100% | Per cent of original cohort remaining after | | | | Per cent of survivors of the nth step remaining after the n + 1st step | | | |
|---|---|---|---|---|---|---|---|---|---|
| | | First Contact | Intake Interview | Intake Conference | Treatment | First Contact | Intake Interview | Intake Conference | Treatment |
| **Sex** | | | | | | | | | |
| Male | 284 | 34.2 | 27.5 | 15.9 | 14.5 | 34.2 | 80.4 | 57.7 | 91.1 |
| Female | 376 | 38.6 | 29.3 | 13.6 | 10.4 | 38.6 | 75.9 | 46.4 | 76.5 |
| Total | 660 | 36.7 | | | | 36.7 | 77.7 | 51.1 | 83.3 |
| **Age** | | | | | | | | | |
| 0-15 | 108 | 40.7 | 33.3 | 15.7 | 13.9 | 40.7 | 81.8 | 47.2 | 88.2 |
| 16-20 | 60 | 23.3 | 18.3 | 11.7 | 10.0 | 23.3 | 78.6 | 63.6 | 85.7 |
| 21-40 | 311 | 38.6 | 31.2 | 17.7 | 14.5 | 38.6 | 80.8 | 56.7 | 81.8 |
| 41-50 | 80 | 43.7 | 30.0 | 11.3 | 10.0 | 43.7 | 68.6 | 37.5 | 88.9 |
| 51 or more | 65 | 43.1 | 26.2 | 12.3 | 9.2 | 43.1 | 60.7 | 47.1 | 75.0 |
| Total | 624 | 38.6 | | | | 38.6 | 77.6 | 51.3 | 83.3 |
| **Social rank of residential census tract** | | | | | | | | | |
| Less than 49 | 31 | 41.9 | 32.3 | 12.9 | 12.9 | 41.9 | 76.9 | 40.0 | 100.0 |
| 50-59 | 81 | 44.4 | 29.6 | 17.3 | 14.8 | 44.4 | 66.7 | 58.3 | 85.7 |
| 60-69 | 94 | 53.2 | 45.7 | 25.5 | 20.2 | 53.2 | 86.0 | 55.8 | 79.2 |
| 70-79 | 147 | 42.2 | 32.7 | 15.0 | 10.9 | 42.2 | 77.4 | 45.8 | 72.7 |
| 80-89 | 116 | 39.7 | 31.0 | 13.8 | 12.9 | 39.7 | 78.3 | 44.4 | 93.7 |
| 90-99 | 50 | 46.0 | 36.0 | 28.0 | 26.0 | 46.0 | 78.3 | 77.8 | 92.9 |
| Total | 519 | 44.3 | | | | 44.3 | 77.8 | 52.5 | 84.0 |
| **Marital Status** | | | | | | | | | |
| Ineligible (16 years old or less) | 117 | 36.8 | 29.9 | 14.5 | 12.0 | 36.8 | 81.4 | 48.6 | 82.4 |
| Single | 134 | 35.1 | 26.1 | 12.7 | 11.9 | 35.1 | 74.5 | 48.6 | 94.1 |
| Married | 263 | 41.8 | 32.3 | 18.6 | 15.2 | 41.8 | 77.2 | 57.6 | 81.6 |
| Separated | 23 | 56.5 | 52.2 | 26.1 | 21.7 | 56.5 | 92.3 | 50.0 | 83.3 |
| Divorced | 32 | 56.3 | 40.6 | 9.4 | 6.3 | 56.3 | 72.2 | 23.1 | 66.7 |
| (Separated & Divorced) | 69 | 58.0 | 46.4 | 18.8 | 14.5 | 58.0 | 80.0 | 40.6 | 76.9 |
| Widowed | 14 | 64.3 | 50.0 | 28.6 | 21.4 | 64.3 | 77.8 | 57.2 | 75.0 |
| Total | 583 | 41.2 | | | | 41.2 | 77.9 | 51.5 | 83.3 |
| **Male age groups** | | | | | | | | | |
| 0-15 | 71 | 43.7 | 35.2 | 16.9 | 15.5 | 43.7 | 80.6 | 48.0 | 91.7 |
| 16-20 | 33 | 12.1 | 12.1 | 12.1 | 12.1 | 12.1 | 100.0 | 100.0 | 100.0 |
| 21-40 | 126 | 36.5 | 28.6 | 19.8 | 18.3 | 36.5 | 78.3 | 69.4 | 92.0 |
| 41-50 | 17 | 11.8 | 11.7 | 0.0 | 0.0 | 11.8 | 100.0 | 0.0 | 0.0 |
| 51 or more | 25 | 52.0 | 40.0 | 16.0 | 12.0 | 52.0 | 76.9 | 40.0 | 75.0 |
| Total | 272 | 156.1 | | | | 156.1 | 435.8 | 257.4 | 358.7 |

## TABLE 6 (cont.)

Attrition of original cohort at successive steps in the tree by selected cohort attributes

| Attributes | Original cohort 100% | Per cent of original cohort remaining after | | | | Per cent of survivors of the nth step remaining after the n+1st step | | | |
|---|---|---|---|---|---|---|---|---|---|
| | | First Contact | Intake Interview | Intake Conference | Treatment | First Contact | Intake Interview | Intake Conference | Treatment |
| **Female age groups** | | | | | | | | | |
| 0-15 | 36 | 36.1 | 30.6 | 13.9 | 11.1 | 36.1 | 84.6 | 45.5 | 80.0 |
| 16-20 | 27 | 37.0 | 25.9 | 11.1 | 7.4 | 37.0 | 70.0 | 42.9 | 66.7 |
| 21-40 | 185 | 40.0 | 34.1 | 16.3 | 11.9 | 40.0 | 85.1 | 47.6 | 73.3 |
| 41-50 | 64 | 51.6 | 34.4 | 14.1 | 12.5 | 51.6 | 66.7 | 40.9 | 88.9 |
| 51 or more | 40 | 37.5 | 17.5 | 10.0 | 7.5 | 37.5 | 46.7 | 57.1 | 75.0 |
| Total | 352 | 41.1 | | | | 41.1 | 75.9 | 46.4 | 76.5 |
| **How first contact was made** | | | | | | | | | |
| Letter | 22 | 22.7 | 22.7 | 13.6 | 13.6 | 22.7 | 100.0 | 60.0 | 100.0 |
| Phone | 412 | 28.4 | 22.3 | 10.9 | 9.2 | 28.4 | 78.6 | 48.9 | 84.4 |
| (Letter + Phone) | 457 | 28.2 | 22.5 | 11.2 | 9.4 | 28.2 | 79.8 | 49.5 | 84.3 |
| In person, referring person alone | 23 | 30.4 | 26.1 | 13.0 | 8.7 | 30.4 | 85.7 | 50.0 | 66.7 |
| In person, alone | 101 | 50.5 | 41.6 | 20.8 | 13.9 | 50.5 | 82.3 | 50.0 | 66.7 |
| In person, accompanied | 55 | 56.4 | 36.4 | 18.2 | 16.4 | 56.4 | 64.5 | 50.0 | 90.0 |
| (In person, alone + accompanied) | 156 | 52.6 | 39.7 | 19.9 | 14.7 | 52.6 | 75.6 | 50.0 | 74.2 |
| Total | 613 | 34.4 | | | | 34.4 | 78.2 | 49.7 | 80.5 |
| **Source of referral** | | | | | | | | | |
| Lay referral other than self | 210 | 20.5 | 15.2 | 6.2 | 5.2 | 20.5 | 74.4 | 40.6 | 84.6 |
| Self referral | 140 | 29.3 | 25.0 | 15.7 | 10.7 | 29.3 | 85.4 | 62.9 | 68.2 |
| Professional medical and psychiatric | 289 | 50.9 | 39.4 | 19.7 | 17.3 | 50.9 | 77.5 | 50.0 | 97.1 |
| Total | 639 | 36.1 | | | | 36.1 | 78.3 | 50.8 | 82.6 |
| **Prior experience with psychiatric remedies** | | | | | | | | | |
| Public hospital | 33 | 18.2 | 12.1 | 3.0 | 3.0 | 18.2 | 66.7 | 25.0 | 100.0 |
| Mixed private and public resources | 37 | 32.4 | 27.0 | 10.8 | 8.1 | 32.4 | 83.3 | 40.0 | 75.0 |
| Private psychiatrist and private hospital | 128 | 43.0 | 34.4 | 17.2 | 14.8 | 43.0 | 80.0 | 50.0 | 86.4 |
| None | 290 | 45.9 | 34.1 | 16.6 | 14.1 | 45.9 | 74.4 | 48.5 | 85.4 |
| Public clinic | 47 | 53.2 | 46.8 | 38.3 | 27.7 | 53.2 | 88.0 | 81.8 | 72.2 |
| Total | 535 | 43.2 | | | | 43.2 | 77.4 | 51.9 | 83.8 |

TABLE 7

Chi square results for comparisons of "in" and "out" populations after first contact, intake interview, and intake conference by attributes (See Appendices I and II)

| Attribute | Table | | After First Contact | | Subtables After Intake Interview | | After Intake Conference | | Selection Program |
|---|---|---|---|---|---|---|---|---|---|
| | $X^2$ | p | $X^2$ | p | $X^2$ | p | $X^2$ | p | |
| Sex | 4.355 (3df) | >0.20 | 1.354 (1df) | >0.10 | 0.680 (1df) | >0.30 | 2.321 (1df) | >0.20 | 1,1,1 |
| Age | 20.046 (12df) | >0.05 | 7.553 (4df) | >0.10 | 9.116 (4df) | >0.05 | 3.378 (4df) | >0.50 | 1,1,1 |
| Social rank of residential census tract | 16.956 (15df) | >0.30 | 4.425 (5df) | >0.30 | 4.947 (5df) | >0.30 | 7.584 (5df) | >0.10 | 1,1,1 |
| Marital status | 15.466 (9df) | >0.05 | 11.087 (3df) | >0.01 | 0.716 (3df) | >0.80 | 3.664 (3df) | >0.30 | 1,1,1 |
| Female age groups | 16.583 (12df) | >0.10 | 3.750 (4df) | >0.30 | 12.284 (4df) | >0.01 | 0.548 (4df) | >0.95 | 1,1,1 |
| Male age groups | 25.517 (12df) | >0.01 | 17.193 (4df) | >0.001 | 0.751 (4df) | >0.90 | 7.573 (4df) | >0.10 | 2,1,1 |
| How first contact was made | 31.179 (3df) | <0.001 | 30.515 (1df) | <0.001 | 0.660 (1df) | >0.30 | 0.005 (1df) | >0.90 | 2,1,1 |
| Source of referral | 56.133 (6df) | <0.001 | 52.320 (2df) | <0.001 | 1.264 (2df) | >0.50 | 2.549 (2df) | >0.20 | 2,1,1 |
| Prior psychiatric experience | 28.607 (12df) | >0.001 | 12.920 (4df) | >0.01 | 3.250 (4df) | >0.50 | 12.437 (4df) | >0.01 | 2,1,2 |

criticism that Robinson made of the use of ecological correlations.[39]

(5) Where researchers use prepared schedules in order to obtain programming information, and most particularly where these schedules are administered by having clinic personnel fill them out to report to the researchers upon their own behavior, the schedules necessarily acquire thereby the important sense of rules governing the clinic reporters' reporting conduct. Both the reliability of their descriptions as well as the validity of the events they are asked to describe thereby become inseparable from the organized daily routines of the clinic's operation that these same persons manage and enforce upon each other. Thus the statements of presumed predictive value remain circumstantial. Their value as predictions depends on precisely the same conditions that are conditional of survival chances and the ways these chances are produced. Such conditions in fact must be presupposed by the researcher if "value" is to be assigned to these predictive statements. Thus, a critical phenomenon which must necessarily be taken into account, along with the experiences with criteria in deciding the question of predictive value, consists in the fact that the criteria are understandable only with respect to a socially controlled process for assembling "in" and "out" populations. The question, therefore, is not whether populations can be programmed, but whether the programming rules are invariant to the particular occasion in which they are being studied.

The search for "predictive criteria" which proceeds without reference to the socially controlled processes for assembling the various populations could easily result in a long catalog of criteria. If reference to the socially controlled processes is omitted, the impression may thereby be obtained that clinic personnel work with the same catalog, and that the circumstances of selection consisted of a morass of minutiae of patients' and clinic personnels' actual circumstances. But when one examines previous studies the interpretive intent clearly is nothing of the sort. Instead one finds an emphasis upon the socially structured use of criteria, *i.e.*, of criteria operating within the constraints of the corporately organized character of the clinic's transactions. Selection criteria are

---

[39] W. S. Robinson, "Ecological Correlations and the Behavior of Individuals," *American Sociological Review*, 15 (June, 1950), 351-357.

thought of by previous authors with the use of a social system as a tacit scheme of interpretation. Thus, the literal use of the Weiss-Schaie advice faces researchers with the dolorous prospect of expanded catalogs of "factors," each assigned its "predictive value," none of which come to grips with the problem of selection criteria.

There remains a final consideration. All previous selection studies, including the one reported in this paper, depend for the sensible character of the question of selection procedures as well as for the sense of their results, upon the assumption that "in" and "out" are *essentially* discrete events. Rosenthal and Frank mention cases that departed from this assumption in their study, but treat such cases as methodological nuisances. We think such cases are more than this.

Consider again that selection criteria can not be described independently of the transactions in which they are used. In our own research we found that "in" and "out" were discrete events only as long as these states were defined by clinic persons with respect to their *administrative* responsibilities in the case. Where, on the other hand, "in" and "out" had to be decided by clinic persons with respect to *medical* responsibilities, the states of "in" and "out" acquired as *essential* features that as of any time a decision had to be made, *that what the case would have turned out to be remained to be seen.* Persons who were medically responsible for the case insisted upon this. As a result the clinic, each month, reported to the State Department of Mental Hygiene an inflated number of persons "in treatment." These included persons for whom active continuing responsibility was assumed, plus an additional and at times very large number of "inactive" cases [40] which were retained in "in-treatment" status because, from the standpoint of clinic persons, to regard them otherwise involved a breach of sanctioned medical practices. Therapists and others were un-

---

[40] A discrepancy of dramatic magnitude between active and "inactive" cases that the U.C.L.A. Clinic reported as "in treatment" occurred at the end of a recent residency training period when 60 persons were transferred from one residency period to the next, whereas an actual count of the in-treatment files showed that 230 cases were being reported to the state. The discrepancy assumed such proportions because with the forthcoming end of the residency period the reporting policy was followed of "evening out" the accumulated cases that had been terminated but not closed over several monthly reports.

willing or unable to recommend administrative closing in these cases because it would breach their medical responsibilities in the case to do so. In order to describe these cases a knowledge was required of the history of the case as well as an assessment of future, possible, but unknown developments, on the part of patients and clinic personnel alike. Clinic personnel were unable to disengage the historical-prospective features from the case in describing its status *for the study.*

When we examined cases at the steps prior to treatment, the identical phenomenon appeared, but with even greater stress upon this peculiar temporal character of the case. We were able to count cases "in" or "out" by disregarding the role of medical responsibility in the case, which is to say by referring the criteria to other clinic transactions than those which were obviously the relevant ones to the study of the processes of selection. When we insisted with clinic personnel that they nevertheless count each case "in" or "out" it was done at the cost of disregarding their complaints. These "decision makers" complained that we were not describing adequately *their* interests in cases and *their* ways of handling clinic affairs.

By treating "ins" and "outs" as essentially discrete events, the researcher may thereby be imposing a characteristic upon the data that is entirely an artifact of his method for describing clinic experiences. Such characteristics may not accord at all with the features of selection procedures. To treat such cases as methodological nuisances may in fact preclude the development of the theory and methods that are necessary for the adequate study of these affairs.

### Con:luding remarks

Although we have been concerned with psychiatric outpatient clinics, the parameters of the selection problem, and the arguments, criticisms, and methods based upon them are general ones, in no way confined by the fact that psychiatric materials were considered. Obvious further applications are to studies of educational and occupational mobility, migration, natural histories, prediction studies of marital adjustment and delinquency, and the like.

The identical arguments of the paper hold wherever the attrition of an original population is attributed by the researcher to the processes of social selection. More generally, the arguments are relevant to studies of the production of careers through the work of social selection, where this involves the progressive attrition of an original cohort of persons, activities, relationships, or indeed any events of social structure whatever, and which are conceived according to the view of the successively accomplished paths of activities whereby social structures are assembled.

## APPENDIX I

### A method for using chi-square to evaluate data involving conditional frequencies

We are indebted to Professor Wilfred J. Dixon, University of California, Los Angeles who devised for us the following method which was used to decide between Rule 1 and Rule 2 at the successive steps in assembling the Selection Programs that are reported in the text. The method is reported here because it permits chi-square to be used to evaluate data in the type of attrition problem represented in this study where the presence of conditional frequencies would otherwise make the use of chi-square incorrect. The method is reported here with Professor Dixon's permission.

### The problem

We were required to compare the "in" and "out" populations at each successive step while using all "ins" and all "outs" at each particular step as column marginals, and all "ins" at the preceding step as the row marginals. However, only the successive out-populations met the conditions for the use of chi-square to evaluate the entire table as well as the subtables. For the successive in-populations, the probability of their appearing at any step was conditional upon their having survived the preceding step. Hence the conditions for the correct use of chi-square could not be satisfied, *i.e.*, that each occurrence be counted only once, and that the compared events occur independently.

Table A is an example of a table that we wanted to evaluate:

TABLE A

OBSERVED NUMBER OF MALES AND FEMALES REMAINING AND TERMINATED
AFTER EACH STEP

|  | Original cohort | First contact | | Intake interview | | Intake conference | | Treatment | |
|---|---|---|---|---|---|---|---|---|---|
|  |  | Out | In | Out | In | Out | In | Out | In |
| Male | 284 | 187 | 97 | 19 | 78 | 33 | 45 | 4 | 41 |
| Female | 376 | 231 | 145 | 35 | 110 | 59 | 51 | 12 | 39 |
| Total | 660 | 418 | 242 | 54 | 188 | 92 | 96 | 16 | 80 |

## The method

Table A was reconstructed as Table B:

TABLE B

OBSERVED NUMBER OF MALES AND FEMALES TERMINATED AFTER EACH STEP

|  | Terminated | | | | |
|---|---|---|---|---|---|
|  | After first contact | After intake interview | After intake conference | Before or after starting treatment | Original cohort |
| Male | 187 | 19 | 33 | 45 | 284 |
| Female | 231 | 35 | 59 | 51 | 376 |
| Total | 418 | 54 | 92 | 96 | 660 |

$X^2_{\text{Table}}$ has 3 degrees of freedom.

Because the in-population at any step consists of the sum of the out-populations at all the succeeding steps, a comparison of the "ins" and "outs" at each step consisted of the appropriate partition of $X^2$ for the table. Figure 2 shows the exact partitions that were required for $2 \times 4$ tables:

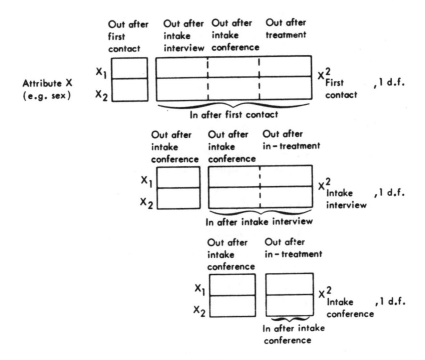

**FIGURE 2.**

Figure 3 shows the exact partitions that were required for tables with more than two rows.

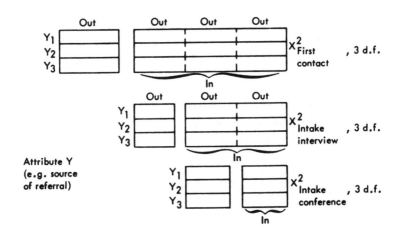

**FIGURE 3.**

## APPENDIX II

### Deciding between rule 1 and rule 2

If chi-square for the table was nonsignificant, Rule 1 was said to describe the observed in and out populations at all steps. Only if the table chi-square was significant were partial chi-squares used to decide between Rules 1 and 2. If chi-square for the table was significant, and if a subtable chi-square was significant, Rule 2 was said to describe the observed in and out populations for that step. If chi-square for the subtable was nonsignificant, Rule 1 was said to describe the two populations at that step.

The procedure for deciding between Rule 1 and Rule 2 is summarized in the following table:

| If the table chi-square was | When the partitioned chi-square was | |
|---|---|---|
| | Significant, the rule assigned to the step was | Nonsignificant, the rule assigned to the step was |
| Significant | Rule 2 | Rule 1 |
| Nonsignificant | Rule 1 | Rule 1 |

A Selection Program was assembled according to the results of the partitioned chi-squares. In the event of a significant chi-square, three decisions were required to assemble the program: one decision for each partition of the table chi-square. For the cases of a nonsignificant table chi-square, one decision defined the Selection Program to consist of the successive application of Rule 1 at each of the three steps.

Table 7 presents the overall and partitioned chi-squares for all attributes considered in this study.

To obtain the chi-squares for subtables, Mosteller's [41] explication

---

[41] From dittoed classroom materials prepared by Professor Charles F. Mosteller, Department of Statistics, Harvard University for Social Relations, 199, Spring, 1959, No. 6, Part II, pp. 4-6.

of Kimball's [42] method for partitioning an $m \times n$ table into an exact set of $2 \times 2$ tables was used. The single degrees of freedom were pooled to obtain chi-squares for subtables with 2 or more degrees of freedom. We were advised by Professor Mosteller [43] that with respect to this procedure no proof exists that the results of pooled chi-squares with single degrees of freedom would be identical with the results of the exact partitioning of a table into subtables with more than one degree of freedom. Therefore the correctness of the decision to pool the single degree of freedom rests on practical grounds.

## ANALYZED STUDIES

Auld, Jr., Frank, and Leonard D. Eron, "The Use of Rorschach Scores to Predict Whether Patients Will Continue Psychotherapy," *Journal of Consulting Psychology,* 17 (1953), 104-109.

Auld, Jr., Frank, and Jerome K. Myers, "Contributions to a Theory for Selecting Psychotherapy Patients," *Journal of Clinical Psychology,* 10 (1954), 56-60.

Brill, Norman Q., and Hugh Storrow, "Social Characteristics of Applicants for Psychiatric Care." Paper presented at the meetings of the Western Division of the American Psychiatric Association, Seattle, September, 1959.

Frank, Jerome D., Lester H. Gliedman, Stanley Imber, Earl H. Nash, Jr., and Anthony R. Stone, "Why Patients Leave Psychotherapy," *A.M.A. Archives of Neurology and Psychiatry,* 77 (1957), 283-299.

Futterman, S., F. J. Kirkner, and M. M. Meyer, "First Year Analysis of Veterans Treated in a Mental Hygiene Clinic of the Veteran's Administration," *American Journal of Psychiatry,* 104 (1947), 298-305.

Garfield, Sol L., and Max Kurz, "Evaluation of Treatment and Related Procedures in 1216 Cases Referred to a Mental Hygiene Clinic," *Psychiatric Quarterly,* 26 (1952), 414-424.

[42] A. W. Kimball, "Short-cut Formulas for the exact partition of $X^2$ in Contingency Table s," *Biometrics,* 10 (December, 1954), 452-458.

[43] Personal communication.

Ginsburg, Sol W., and Winifred Arrington, "Aspects of Psychiatric Clinic Practice," *American Journal of Orthopsychiatry*, **18** (April, 1948), 322-333.

Hollingshead, August B., and Frederick C. Redlich, *Social Class and Mental Illness*. New York: John Wiley & Sons, Inc., 1958.

Imber, Stanley D., Earl H. Nash, and Anthony R. Stone, "Social Class and Duration of Psychotherapy," *Journal of Clinical Psychology*, **11** (1955), 281-284.

Kadushin, C., "Decisions to Undertake Psychotherapy," *Administrative Science Quarterly*, **31** (1958), 379-411.

Katkov, B., and A. Meadow, "Rorschach Criteria for Predicting Continuation in Individual Psychotherapy," *Journal of Consulting Psychology*, **17** (1953), 16-20.

Katz, Jay, and Rebecca A. Solomon, "The Patient and His Experience in an Outpatient Clinic," *A.M.A. Archives of Neurology and Psychiatry*, **80** (1958), 86-92.

Kurland, Shabse, "Length of Treatment in a Mental Hygiene Clinic," *Psychiatric Quarterly Supplement*, **30** (1956), 83-90.

Mensh, Ivan N., and Janet M. Golden, "Factors in Psychotherapeutic Success," *Journal of the Missouri Medical Association*, **48** (1951), 180-184.

Myers, Jerome K., and Leslie Schaffer, "Social Stratification and Psychiatric Practice: A Study of an Outpatient Clinic," *American Sociological Review*, **19** (1954), 307-310.

Myers, Jerome K., and Frank Auld, Jr., "Some Variables Related to Outcome of Psychotherapy," *Journal of Clinical Psychology*, **11** (1955), 51-54.

Rogers, Lawrence S., "Drop Out Rates and Results of Psychotherapy in Government Aided Mental Hygiene Clinics," *Journal of Clinical Psychology*, **16** (1960), 89-92.

Rosenthal, David, and Jerome D. Frank, "The Fate of Psychiatric Outpatients Assigned to Psychotherapy," *The Journal of Nervous and Mental Diseases*, **127** (1958), 330-343.

Rubenstein, Eli A., and Maurice Lorr, "A Comparison of Terminators and Remainders in Outpatient Psychotherapy," *Journal of Clinical Psychology*, **12** (1956), 345-349.

Schaffer, Leslie, and Jerome K. Myers, "Psychotherapy and Social Stratification: An Empirical Study of Practices in a Psychiatric Outpatient Clinic," *Psychiatry*, **17** (1954), 83-93.

Storrow, Hugh A., and Norman Q. Brill, "A Study of Psychotherapeutic Outcome: Some Characteristics of Successfully and Unsuccessfully Treated Patients." Paper presented at the meetings of the California Medical Association, San Francisco, February, 1959.

Tissenbaum, M. J., and H. M. Harter, "Survey of a Mental Hygiene Clinic—21 Months of Operation," *Psychiatric Quarterly*, 24 (1950), 677-705.

Weiss, James M. A., and K. Warner Schaie, "Factors in Patients' Failure to Return to Clinic," *Diseases of the Nervous System,* 19 (1958), 429-430.

Winder, Alvin E., and Marvin Hersko, "The Effect of Social Class on the Length and Type of Psychotherapy in a Veteran's Administration Mental Hygiene Clinic," *Journal of Clinical Psychology*, 11 (1955), 77-79.

# EIGHT

# The rational properties of scientific and common sense activities

The program of his discipline requires that the sociologist scientifically describe a world that includes as problematical phenomena not only the other person's actions, but the other person's knowledge of the world. As a result, the sociologist cannot avoid *some* working decision about the various phenomena intended by the term "rationality."

Commonly, sociological researchers decide a definition of rationality by selecting one or more features from among the properties of scientific activity as it is ideally described and understood.[1] The definition is then used methodologically to aid the researcher in deciding the realistic, pathological, prejudiced, delusional, mythical, magical, ritual, and similar features of everyday conduct, thinking, and beliefs.

But because sociologists find with such overwhelming frequency that effective, persistent, and stable actions and social structures occur despite obvious discrepancies between the lay person's and the ideal scientist's knowledge and procedures, sociologists have

[1] One definition that enjoys current favor is known as the rule of empirically adequate means. A person's actions are conceived by the researcher as steps in accomplishing tasks whose possible and actual accomplishment is empirically decidable. Empirical adequacy is then defined in terms of the rules of scientific procedure and the properties of the knowledge that such procedure produces.

found the rational properties that their definitions discriminated empirically uninteresting. They have preferred instead to study the features and conditions of nonrationality in human conduct. The result is that in most of the available theories of social action and social structure rational actions are assigned residual status.

With the hope of correcting a trend, it is the purpose of this paper to remedy this residual status by reintroducing as a problem for empirical inquiry (a) the various rational properties of conduct, as well as (b) the conditions of a social system under which various rational behaviors occur.

### Rational behaviors

"Rationality" has been used to designate many different ways of behaving. A list of such behaviors can be made without necessarily exercising the theorist's choice of treating any one or more as definitive of the term "rationality." Alfred Schutz' classical paper on the problem of rationality [2] inventories these meanings and is therefore our point of departure.

When the various meanings of the term which Schutz inventoried are phrased as descriptions of conduct, the following list of behaviors results. In the remainder of the paper, these behaviors will be referred to as "the rationalities."

(1) *Categorizing and comparing.* It is commonplace for a person to search his experience for a situation with which to compare the one he addresses. Sometimes rationality refers to the *fact* that he searches the two situations with regard to their comparability, and sometimes to his *concern* for making matters comparable. To say that a person addresses the tasks of comparison is equivalent to saying that he treats a situation or a person or a problem as an instance of a type. Thereby the notion of a "degree of rationality" is encountered for the extensiveness of a person's concern with classification, the frequency of this activity, the success with which he engages in it are frequently the behaviors meant by saying that one person's activities are more rational than another's.

(2) *Tolerable error.* It is possible for a person to "require"

2 Alfred Schutz, "The Problem of Rationality in the Social World," *Economica,* Vol. 10, May, 1953.

varying degrees of "goodness of fit" between an observation and a theory in terms of which he names, measures, describes, or otherwise intends the sense of his observation as a datum. He may pay a little or a lot of attention to the degree of fit. On one occasion he will allow a literary allusion to describe what has occurred. On another occasion and for the same occurrences he may search for a mathematical model to order them. It is sometimes said, then, that one person is rational while another is not or is less so, by which is meant that one person pays closer attention than does his neighbor to the degree of fit between what he has observed and what he intends as his finding.

(3) *Search for "means."* Rationality is sometimes used to mean that a person reviews rules of procedure which in the past yielded the practical effects now desired. Sometimes it is the fact that a person seeks to transfer rules of practice which had a pay-off in situations of like character; sometimes it is the frequency of this effort; at other times the rational character of his actions refers to the person's ability or inclination to employ in a present situation techniques that worked in other situations.

(4) *Analysis of alternatives and consequences.* Frequently the term rationality is used to call attention to the fact that a person in assessing a situation anticipates the alterations which his actions will produce. Not only the fact *that* he "rehearses in imagination" the various courses of action which will have occurred, but the care, attention, time, and elaborateness of analysis paid to alternative courses of action are frequent references. With respect to the activity of "rehearsing in imagination," the competing lines of actions-that-will-have-been-completed, the clarity, extent of detail, the number of alternatives, the vividness, and the amount of information which fills out each of the schemata of competing lines of action are often the intended features in calling a person's actions "rational."

(5) *Strategy.* Prior to the actual occasion of choice a person may assign to a set of alternative courses of action the conditions under which any one of them is to be followed. Von Neumann and Morgenstern have called the set of such decisions a player's strategy.[3] The set of such decisions can be called the strategy character of

---

[3] John von Neumann and Oskar Morgenstern, *Theory of Games and Economic Behavior* (Princeton, N.J.: Princeton University Press, 1947), p. 79.

the actor's anticipations. A person whose anticipations are handled under the trust that his circumstances tomorrow will be like those he has known in the past is sometimes said to be acting with less rationality than the one who addresses alternatively possible future states of his present situation by the use of a manual of "what-to-do-in-case-of's."

(6) *Concern for timing*. When we say that a person intends through his behaviors to realize a future state of affairs, we frequently mean by such an intention that the person entertains an expectation of the scheduling of events. The concern for timing involves the extent to which he takes a position with regard to the possible ways in which events can temporally occur. A definite and restricted frame of scheduled possibilities is compared with a "lesser rationality" that consists of the person orienting the future fall of events under the aspect of "anything can happen."

(7) *Predictability*. Highly specific expectations of time scheduling can be accompanied by the person's paying concern to the predictable characteristics of a situation. He may seek preliminary information about it in order to establish some empirical constants or he may attempt to make the situation predictable by examining the logical properties of the constructs he uses in "defining" it or by reviewing the rules that govern the use of his constructs. Accordingly, making the situation predictable means taking whatever measures are possible to reduce "surprise." Both the desire for "surprise in small amounts" as well as the use of whatever measures yield it are frequently the behaviors intended by the term rationality in conduct.

(8) *Rules of procedure*. Sometimes rationality refers to rules of procedure and inference in terms of which a person decides the correctness of his judgments, inferences, perceptions, and characterizations. Such rules define the distinct ways in which a thing may be decided to be *known*—distinctions, for example, between fact, supposition, evidence, illustration, and conjecture. For our purposes two important classes of such rules of correct decisions may be distinguished: "Cartesian" rules and "tribal" rules. Cartesian rules propose that a decision is correct because the person followed the rules without respect for persons, *i.e.*, that the decider decided as "any man" would do when all matters of social affiliation were treated as specifically irrevelant. By contrast,

"tribal" rules provide that a decision is correct or not according to whether certain interpersonal solidarities are respected as conditions of the decision. The person counts his decision right or wrong in accordance with whom it is referentially important that he be in agreement.

The term rationality is frequently used to refer to the application of Cartesian rules of decision. Because conventions may impose constraints on such decision-making, the extent to which the constraints are suppressed, controlled, or rendered ineffective or irrelevant is another frequent meaning of rationality.

(9) *Choice.* Sometimes the fact that a person is aware of the actual possibility of exercising a choice and sometimes the fact that he chooses are popular meanings of rationality.

(10) *Grounds of choice.* The grounds upon which a person exercises a choice among alternatives as well as the grounds he uses to legitimize a choice are frequently pointed out as rational features of an action. Several different behavioral meanings of the term "grounds" need to be discriminated.

(a) Rational grounds sometimes refer exclusively to the scientific *corpus* [4] of information as an inventory of propositions which is treated by the person as correct grounds of further inference and action.

(b) Rational grounds sometimes refer to such properties of a person's knowledge as the "fine" or "gross" structure of the characterizations he uses, or whether the "inventory" consists of a set of stories as compared with universal empirical laws, or the extent to which the materials are codified, or whether the *corpus* in use accords with the *corpus* of scientific propositions.

(c) Insofar as the grounds of choice are the strategies of action, as was noted before in point 5, another sense of rationality is involved.

(d) Grounds of a person's choice may be those which he quite literally *finds* through retrospectively interpreting a present outcome. For example, a person may realize such grounds in the course of historicizing an outcome in the effort to determine what was "really" decided at a prior time. Thus, if a present datum

---

[4] The concept of the *corpus* of knowledge is taken from Felix Kaufmann, *Methodology of the Social Sciences* (New York: Oxford University Press, 1944), especially pp. 33-66.

is treated as an-answer-to-some-question, the datum may motivate the question that the person seeks it to be the answer to. Selecting, arranging, and unifying the historical context of an action after its occurrence so as to present a publicly acceptable or coherent account of it is a familiar meaning of "rationalization."

(11) *Compatibility of ends-means relationships with principles of formal logic.* A person may treat a contemplated course of action as an arrangement of steps in the solution of a problem. He may arrange these steps as a set of "ends-means" relationships but count the problem solved only if these relationships are accomplished without violating the ideal of full compatibility with the principles of formal scientific logic and the rules of scientific procedure.[5] The fact that he may do so, the frequency with which he does so, his persistence in treating problems in this way, or the success that he enjoys in following such procedure are alternative ways of specifying the rationality of his actions.

(12) *Semantic clarity and distinctness.* Reference is often made to a person's attempt to treat the semantic clarity of a construction as a variable with a maximum value which must be approximated as a required step in solving the problem of constructing a credible definition of a situation. A person who witholds credence until the condition of approximate maximum value has been met is frequently said to be more rational than another who will lend credence to a mystery.

A person may assign a high priority to the tasks of clarifying the constructs which make up a definition of a situation and of deciding the compatibility of such constructs with meanings intended in terminologies employed by others. On the other hand, the person may pay such tasks little concern. The former action is sometimes said to be more rational than the latter.

(13) *Clarity and distinctness "for its own sake."* Schutz points out that a concern for clarity and distinctness may be a concern for distinctness that is adequate for the person's purposes. Different possible relationships, ideal or actual, between (a) a concern for clarity and (b) the purposes which the clarity of the construct serves reveal additional behavioral meanings of rationality. Two variables are involved: (1) the respect required for the tasks of

[5] When treated as a rule for defining descriptive categories of action, this property is known as the rule of the empirical adequacy of means.

clarification and (2) the value assigned by the person to the accomplishment of a project. One relationship between these variables makes the task of clarification itself the project to be accomplished. This is the meaning of "clarification for its own sake." But the relationship between the two variables may be treated by a person as consisting in some degree of independent variability. Such a relationship would be meant when treating as an ideal, "clarification that is sufficient for present purposes." Rationality frequently means a high degree of dependence of one upon the other. Such a dependence when treated as a rule of investigative or interpretive conduct is sometimes meant in the distinction between "pure" and "applied" research and theory.

(14) *Compatibility of the definition of a situation with scientific knowledge.* A person can allow what he treats as "matters of fact" to be criticized in terms of their compatibility with the body of scientific findings. As a description of a person's actions, the "allowed legitimacy of such criticism" means that in the case of a demonstrated discrepancy that what the person treats as correct grounds of inference and action (a meaning of "fact") will be changed by him to accommodate what is scientifically the case. Frequently, a person's actions are said to be rational to the extent that he accommodates or is prepared to accommodate in this fashion to what is scientifically the case.

Frequently rationality refers to the person's feelings that accompany his conduct, *e.g.* "affective neutrality," "unemotional," "detached," "disinterested," and "impersonal." For the theoretical tasks of this paper, however, the fact that a person may attend his environment with such feelings is uninteresting. It is of interest, however, that a person uses his feelings about his environment to recommend the sensible character of the thing he is talking about or the warrant of a finding. There is nothing that prohibits a scientific investigator from being passionately hopeful that his hypothesis will be confirmed. He is prohibited, however, from using his passionate hope *or* his detachment of feeling to recommend the sense or warrant of a proposition. A person who treats his feelings about a matter as irrelevant to its sense or warrant is sometimes said to be acting rationally, while a person who recommends sense and warrant by invoking his feelings is said to act with less rationality. This holds, however, only for ideally described scientific activities.

### Scientific rationalities

The foregoing rationalities may be used to construct an image of a person as a type of behavior. A person can be conceived who may [6] search a present situation for its points of comparability to situations that he knew in the past and may search his past experience for formulas that appear in his present view to have yielded the practical effect in the past that he now seeks to bring about. In going about this task he may pay close attention to these points of comparability. He may anticipate the consequences of his acting according to the formulas that recommend themselves to him. He may "rehearse in imagination" various competing lines of action. He may assign to each alternative, by a decision made prior to the actual occasion of choice, the conditions under which any one of the alternatives is to be followed. Along with such structurings of experience as these, the person may intend through his behaviors to realize a projected outcome. This may involve his paying specific attention to the predictable characteristics of the situation that he seeks to manipulate. His actions may involve the exercise of choice between two or more means for the ~ame ends or of a choice between ends. He may decide the correctness of his choice by invoking empirical laws and so on.

In extending the features· of this behavioral type to incorporate all of the preceding rationalities, a distinction between the interests of everyday life and the interests of scientific theorizing intrudes upon this list. Where a person's actions are governed by the "attitude of daily life," all of the rationalities can occur *with four important exceptions*. Phrased as ideal maxims of conduct, these excepted rationalities state that the projected steps in the solution of a problem or the accomplishment of a task, *i.e.*, the "means-ends relationships," be constructed in such a way (1) that they remain in full compatibility with the rules that define scientifically correct decisions of grammar and procedure; (2) that all the elements be conceived in full clearness and distinctness; (3) that the clarification of both the body of knowledge as well as the rules of investiga-

---

[6] By "may" 'is meant available as one of a set of alternatives. It does not mean likelihood.

tive and interpretive procedure be treated as a first priority project; and (4) that the projected steps contain only scientifically verifiable assumptions that have to be in full compatibility with the whole of scientific knowledge. The behavioral correlates of these maxims were described before as rationalities (11) through (14). For ease of reference, I shall refer to these four as "the scientific rationalities."

It is the crux of this paper and of the research program that eventuates if its arguments are correct, that *the scientific rationalities, in fact, occur as stable properties of actions and as sanctionable ideals only in the case of actions governed by the attitude of scientific theorizing. By constrast, actions governed by the attitude of daily life are marked by the specific absence of these rationalities either as stable properties or as sanctionable ideals.* Where actions and social structures that are governed by the presuppositions of everyday life are concerned, any attempts to stabilize these features or to compel adherence through socially systematic administration of rewards and punishments are the operations required to multiply the anomic features of interaction. All of the other rationalities, (1) through (10), however, can occur in actions governed by either attitude both as stable properties and sanctionable ideals. This critical point is restated in detail in Table 1.

The preceding assertions are meant as empirical matters, not as doctrinal ones. The reconstruction of the "problem of rationality"[7] proposed by this paper depends upon the warranted character of these assertions. Their test depends upon a viable distinction between the "attitude of daily life" and the "attitude of scientific theorizing." It is necessary, therefore, that the different presuppositions that make up each attitude be briefly compared. After this is done, we shall return to the main thread of the argument.

---

[7] For the sociological theorist, the "problem of rationality" can be treated as consisting of five tasks: (1) clarifying the various referents of the team "rationality" which includes stating the behavioral correlates of the various "meanings" of rationality as (a) the individual's actions as well as (b) the "system's" characteristics; (2) deciding on the ground of the examination of experience rather than by an election of theory which of the behavioral designata go together; (3) deciding an allocation of behavioral designata between definitional and empirically problematical status; (4) deciding the grounds for justifying any of the many possible allocations that he may finally choose to make; and (5) showing the consequences of alternative sets of decisions for sociological theorizing and investigation.

TABLE I

A SUMMARY OF THE PROPOSITIONS RELATING THE RATIONALITIES
TO THE CONDITIONS OF THEIR OCCURRENCE

| | For all actions that are governed by the rules of relevance of daily life can the rationalities occur IF | | | For all actions that are governed by the rules of relevance of scientific theorizing can the rationalities occur IF | | |
|---|---|---|---|---|---|---|
| | Considered as an ideal standard of action? | Considered as an operative standard of action? | Considered as a property of actual practice? | Considered as an ideal standard of action? | Considered as an operative standard of action? | Considered as a property of actual practice? |
| 1. Categorizing and comparing | Yes | Yes | Yes | Yes | Yes | Yes |
| 2. Tolerable error | Yes | Yes | Yes | Yes | Yes | Yes |
| 3. Search for "means" | Yes | Yes | Yes | Yes | Yes | Yes |
| 4. Analysis of alternatives and consequences | Yes | Yes | Yes | Yes | Yes | Yes |
| 5. Strategy | Yes | Yes | Yes | Yes | Yes | Yes |
| 6. Concern for timing | Yes | Yes | Yes | Yes | Yes | Yes |
| 7. Predictability | Yes | Yes | Yes | Yes | Yes | Yes |
| 8. Rules of procedure | Yes | Yes | Yes | Yes | Yes | Yes |
| 9. Choice | Yes | Yes | Yes | Yes | Yes | Yes |
| 10. Grounds of choice | Yes | Yes | Yes | Yes | Yes | Yes |
| 11. Compatibility of ends-means relationships with formal logic | No | No | No | Yes | Yes | Yes |
| 12. Semantic clarity and distinctness | No | No | No | Yes | Yes | Yes |
| 13. Clarity and distinctness "for its own sake" | No | No | No | Yes | Yes | Yes |
| 14. Compatibility of the definition of a situation with scientific knowledge | No | No | No | Yes | Yes | Yes |

"Yes" is to be read, "Is empirically possible either as a stable property and/or a *sanctionable* ideal."

"No" is to be read, "Is empirically possible only as an unstable property and/or an *unsanctionable* ideal." By this is meant that attempts to stabilize the feature or to compel adherence through systematic administration of rewards and punishments, are the operations required to multiply the anomic features of the interaction.

What these propositions state for the rationalities when considered singly, they state as well for the set of them taken in any combination.

### Presuppositons of the two attitudes

The attitudes of daily life and scientific theorizing [8] were described by Alfred Schutz [9] in his studies of the constitutive phenomenology of common sense situations.[10] Because the arguments of this paper depend upon the assumption that these attitudes do not shade into each other, it is necessary that the presuppositions that comprise each be briefly compared.

(1) Schutz finds that in everyday situations the "practical theorist" achieves an ordering of events while seeking to retain and sanction the presupposition that the objects of the world are as they appear. The person coping with everyday affairs seeks an interpretation of these affairs while holding a line of "official neutrality" toward the interpretive rule that one may doubt that the objects of the world are as they appear. The actor's assumption consists in the expectation that a relationship of undoubted correspondence exists between the particular appearances of an object and the intended-object-that-appears-in-this-particular-fashion. Out of the set of possible relationships between the actual appearances of the object and the intended object, as for example, a relationship of *doubtful* correspondence between the two, the person expects that the presupposed undoubted correspondence is the sanctionable one. He expects that the other person employs the same expectancy in a more or less identical fashion, and expects that just as he expects the relationship to hold for the other person the other person expects it to hold for him.

In the activities of scientific theorizing quite a different rule of

[8] To avoid misunderstanding I want to stress that the concern here is with the attitude of scientific *theorizing*. The attitude that informs the activities of actual scientific inquiry is another matter entirely.

[9] Alfred Schutz, "The Stranger," *American Journal of Sociology*, Vol. 49, May, 1944; "The Problem of Rationality in the Social World," *Economica*, Vol. 10, May, 1943; "On Multiple Realities," *Philosophy and Phenomenological Research*, Vol. 4, June, 1945; Choosing among Projects of Action," *Philosophy and Phenomenological Research*, Vol. 12, December, 1951; "Common Sense and Scientific Interpretation of Human Action," *Philosophy and Phenomenological Research*, Vol. 14, September, 1953.

[10] In accordance with the program, attitude and method of Husserlian phenomenology he sought the presuppositions and the corresponding environmental features intended by them that were invariant to the specific contents of actions and their objects. The list is not exhaustive. Further research should reveal others. Like any product of observation they have the provisional status of "so until demonstrated to be otherwise."

interpretive procedure is used. It provides that interpretation be conducted while holding a position of "official neutrality" toward the *belief* that the objects of the world are as they appear. The activities of everyday life, of course, permit the actor's doubt that the objects are as they appear; but this doubt is in principle a doubt that is limited by the theorist's "practical considerations." Doubt for the practical theorist is limited by his respect for certain valued, more or less routine features of the social order as "seen from within," that he specifically does not and will not call into question. By contrast, the activities of scientific theorizing are governed by the strange ideal of doubt that is in principle unlimited and that specifically does not recognize the normative social structures as constraining conditions.

(2) Schutz refers to a second assumption as the person's practical interest in the events of the world. The relevant features of events that his interest in them selects, carry along for the person as their invariant feature that they can actually and potentially affect the actor's actions and can be affected by his actions. Under this presupposed feature of events, the accuracy of his orderings of events is assumed by the person to be tested and testable without suspending the relevance of what he knows as fact, supposition, conjecture, fantasy, and the like by virtue of his bodily and social positions in the real world. Events, their relationships, their causal texture, are not for him matters of theoretic interest. He does not sanction the notion that in dealing with them it is correct to address them with the interpretive rule that he knows nothing, or that he can assume that he knows nothing "just to see where it leads." In everyday situations what he knows is an integral feature of his social competence. What he knows, in the way he knows it, he assumes personifies himself as a social object to himself as well as to others as a bona fide member of the group. He sanctions his competence as a bona fide member of the group as a condition for his being assured that his grasp of meanings of his everyday affairs is a realistic grasp.

By contrast, the interpretive rules of the attitude of scientific theorizing provide that the sense and accuracy of a model is to be tested and decided while suspending judgment on the relevance of what the theorizer knows by virtue of his social and bodily positions in the real world.

(3) Schutz describes the time perspective of daily life. In his

everyday activities the person reifies the stream of experience into "time slices." He does this with the use of a scheme of temporal relationships that he assumes he and other persons employ in an equivalent and standardized fashion. The conversation that he is having consists for him not only of the events of his stream of experience but of what was, or may be said at a time that is designated by the successive positions of the hands of the clock. The "sense of the conversation" is not only progressively realized through a succession of realized meanings of its thus-far accomplished course but every "thus-far" is informed by its anticipations. Further, as of any Here-and-Now, as well as over the succession of Here-and-Nows, the conversation for him has both its retrospective and prospective significances. These include the Here and Now references to beginnings, duration, pacing, phasing, and termination. These determinations of the "inner time" of the stream of experiences are coordinated with a socially employed scheme of temporal determinations. He uses the scheme of standard time as a means of scheduling and coordinating his actions with those of others, of gearing his interests to those of others and of pacing his actions to theirs. His interest in standard time is directed to the problems such specifications solve in scheduling and coordinating interaction. He assumes too that the scheme of standard time is entirely a public enterprise, a kind of "one big clock identical for all."

There are other and contrasting ways of temporally punctuating the stream of experience so as to produce a sensible array of events in the "outer world." When the actor is engaged in the activities of scientific theorizing, standard time is used as a device for constructing one out of alternative empirically possible worlds (assuming of course that the theorizer is interested in matters of fact). Thus, what would from his interests in the mastery of practical affairs involve the actor's use of time to gear his interests to the conduct of others, is for his interests as a scientific sociological theorist a "mere" device for solving his scientific problem which consists of clearly formulating such programs of coordinated actions in the fashion of relationships of cause and effect. Another contrasting use of time occurs in appreciating the events portrayed "within the theater play." The interests in standard time are put aside as irrelevant. When he attends the social structures portrayed in a novel like *Ethan Frome*, for example, he allows the lovers' fate to come before and as a condition for appreciating the sequence of steps that led up to it.

(4) The person in managing his daily affairs assumes a commonly entertained scheme of communication in a different manner than does the scientific theorist. The man in daily life is informed as to the sense of events by using a presupposed background of the "natural facts of life" that from his point of view "Any of Us" is obligated to know and give credence to. The use of such natural facts of life is a condition of continued bona fide membership in the group. He assumes that such a background is used by himself and others in the manner of morally enforceable "coding rules." In their terms he decides the correct correspondence between the actual appearance of an object and the intended-object-that-appears-in-a-particular-way.

This assumption of a common intersubjective world of communication is startlingly modified in the actions of scientific theorizing. The "relevant other persons" for the scientific theorizer are universalized "Anymen." They are, in the ideal, disembodied manuals of proper procedures for deciding sensibility, objectivity and warrant. Specific colleagues are at best forgiveable instances of such highly abstract "competent investigators." The scientific theorizer is obligated to know only what he has decided to lend credence to. It is his mere option to trust the findings of colleagues on the grounds of membership in a professional or any other society. If he witholds credence, he is permitted to justify this by invoking as grounds his impersonal subscription to a community of "competent investigators" who are anonymous with respect to collectivity membership and whose actions conform to norms of the manual of procedures. By such actions he may risk criticism for unreasonable rigor. But such actions in daily life would risk a change in status to criminality, sickness, or incompetence.

(5) The person assumes a particular "form of sociality." Among other things the form of sociality consists of the person's assumption that some characteristic disparity exists between the "image" of himself that he attributes to the other person as that person's knowledge of him, and the knowledge that he has of himself in the "eyes" of the other person. He assumes too that alterations of this characteristic disparity remain within his autonomous control. The assumption serves as a rule whereby the everyday theorist groups his ex-

periences with regard to what goes properly with whom. There corresponds, thereby, to the common intersubjective world of communication, unpublicized knowledge which in the eyes of the actor is distributed among persons as grounds of their actions, *i.e.*, of their motives or, in the radical sense of the term, their "interests," as constituent features of the social relationships of interaction. He assumes that there are matters that one person knows that he assumes others do not know. The ignorance of one party consists in what another knows that is motivationally relevant to the first. Thereby matters that are known in common are informed in their sense by the personal reservations, the matters that are selectively withheld. Thus the events of everyday situations are informed by this integral background of "meanings held in reserve," of matters known about self and others that are none of somebody else's business; in a word, the private life.

This assumption is heavily modified in the rules that govern the actions of scientific theorizing. In the sociality of scientific *theorizing* no disparity exists between a public and private life as far as decisions of sense and warrant are concerned. All matters that are relevant to his depiction of a possible world are public and publicizable.

There are additional presuppositions but for the purposes of this paper it is enough to establish only the fact of the distinction between these "attitudes."

These two sets of presuppositions do not shade into each other, nor are they distinguishable in degree. Rather, passing from the use of one set to the use of another—from one "attitude" to another —produces a radical alteration in the person's scenic structurings of events and their relationships. In the literal mathematical sense the two attitudes produce logically incompatible sets of events. The nature of the difference between the systems of events that are constituted by the two sets of interpretive presuppositions may be illustrated by comparing the related events that a viewer witnesses on his television screen when he attends the events of "the story" with the events he witnesses when he attends the scene as a set of effects accomplished by a set of professional actors behaving in accordance with instructions from a moving picture producer. It would be the grossest philosophical didacticism to say that the viewer has seen "different aspects of the same thing," or that the events of the story are "nothing but" uncritically appreciated events of the production.

## Methodology

It is the scientific rationalities to which writers on social organization and decision making commonly refer as features of "rational choice." It is proposed here, however, that the scientific rationalities are neither properties of nor sanctionable ideals of choices exercised within the affairs governed by the presuppositions of everyday life. If the scientific rationalities are neither stable properties nor sanctionable ideals of choices exercised within the affairs governed in their sense by the presuppositions of everyday life, then the troubles encountered by researchers and theorists with respect to the concepts of organizational purposes, the role of knowledge and ignorance in interaction, the difficulties in handling meaningful messages in mathematical theories of communication, the anomalies found in studies of betting behavior, the difficulties in rationalizing the concept of abnormality in light of cross-cultural materials may be troubles of their own devising. The troubles would be due not to the complexities of the subject matter, but to the insistence on conceiving actions in accordance with scientific conceits instead of looking to the actual rationalities that persons' behaviors in fact exhibit in the course of managing their practical affairs.

Schutz tells us what it means to say that an actor has rational choice [11]:

"Rational choice would be present if the actor had sufficient knowledge of the end to be realized as well as the different means apt to succeed. But this postulate implies:

"1. Knowledge of the place of the end to be realized within the framework of the plans of the actor (which must be known by him too).

"2. Knowledge of its interrelations with other ends and its compatibility or incompatibility with them.

"3. Knowledge of the desirable and undesirable consequences which may arise as by-products of the realization of the main end.

[11] Schutz, "The Problem of Rationality in the Social World," pp. 142-143.

"4. Knowledge of the different chains of means which technically or even ontologically are suitable for the accomplishment of this end regardless of whether the actor has control of all or several of these elements.

"5. Knowledge of the interference of such means with other ends of other chains of means including all their secondary effects and incidental consequences.

"6. Knowledge of the accessibility of these means for the actor, picking out the means which are within his reach and which he can and may set going.

"The aforementioned points do not by any means exhaust the complicated analysis that would be necessary in order to break down the concept of rational choice in action. The complications increase greatly when the action in question is a social one. . . . In this case the following elements become additional determinants for the deliberation of the actor. First, the interpretation or misinterpretation of his own act by his fellow man. Second, the reaction by the other people and its motivation. Third, all the outlined elements of knowledge (1) to (6) which the actor rightly or wrongly attributes to his partners. Fourth, all the categories of familiarity and strangeness, of intimacy and anonymity, of personality and type which we have discovered in our inventory of the organization of the social world." But, then, asks Shutz, where is this system of rational choice to be found? ". . . the concept of rationality has its native place not at the level of everyday conceptions of the social world but at the theoretical level of the scientific observation of it, and it is here that it finds its field of methodological application."

Schutz concludes that it is found in the logical status, the elements, and the uses of the model which the scientist decides on and uses as a scheme for interpreting the events of conduct.

"This does not mean that rational choice does not exist within the sphere of everyday life. Indeed it would be sufficient to interpret the terms clearness and distinctness in a modified and restricted meaning, namely, as clearness and distinctness adequate to the requirements of the actor's practical interest. . . . What I wish to emphasize is that the ideal of rationality is not and cannot be a *peculiar* feature of everyday thought nor can it therefore be a methodological principle of the interpretation of human sets in daily life."

Reconstructing the problem of rationality so as to hand it back to researchers consists in the proposal that sociologists cease treating the scientific rationalities as a methodological rule for interpreting human actions.

Procedurally speaking, how would an investigator act once he has ceased to treat the scientific rationalities as a methodological rule?

### Norms of conduct

When the beforementioned rational properties of action are conceived as norms of proper conduct, four meanings of such norms can be distinguished.

First, the norms may consist of the rationalities to which scientific observers subscribe as *ideal norms* of their activities as scientists. Second, the term may refer to rationalities as operative norms of actual scientific work. Empirically, the two sets of norms do not show point for point correspondence. For example, there is a routinization of problem design and solution as well as a trust of other investigators found in actual investigative operations which textbooks in methodology generally ignore. Third, the term may refer to a socially employed and socially sanctioned ideal of rationality. Here the reference is to those rationalities as standards of thought and conduct that remain in accord with a respect for the routine orders of action of everyday life. Such standards are referred to in everyday language as "reasonable" thinking and conduct. Fourth, there are the rationalities as operative norms of actual activities of daily life.

To use the rationalities as a methodological principle for the interpretation of human actions in daily life means to proceed as follows:

(1) The ideal characteristics that scientific observers subscribe to as the ideal standards of their investigative and theorizing conduct are used to construct the model of a person who acts in a manner governed by these ideals. Von Neumann's game player, for example, is such a construction.[12]

[12] Consider his characteristics. He never overlooks a message; he extracts from a message all the information it bears; he names things properly and in proper time; he never forgets; he stores and recalls without distortion; he never acts on principle but only on the basis of an assessment of the consequences of a line of conduct for the problem of maximizing the chances of achieving the effect he seeks.

(2) After describing actual behaviors, one looks to the model, seeking through the comparison for the discrepancies between the way in which a person so constructed would have acted and the way the actual person has acted. Questions like the following are then asked: Compared with the model, how much distortion is there in recall? What is the efficiency of the means that the actual person employed when they are viewed with reference to the observer's wider knowledge, this observer's wider knowledge being typified as "The current state of scientific information"? What constraints are there upon the use of norms of technical efficiency in the attainment of ends? How much and what kind of information is needed for decisions that are predicated on the consideration of all the scientifically relevant parameters of the problem and how much of this information did the actual person have?

In a word, the model furnishes a way of stating the ways in which a person would act were he conceived to be acting as an ideal scientist. The question then follows: What accounts for the fact that actual persons do not match up, in fact rarely match up, even as scientists? In sum, the model of this rational man as a standard is used to furnish the basis of ironic comparison; and from this one gets the familiar distinctions between rational, nonrational, irrational, and arational conduct.[13]

But this model is merely one among an unlimited number that might be used. More importantly, *no necessity dictates its use.* To be sure, *a model* of rationality is necessary, but only for the task of deciding a definition of credible knowledge and then *only but unavoidably for scientific theorizing. It is not necessary and it is avoidable in theorizing activities employed in coming to terms with the affairs of everyday life.*

It is necessary for scientific theorizing but *not* because of any ontological characteristic of the events that scientists seek to conceive and describe.

It is necessary because the rules that govern the use of their propositions as correct grounds for further inference, *i.e.*, the very definition of credible knowledge, describe such sanctionable procedures as, for example, not permitting two incompatible or con-

[13] Vilfredo Pareto, *The Mind and Society,* ed. Arthur Livingston (New York: Harcourt Brace & World, Inc., 1935), especially Vol. I. Marion J. Levy, Jr., *The Structure of Society* (Princeton, N.J.: Princeton University Press, 1952).

tradictory propositions both to be used as legitimate grounds for deducing the warrant of another proposition. Since the definition of credible knowledge, scientific or otherwise, consists of the rules that govern the use of propositions as grounds of further inference and action, the necessity of the model is provided by the decision in the first place to act in conformity with these rules.[14] The model of rationality for scientific theorizing literally consists of the theorizer's ideal that the meanings of these rules can be clearly explicated.

It is a consequence of the fact that actions of inquiry and interpretation are governed by what to common sense are the outlandish rules of scientific activities that the decision to use a proposition as grounds of further inference varies independently of whether or not the user can expect to be *socially* supported for using it. But in activities governed by the presuppositions of daily life the body of credible knowledge is not subject to such rigid restrictions regarding the use of propositions as legitimate grounds for further inference and action. Within the rules of relevance of everyday life a correctly used proposition is one for whose use the user specifically expects to be socially supported and by the use of which he furnishes others evidence of his bona fide collectivity status.

### Rationalities as data

No necessity dictates that a definition of rational action be decided in order to conceive a field of observable events of conduct. This result has the important and paradoxical consequence of permitting us to study the properties of rational action more closely than ever before.[15] Instead of using the vision of the ideal scientist as a means for constructing descriptive categories of behavior—and rational, nonrational, irrational and arational are such categories— the rational characteristics of activities may be addressed with the empirical task of describing them as they are found separately in the above list of rationalities or in clusters of these characteristics. The user, then, would look to the conditions of the actor's make-up

[14] Kaufmann, *op. cit.*, pp. 48-66.

[15] It is through the absence of the "scientific rationalities" in the actions that constitute the routine social structures that rational action becomes problematical in the ways intended in Max Weber's neglected distinction between formal and substantive rationality.

and to his characteristic relationships to others as factors that might account for the presence of these rationalities, but without ironic comparison.

*Instead of the properties of rationality being treated as a methodological principle for interpreting activity, they are to be treated only as empirically problematical material. They would have the status only of data and would have to be accounted for in the same way that the more familiar properties of conduct are accounted for.* Just as we might ask how the properties of a status arrangement are relevant to the incidence of striving behavior, or organized dissent, or scapegoating, or to the chances of occupational mobility or whatever, so we might ask how the properties of a status arrangement are determinative of the extent to which the actions of the actors show the rationalities. Questions such as the following, then, press for answers: Why are rationalities of scientific theorizing disruptive of the continuities of action governed by the attitude of daily life? What is there about social arrangements that makes it impossible to transform the two "attitudes" into each other without severe disruptions of the continuous activity governed by each? What must social arrangements be like in order that large numbers of persons, as we know them in our society today, can not only adopt the scientific attitude with impunity, but can, for their success in employing it, make substantial claims for a living upon those to whom the attitude is foreign and in many cases repugnant? In a word, the rational properties of conduct may be removed by sociologists from the domain of philosophical commentary and given over to empirical research.

It is possible to state a general rule which subsumes innumerable research problems: *Any factor that we take to be conditional of any of the properties of activities is a factor that is conditional of the rationalities.* This rule sets up the claim that such factors, for example, as territorial arrangements, the number of persons in a net, rates of turnover, rules governing who can communicate with whom, timing patterns of messages, the distributions of information as well as the operations for altering these distributions, the number and location of information "transformation" points, the properties of coding rules and languages, the stability of social routines, the structured or *ad hoc* incidence of strain in a system, the properties of prestige and power arrangements, and so on are to be considered determinative of the rational properties of actions governed by the attitude of daily life.

### Conclusion

It has been the purpose of this paper to recommend the hypothesis that the scientific rationalities can be employed only as ineffective ideals in the actions governed by the presuppositions of everyday life. The scientific rationalities are neither stable features nor sanctionable ideals of daily routines, and any attempt to stabilize these properties or to enforce conformity to them in the conduct of everyday affairs will magnify the senseless character of a person's behavioral environment and multiply the disorganized features of the system of interaction.

# Appendix to chapter five

In February, 1967, after this volume was in press, I learned from my collaborator, Robert J. Stoller, M.D., that Agnes, in October, 1966, had disclosed to him that she was not a biologically defective male. With his permission I quote the relevant passage from the recently completed manuscript of his book, *Gender Identity:*

"Eight years ago, when this research project was only a year old, a patient was seen who was found to be a unique type of a most rare disorder: testicular feminization syndrome, a condition in which it is felt that the testes are producing estrogens in sufficient amount that the genetically male fetus fails to be masculinized and so develops female genitalia and in puberty female secondary sex characteristics. This particular case was unique in that the patient was completely feminized in her secondary sex characteristics (breasts and other subcutaneous fat distribution; absence of body, facial, and limb hair; feminization of the pelvic girdle; and very feminine and soft skin) with a nonetheless normal-sized penis and testes. Abdominal contents were normal male. Following extensive workup, including examination of testicular tissue by microscope, it was decided that the findings were compatible with estrogen production by the testes. A report of these findings was published. [See footnote, p. 152.] At the time of this workup the patient was 19 years old and had been living undetected as a young woman for about two years. As far back as her memory reached, she had wanted to be a girl and had felt herself to be a girl though she was fully aware that she was anatomically a male and was treated by her family and by society as a boy. Consideration was given to the possibility that she had been taking estrogens on her own, but it was finally decided that this was not the case for the following reasons: (1) she very clearly denied taking such estrogens at the time that she revealed many other parts of her past history which would seem to be equally embarrassing to reveal; (2) even after successfully getting the operation she wanted, she still denied taking estrogens; (3) in order to have effected the biological changes found on physical examination and laboratory tests, she would have had to take just the right drug in just the right amounts starting at just the right time at puberty in order to have converted her body to the state in which it was found at age 19, and it was felt that this amount of information about endocrinology and sophistication about womanhood was beyond the possibilities of this person when 12 years old. There are no cases in the endocrinological literature of a male taking massive doses of estrogens exogenously from puberty on; (4) she was closely observed during hospitalization pre-operatively and her belongings searched; no estrogens were found; shortly after the testes were removed, she developed a menopause, which was considered good evidence that the testes were the source of estrogens; (5) when the testes were examined microscopically and sent to experts in other medical centers for confirmation, the tissue was considered as capable of producing testicular feminization syndrome; (6) the testes, examined postoperatively, were found to contain over twice as much estradiol as is present in the normal adult male.

"Not being considered a transsexual, her genitalia were surgically transformed so that she now had the penis and testes removed and an artificial vagina constructed from the skin of the penis. She subsequently married, moved away, and lived a very full life as a woman. She remained in contact over the years, and infrequently I would have a chance to talk to her and find out how her life was going.

"Five years later she returned. She had been passing successfully as a woman, had been working as a woman, and had been leading a very active, sexually gratifying life as a beautiful and popular young woman. Over the years, she had carefully observed the behavior of her women friends and had learned all the fine details of the expressions of femininity of a woman of her social class and age. Bit by bit, she had reassured herself on any of the possible defects in her femininity, the most important confirmations coming from the men who made love to her, none of whom complained that her anatomy was in the slightest bit suspicious. However, she still was not certain that her vagina was normal enough, and so I arranged for her to see a urologist who, because of his reputation, was in an outstanding position to speak to her as an authority; he told her unequivocally that her genitalia were quite beyond suspicion. . . .

"During the hour following the welcome news given her by the urologist, after having kept it from me for eight years, with the greatest casualness, in mid-sentence, and without giving the slightest warning it was coming, she revealed that she had never had a biological defect that had feminized her but that she had been taking estrogens since age 12. In earlier years when talking to me, she had not only said that she had always hoped and expected that when she grew up she would grow into a woman's body but that starting in puberty this had spontaneously, gradually, but unwaveringly occurred. In contrast, she now revealed that just as puberty began, at the time her voice started to lower and she developed pubic hair, she began stealing Stilbestrol from her mother, who was taking it on prescription following a panhysterectomy. The child then began filling the prescription on her own, telling the pharmacist that she was picking up the hormone for her mother and paying for it with money taken from her mother's purse. She did not know what the effects would be, only that this was a female substance, and she had no idea how much to take but more or less tried to follow the amounts her mother took. She kept this up continuously throughout adolescence, and because by chance she had picked just the right time to start taking the hormone, she was able to prevent the development of all secondary sex characteristics that might have been produced by androgens and instead to substitute those produced by estrogens. Nonetheless, the androgens continued to be produced, enough that a normal-sized adult penis developed with capacity for erection and orgasm till sexual excitability was suppressed by age 15. Thus, she became a lovely looking young 'woman,' though with a normal-sized penis. . . .

"My chagrin at learning this was matched by my amusement that she could have pulled off this coup with such skill. Now able to deal openly with me, for the first time she reported much that was new about her childhood and permitted me to talk with her mother, something that had been forbidden for those eight years."

This news turned the article into a feature of the same circumstances it reported, *i.e.*, into a situated report. Indeed, if the reader will re-read the article in light of these disclosures, he will find that the reading provides an exhibit of several prevailing phenomena of ethnomethodological study: (1) that the recognizedly rational accountability of practical actions is a member's practical accomplishment, and (2) that the success of that practical accomplishment consists in the work whereby a setting, in the same ways that it consists of a recognized and familiar organization of activities, masks from members' relevant notice members' practical ordering practices, and thereby leads the members to see a setting's features, which include a setting's accounts, "as determinate and independent objects."

Following Agnes' disclosures, Stoller exploited the break by tape recording 15 hours of interviews with her and her mother. A subsequent study will be done using the particulars of the disclosures to study the above phenomena. We plan, with the use of the new materials, to re-listen to the earlier taped conversations, to inspect our subsequent records, and to re-read this article. To mark this prospect the original article is called *Part 1*.